Table of Contents

To the Cream of My Crop

I am blessed to have a wonderful wife, Paula,
who has been my partner and associate editor
for this and other writing projects.

And

David C. Cummings, left, and
John B. Cummings, III

Our sons of whom we are
very proud are hardworking,
good husbands and great fathers.

And

Our grandchildren who have
provided us joy and happiness.

Max, Lucy (who has been a big help proofing this
book), Jamie and Chloe Cummings

i

PREFACE

The seed for this project was planted years ago when I was driving through Fall River listening, as I did and still do, to local talk radio station WSAR. The host of the show was asking for names of successful people who came from Fall River. Callers provided names but very few were mentioned other than the most well-known, like Emeril Lagasse and Jerry Remy.

I knew far more names than were presented and the talk show host gave names of people who did not qualify, like the late former Congressman Joe Martin. As I drove along, I wracked my brain for other names like Dean and Mullaney, Buda and Raposo, Reitzas and Gibson, to name just a few. I knew many as a result of my previous careers.

Over the years the idea germinated, and I conceived the idea for *Cream of the Crop*. As I researched individuals for this book I found the famous and not so famous.

Early on in the research I encountered a dilemma: whom to include? Whom to omit? I made a decision: *ONLY THOSE WHO RECEIVED SOME EDUCATION IN FALL RIVER WOULD BE INCLUDED*. Some from the suburbs would be referenced and others who made significant contributions to the local quality of life would also deserve inclusion. Primarily, this is a book about the cream of the crop who were educated in Fall River. Some were born here and some moved early in life out of the area or to the suburbs. Others lived in the suburbs but attended Fall River schools. I have included teams who were either state champions or undefeated in their particular sport. Mayors, judges, school superintendents, police, and fire chiefs as well deserve a mention, all with the same prerequisite: **that they experienced some schooling in our city**.

Other cities and towns in the Commonwealth of Massachusetts have their own well-known and successful residents—Leno, Bloomberg, Kerrigan, Marciano, Damon and Affleck. Fall River is the soil and the schools provided the nourishment that guided hundreds of stars from different fields of endeavor-—arts, business, military, religion, government, media and sports. They come from all of Fall River's many diverse neighborhoods.

They walked the same streets, played in the same parks, had many of the same teachers and they had a vision. They graduated from high school or in some cases parochial or preparatory school and went on to further their education (many were first generation in their family to attend college) and achieved heights that even their parents could only hope for. They made their parents and our city proud.

Included in these pages are parents and children, siblings and only children of hard working and, in many cases, immigrant parents who wanted the best for their offspring. The adults encouraged education; both parents worked and sacrificed to make success a reality. Our "cream" is truly representative of the melting pot our city was and still is. The common denominator was family values. When asked who or what was their greatest influence when growing up the majority answered "parents." Some teachers garnered a shout out but mostly it was Mom and/or Dad. Most had good memories of the safe city and neighborhoods where friends met to play pick-up ball after school or enjoyed weekend activities.

Receiving a prominent place in this book are our "heroes"—departed soldiers from our wars from 1850 to the present. They gave of themselves so that we may enjoy the freedoms we currently enjoy. Many, but not all, of our crop joined the military. Some made it a career. What the majority agreed upon was that Fall River offered them little future. Despite the fondness for the city and its people, most felt the need to sew their oats in other locations. They all possessed the same Fall River DNA

but many needed a different environment. They gave up chow mein sandwiches, Coney Island Hot Dogs and booths at Rector's Spa and the Granite Block Spa, where they did their homework from Durfee or one of the two all-boys schools or five all-girls schools, barracuda jackets, saddle shoes, white bucks and desert boots and more purchased at the Hub or Paul Woltman's, Empire or Tom Ellison's. Some of the girls were outfitted at Lenor's or Wilbur's to attend a movie at one of multiple city theaters or drive-ins in the area or go to a dance at CYO, Club Cal or Forresters or the YMCA. Hitchhiking to the Boston Garden or to Horseneck Beach was not unusual. Upon return they would sneak down to Columbus Park to Marzillis for a piece of pizza or a grinder. Some would even go to excess with two pork pies or chourico and chip sandwich along with a fifteen cent cold one to wash it down or perhaps, even a Frosty Beverage or a cream soda from White Eagle. Many continue to go to Sam's Bakery when they get back for a visit because Sam's is still around, make it last! Some would head to Lincoln Park for one more ride on the Comet Coaster or a view of the dance hall where courting took place.

Rector's Spa photo courtesy of
Maryellen Kurkulos

Many of those included herein would fit nicely into multiple categories. Future leaders developed skills on Fall River athletic fields or in its gymnasiums and then blossomed in their careers. Most have been kind enough to provide personal information for this book. For most, the public domain provided me with ample information. The Internet is a remarkable tool that has given me access to information on many levels and provided images as well. Such an undertaking as this would be virtually impossible without this tool and my sources are listed in the book. They deserve note because without them this undertaking would have been impossible.

The book is divided into two eras. The section 1850 to 1925 represents the city in its glory. Fall River was the "Cotton King" with factories humming and employment at peak levels. The second period in our city's history, 1926 to the present, has been a sad time. Factories departed for the South and the economy was hit with high unemployment. Many efforts were made to turn things around. A new industrial park was developed but it has been spinning its wheels for more than 50 years as major employers have come and gone. The city was cut in half by a highway and a new high school was built in an underpopulated section of the city.

It is my hope that this book will not only serve as a valuable historical document for future generations of Fall Riverites but also an inspiration for generations of young residents. I did not set out to create heroes. I set out to find former or current residents who were motivated to be the best they could be in their specific field of interest, which eventually became their expertise. Unfortunately, names will not appear that I am sure should. Those listed here are not the only cream of Fall River's crop but they are certainly deserving to be so listed. With apologies in advance to family and friends of those who were subject to oversight, the author looks forward to hearing in writing about others from those so inclined.

Meet Fall River's *Cream of the Crop* from the last 160 plus years. Who will come next?

John B. Cummings, Jr.
Westport, Massachusetts
May 8, 2014

FOREWORD

The idea to write a compilation of biographies of Fall Riverites is not without precedent, yet *Cream of the Crop* represents a first for Fall River and constitutes a major contribution to the genre.

Throughout the nineteenth and early-twentieth centuries, when Fall River, Massachusetts, the so-called "Spindle City," was a major textile center at its economic peak, several biographical publications, among them A. Forbes and J.W. Greene's 1851 work, *The Rich Men of Massachusetts,* and J.H. Beers' 1912 book *Representative Men and Old Families of Southeastern Massachusetts,* were published, extolling the virtues and accomplishments of the individuals whose particulars were contained within. The main criteria for inclusion in these volumes and myriad others like them, which were intended for an elite audience, was largely based on one's wealth or social position, and the ability to pay—for these volumes were produced solely by subscription. For an additional fee, one could procure a handsomely bound deluxe edition on fine paper, its book block finished in gilt, profusely illustrated with portrait engravings, including, of course, their own image. The age-old agenda was simple—payment warranted inclusion, and the more one was willing to expend, the more one received in-kind.

For John B. (Red) Cummings, Jr., there would be no such agenda. His requirements for inclusion in *Cream of the Crop* were brilliant in their simplicity: One had to receive a portion of their education in Fall River and had to have excelled in his or her particular field.

And what is success? According to the *Oxford English Dictionary,* it is "the prosperous achievement of something attempted; the attainment of an object according to one's desire." But what drives one to achieve success is far more difficult to define, being as unique in each case as is the individual. For some, perhaps, it is the desire for fame, the accumulation of wealth or power, or the hope to contribute to the betterment of mankind—the list endless, the reasons personal. But regardless the motivation, all of the individuals profiled in these pages brought their dreams to fruition and success was achieved.

John's subjects are the products of various socioeconomic backgrounds. For some, the path to personal success was eased by virtue of being the children of prominent, well-educated parents; the ability to acquire an education was encouraged and readily accessible, doors were opened and fewer barriers remained to stymie the path to success. For many, however, the opposite was the case. The progeny of immigrants who traveled to Fall River to seek a better life, they were the children of struggle and sacrifice, and some of poverty, to whom little could be taken for granted. An education was in itself a major achievement and a path to the opportunity for betterment that had never been available to their parents. All, in one way or another, aspired to and achieved the American Dream.

In each of the profiles here presented, ambition took flight and soared, in some cases to unimaginable heights. Some individuals were gifted with superior intellect, or athletic prowess, or business savvy, or creativity on varying levels—their skills came to the forefront. Undoubtedly, in some cases, fortune smiled and luck played a part. But the common denominator in each of these stories is the hope, the ability to dream, the aspiration for something better.

Some of the people whose stories are told here I have had the privilege of knowing personally and considered friends, others I knew slightly or met in passing, and one of them, my closest friend and mentor, made a strong impact on my life and changed its direction—her success, her passion, she willingly shared with me, and for that, I am forever indebted.

In response to a letter I once wrote to Malcolm Pratt Aldrich, Sr.—Mac to his friends but always, out of respect, Mr. Aldrich to me—thanking him for a personal kindness, he responded:

I have met many powerful men and women in my life ... some of them I have liked more than others, but I've admired most of them for the impact they've had on the lives of others. Success gives you that, the ability to have impact. Someone helped me once, and because of that I can do the same.

A gentleman of the old school and one of the finest men I have ever had the privilege of knowing, Mr. Aldrich took the maxim *noblesse oblige* to heart, and spent a lifetime giving back. For him, success and responsibility functioned in tandem, and his belief that success brings with it the ability to impact the lives of others was a mantra by which he lived his life. Though he made his career elsewhere, he was a Fall River boy born and bred, and always considered his native city "home" and as such, he often gave back. It was a trait that he shared with a good number of those represented in these pages.

But the vast majority of individuals profiled here were unknown to me, and I found the particulars of their lives and accomplishments fascinating and, in many cases, inspiring. Though some names are well known and others ring familiar, some are equally obscure, yet this in no way diminishes their accomplishments.

And their profiles in *Cream of the Crop* make for fascinating reading.

John is uniquely qualified to undertake this work: The scion of a family steeped in Fall River's political, business, and social history, he spent a career "downtown" in banking and non-profit philanthropic work, and served on the boards of numerous organizations. As such, he came into contact with a wide range of people, forming the impetus for this work. The nucleus was formed and, through extensive research, he painstakingly ferreted out additional names.

When I was asked to write this foreword, I asked John what he hoped to accomplish in undertaking this work. Unhesitatingly, he responded:

> When I first conceived the idea for this book, I just wanted it to be a shout-out to Fall Riverites who did exceedingly well. As time passed and more and more names came to light, I felt that this would be a real positive image improvement vehicle for Fall River. And finally, I am bursting with pride that our city has produced so many outstanding, successful individuals from all walks of life. I hope this will serve as a motivator to current and future generations, that anything is within the realm of possibility for anyone. I view it as achievements and inspiration. Achievement for former students and inspiration for present and future students.

Points well said.

I viewed the work in an additional light. In my estimation, *Cream of the Crop* represents an important historical record, a source of material for researchers delving into the lives of successful Fall Riverites and the history of their city. Indeed, many of the individuals profiled herein warrant full-length biographies in their own right; thanks to John's groundbreaking work in bringing their stories to light, this may some day come to pass.

For each of the individuals profiled within these pages, "We'll Try," the motto adopted by the residents of Fall River following a devastating conflagration in 1843 rings true—they tried, and they succeeded.

Michael Martins
Curator
Fall River Historical Society
March, 2014

Achievement

---◆◆---

Success is to be measured

not so much by the position that one has reached in life

as by the obstacles

which he has overcome while trying to succeed.

---◆◆---

Booker T. Washington

1850-1925

Arts

———— ·•·•· ————

An artist cannot fail; it is a success to be one.

———— ·•·•· ————

Charles Horton Cooley

HERBERT R. ANTHONY
Composer

Profile

Herbert (Bert) Anthony was born in 1876 and died in 1923. He and his brother Howard were born in Fall River to William and Amelia (Wood) Anthony. He never married nor did he have any children.

Experience

Bert Anthony was widely known as a musician and composer of instrumental music, but he began his career as a floor sweeper in the Munroe Music Store in downtown Fall River.

He maintained a teaching studio in Fall River with his brother Howard. In the late part of his career he devoted significant time to developing compositions to be taught to youth. Eventually, the composer established Anthony Bros. Music Publishing Co. in association with his brother.

As well as a composer, Anthony connected with the best known bands and orchestras in the area.

His first known compositions were published in 1899 and continued after his death in 1923 at the young age of 47. Bert was a composer of at least 60 songs, many highly acclaimed.

Education

Educated in Fall River schools.

Skills

His best known musical pieces were "Fan Tan" (1902), "I Love You So" (1899) and "Dancing With Ma Baby" (1899). "A Warm Reception" (1899) was famous composer, John Philip Sousa's, favorite ragtime march. Sousa called the piece, "A very clever composition; will surely find its way to the front." He also composed a number of other popular instrumental pieces.

Information and sheet music cover gathered from *Wikipedia*, the *Fall River Globe* and correspondence from Erroll Crowl

HERBERT CASH
Artist

Profile
Born in England in 1864, Herbert Cash moved to Fall River at age nine in 1873. He was the son of Martha Dimlow and Samuel Cash and was one of five children. He married Elizabeth Shovelton. Very little information is known about Cash but he died in 1914.

Experience
A well-known member of the Fall River Evening Drawing School, Cash not only painted wonderful still-lifes but also detailed landscapes like the one here. Still-lifes of vegetables and fruits from Cash and his fellow Fall River painters were often considered masterpieces.

In 1906, Cash went abroad to study in England and later in Paris. His exhibitions of his collection of paintings, etchings and watercolors, especially his English scenes were considered noteworthy.

Education
He attended Fall River schools and then enrolled in the Fall River Evening Drawing School. After that he studied at the Art Students League in New York.

Skills
Cash, an accomplished draftsperson, was a teacher of drawing and textile ornamentation at Durfee Technical College. His technique included easel paintings of all genre, including still life.

Also of Note
His work is on display at the Fall River Public Library, the Fall River Historical Society and in many private collections.

Information gathered from *Ask Art: The Artist Bluebook*, the Fall River Historical Society and *Fall River Evening News*—photo courtesy of the Fall River Historical Society collection

BRYANT CHAPIN
Artist

Profile
Bryant Chapin was born in 1859, the son of Louise Bigelow and Daniel A. Chapin. He had a brother, Herbert. He died in 1927 and the family is buried in Oak Grove Cemetery in Fall River.

Experience
Chapin taught at the Evening Drawing School, which was part of the Fall River Evening Drawing School of Massachusetts painters. He studied with Robert S. Dunning (see Dunning) and his early work reflects Dunning's influence.

Chapin's style is fluid and soft. Many of his paintings are of berries in and falling out of wooden berry boxes. He was both a railroad engineer and bank clerk before taking up art and opening a studio on Purchase Street in Fall River.

Education
Local Fall River schools. Also, Chapin served as an art lecturer during his 40-year career.

Skills
Chapin is known for his many still-life paintings, particularly fruit as seen above. Many painting are of berries, some on the ground and others in berry boxes. Most of his works were set on highly polished tables to best reflect the subject matter. He also painted landscapes and traveled to Europe on several occasions to paint European landscapes.

Also of Note
Many of his works can be found in the Fall River Public Library, the Fall River Historical Society and in private collections both locally and nationally.

ROBERT SPEAR DUNNING
Artist

Profile

Robert Spear Dunning was born in Brunswick, Maine, in 1829 and died in Westport Harbor at his summer home and studio in 1905. He is buried in Oak Grove Cemetery. Dunning was the son of Joseph and Rebecca Spear Dunning. He married Mehitable Hill of Fall River, they had no children. Robert Spear was survived by his brother, Marillo B. Dunning of New York.

Experience

Dunning was the co-founder of the Fall River School of Still Life Painting. After working as a youth in both a mill and later in coastal shipping, Dunning studied art. At age 30, he partnered with John E. Grouard to create the firm of Grouard and Dunning, artists.

In 1850, he exhibited his works at the National Academy of Design and the American-Art Union, returning to Fall River in 1852. He taught in his studio at 6 North Main Street.

Fall River became an important center of American still-life painting with its small but influential group of students including Cash, Chapin, Fish, Miller and Zuill.

In 1865, Dunning began to concentrate on still life painting but also made frequent trips to New Hampshire to paint landscapes. He was also a well-known portraitist.

Education

Local Fall River schools, James Roberts in Thomaston, Maine, and the National Academy of Design. In 1870, he co-founded the Fall River Evening Drawing School with John Grouard. Both men could also be classified in the Education section of this book.

Skills

Dunning was recognized for his paintings of fruit in silver or glass on highly polished surfaces. He painted in detail, using bright colors often with honeycombs borrowing style from the Dutch and the English as well as his own attention to detail. He did, however, paint portraits and one of his finest may have been of his longtime friend, Franklin H. Miller (see Miller). His media were oils and water colors.

Also of Note

His works can be found at the National Museum of Art, the Fall River Historical Society and Fall River Public Library as well as a portrait of the Honorable Frank S. Stevens in the Swansea, Massachusetts Town Hall.

Information gathered from *Wikipedia*; Fall River Historical Society, White Mountain Art and Artist; and *Victorian Vistas Fall River 1901-1911*

HERBERT A. FISH
Artist

Profile
Herbert Fish was born in 1855, the son of Sarah Crosby and John S. Fish. He died in 1932.

Experience
Very little seems to be known about Fish. His style of painting reflects the Fall River Evening Drawing School. Many of his landscape works in oils, watercolors and pastel still-life depict berries and many show the fruits coming out of baskets.

Education
Educated in Fall River schools and the Fall River Evening Drawing School under the tutelage of R.S. Dunning and F.H. Miller.

Skills
Before his career as an artist, Fish spent time as a tailor and in retail as a candy salesperson before taking a position weighing and sampling cotton.

Also of Note
Many of his works can be found in the Fall River Public Library, the Fall River Historical Society and in private collections both locally and nationally.

Information gathered from *Ask Art: The Artist Bluebook*
—photo taken by the author courtesy of Bernard A.G. Taradash Collection

GEORGE A. HOLT
Actor and Film Director

Profile
Son of Stephen and Adee Holt, George A. Holt was born in Fall River in 1878 and died in California at age sixty-five in 1944. He was married to Mary Holt and they had a son and a daughter.

Experience
His acting and directing occurred during film's silent era between 1913 and 1935. He appeared in 64 films and directed 24 between 1919 and 1924.

Some of his films include:

The Proof of the Man (1913)

His Buddy (1919)

The Lone H (1919)

The Trail of the Holdup Man (1919)

Kingdom Come (1919)

Ace High (1919)

Education
Local Fall River schools and B.M.C. Durfee High School.

Skills
Holt served his country as part of the Battery A Rhode Island Infantry in 1916 and was in pursuit of the famed Pancho Villa from June through October. He was stationed at Camp Pershing in Columbus, New Mexico.

MARY LIZZIE MACOMBER
Artist

Profile
Mary Lizzie Macomber was born in 1861 and died in 1916. She is buried in Oak Grove Cemetery with other family members.

Experience
Ill health cut short Macomber's art studies in Boston but after her recovery she studied briefly with Frank Duveneck and then opened a studio in Boston.

In 1913, her painting, Ruth, was exhibited in the National Academy Design Show in New York City. Over the next 13 years Macomber exhibited 25 more paintings in the National Academy as well as other major museums and galleries.

Some of her more admired works are "Love Awakening Memory" (1892), "Love's Lament" (1893), "St. Catherine" (1897, see above), "The Hour Glass" (1900) and the "Lace Jabot" (1900; a self portrait). In her later years, a great deal of her time was devoted to portraiture.

Education
Local Fall River schools and The Boston Museum of Fine Arts School.

Skills
Macomber's paintings of beautiful women were highly acclaimed and she painted in a style of the pre-Raphaelite school.

Currently hanging in the atrium of the Fall River Public Library is Macomber's work, "Marconi." The painting depicts an angel-like woman looking out over the ocean trying to hear any response to the SOS (Marconi's invention of the wireless) from the *Titanic* to the rescue ship the *Carpathia*, which saved more than 700 passengers. (A detailed exhibit on the *Titanic* can be viewed at the Fall River Marine Museum on Water Street.) At the extreme point of the canvas sparks can be seen over the water, a tribute to Marconi and his invention.

Also of Note
Macomber's works may be seen at the Fall River Public Library, the Boston Museum of Fine Arts and in private collections. She exhibited at the 1892 Chicago Columbian Exposition.

Information gathered from *Architectural Elements, Art & Architecture* and the
Encyclopedia Britannica—photo of Miss Macomber courtesy of the Fall River Historical Society collection

FRANKLIN HARRISON MILLER
Artist

Profile
The son of Estes Peckham and Southard Miller, Franklin Miller was born in 1843 and died in 1911 of throat cancer. There is no record of Miller marrying or having any children; he lived his entire life in Fall River.

Experience
F.H. Miller was a contemporary of R.S. Dunning and a student of still-life art espoused by teachers of the Fall River Evening Drawing School. Miller's work most resembles Dunning and Chapin but is considered more informal. He shared a studio in the Borden Block with Dunning.

Education
Local Fall River schools as well as schools in Boston and Paris. Miller was tutored by Benjamin Champney and George Innes, a leading New England landscape artist.

Skills
Miller and his friend and Fall River Evening School of Drawing co-founder, R.S. Dunning, both became recognized as still-life and landscape painters from the Fall River Evening Drawing School.

Also of Note
Examples of his work may be found at the Fall River Historical Society and in private collections.

Information gathered from *Ask Art: The Artist Bluebook* and the
Fall River Historical Society—image courtesy of the Fall River Historical Society collection

FREDERICK OAKES SYLVESTER
Artist, Poet and Educator

Profile
Frederick Oakes Sylvester was born in Brockton, Massachusetts, in 1869 and came with his parents, Charles Frederick and Mary Kilburn, to Fall River when he was thirteen years old. Frederick married Florence Gerry and they had two children together. He died in St. Louis in 1915 from pneumonia. From 1908 until his passing, Sylvester maintained a summer cottage on the western bluffs in Elsah, Missouri, overlooking the river where many of his paintings were created.

Experience
After his graduation from Massachusetts Art School, Sylvester became Director of Art at Sophie Newcomb College, which is part of Tulane University in New Orleans. From there he moved to Saint Louis.

Eads Bridge on the River

As well as teaching at St. Louis schools for 23 years and Principia School after it was founded in 1901, Sylvester found time to continue to paint and write poetry. Sylvester often referred to himself as "The Painter Poet." One of his finest works was a large mural of the clubhouse commissioned by the St. Louis Country Club, but it was either painted over or destroyed.

His *Principia Collection* was published in book form in 1988 by The Principia Corporation. Many of his paintings centered on the Mississippi, *The Great River*, from where most of his poetry also originates. His book was the culmination of his dream and his artistic talents. Sylvester was known as an American Impressionist and Post-Impressionist. Much of his poetry and art reflects his deeply religious beliefs and convictions.

Education
Local Fall River schools and B.M.C. Durfee High School class of 1888, he then attended Massachusetts Art School in Boston.

Skills
Sylvester first gained official recognition as an artist when he was elected to associate membership in the Society of Western Artists in 1899. He then was elected a full member and vice president of the group. Exhibitions of his work were held in Illinois and Missouri.

Also of Note
Sylvester exhibited his works at the St. Louis Louisiana Purchase Exposition, where he was awarded a bronze medal, and the 1904 St. Louis World's Fair. He was awarded a silver medal in the Portland Exposition.

His works may be found in private collections in the Midwest as well as the Missouri Historical Society, Principia College, The St. Louis Art Museum, the St. Louis Athletic Club and in public libraries.

Information gathered from Early Painters of Fall River, the Fall River Historical Society and The Principia Collection—images courtesy of *Wikipedia* and The Principia Collection

ABBIE LUELLA ZUILL
Artist

Profile
Abbie Luella Zuill was the daughter of Hannah Vickery and George F. Allen. She was born in 1856 and died in 1921. Married, she had a son named Robert and lived most of her life in the Pottersville section of Somerset.

Experience
Zuill was considered a still-life specialist. She preferred to paint roses, but whatever she painted she liked her subjects to appear on polished table tops with carved edges (see above). Most of her work was done with soft, luminous light. Zuill painted some landscapes and occasionally depicted hanging bananas, a rare subject for any still-life artist.

Education
Local Fall River schools and the Fall River Evening Drawing School.

Skills
Another member and teacher in the Fall River Evening Drawing School founded by R.S. Dunning and F. H. Miller, Zuill was believed to be most faithful to Dunning's teaching. So much so that after Dunning died in nearby Westport Harbor in 1905, she was called upon to complete many of his unfinished works. Since she was a more recent student and much younger, her works are not as bright and her fruit is not as sharply defined as her mentor's.

Also of Note
Her works can be seen at the Fall River Historical Society and in many private collections.

Information gathered from *Ask Art: The Artist Bluebook*, American Still Life Painting and *Fall River Evening Herald*—image courtesy of the Fall River Historical Society collection

1850-1925

Business

Invitation Ode

One hundred years ago,
to crude machines we owe
a tribute grand.
Unfailing progress came,
weaving both cloth and fame,
wafting Fall River's name
through every land.
Fall River bids you come,
four million spindles hum
your welcome here.
Join us in rosy June,
come morning night or noon,
come with your hearts atune
with festal cheer.

J. Edmund Estes (1911)

CORNELIUS NEWTON BLISS
Merchant
Secretary of the Interior

Profile
Cornelius Newton Bliss was the son of Ashael Newton Bliss and Irene Borden Luther. Bliss was born in 1833. He was the spouse of Mary Elizabeth Plummer and the father of two children, Lillie P. Bliss, one of the founders of the Museum of Modern Art in New York City, and financier, Cornelius Newton Bliss, Jr. Cornelius Newton, Sr., died in 1911 and is buried in Woodlawn Cemetery in the Bronx, New York.

Experience
Launching his career in his stepfather William Keep's counting house at age 16, Bliss became clerk and a junior partner in a Boston commercial house. Moving to New York, Bliss opened a division of the firm, adding the names Bliss and Fabyan to the original name of Wright and Wyman. In 1881, the firm was called Bliss and Fabyan & Company. It was a wholesale dry goods firm, one of the largest in the nation at the time. The firm did considerable business with M.C.D. Borden, also known as "The Calico King," who operated the Fall River Iron Works and The American Printing Company in Fall River (see M.C.D. Borden).

Bliss was so highly regarded that President William McKinley offered him the position of Secretary of the Treasury and later Vice President, both of which he declined. The latter was accepted by Theodore Roosevelt, who famously became president after McKinley's assassination.

Bliss served as the 21st United States Secretary of the Interior from 1897 to 1899. He was also an incorporator of the American Red Cross.

Education
Local Fall River schools, Fiske Private School on Franklin Street in Fall River and later in New Orleans.

Skills
Bliss was one of the founders of the New York Chamber of Commerce and was a director of many highly regarded New York financial institutions. He served as treasurer of the Republican National Committee from 1892 to 1904.

Also of Note
He was a member of the Jekyll Island Club in Georgia, also known as The Millionaires' Club.

Information gathered from *Wikipedia* and *Victorian Vistas-Fall River 1890-1900* and *Parallel Lives*
—photo courtesy of *Wikipedia*

MATTHEW CHALONER DURFEE BORDEN
Industrialist

Profile
Matthew Chaloner Durfee Borden was born in 1842 to Colonel Richard and Abby Durfee Borden. He married his relative Harriett M. Durfee and they had seven children. Borden died at his summer home in Oceanic, New Jersey, in 1912.

Experience
He was referred to as M.C.D. Borden or by his nickname, "The Calico King." In 1865 he became a stock boy in a leading New York dry goods house. Within three years he had become a partner in a commission house where he represented American Print Works as a selling agent before its failure in 1879. Together with his older brother, Thomas, he reorganized the firm under the name of The American Printing Company. In 1887, the Calico King bought out his brother and built three large print mills, the Iron Works, on 20 acres along the Taunton River (years later to be the site of two major Firestone fires). Eventually, the property was bought by Tillotson Corporation and Borden Remington, which owns the site to this date. The Iron Works produced 70,000 pieces of print cloth per week.

Education
Local Fall River schools, Phillips Academy Andover and Yale University.

Skills
The Calico King was considered the largest manufacturer and printer of calico cloth in the world.

Also of Note
Borden's father, Colonel Richard Borden, founded Fall River Iron Works and was the first president of the Fall River National Bank in 1825. In 1893, while "another" Borden was being charged with brutal murders, it was M.C.D. who was making the greatest impact upon the Spindle City as the textile capital of the world.

In 1898, the Fall River Boys Club was dedicated as a result of a generous gift by Borden who was unable to attend. At the time, it was called by many "the finest building of its kind in the country, yes, in the world." When Borden died in 1912 during the Fall River Cotton Centennial, his estate was valued at more than $5 million. All of it but $250,000 (a bequest to Yale) went to his sons.

Information gathered from *Wikipedia* and *Victorian Vistas-Fall River 1890-1900*—photo courtesy of *Wikipedia*

SPENCER BORDEN
Manufacturer and Chemist

Profile

Spencer Borden was the son of Jefferson and Susan Easton Borden. Born in 1848, he was the husband of Effie Brooks and father of Spencer Borden, Jr., and Brooks Borden. Brooks Borden was killed when a train hit a sleigh full of high school students on January 31, 1894, on Brownell Street in the North End. Spencer was also the father of two daughters, Leonora and Florence. He died in 1921 and is buried with other family members in Oak Grove Cemetery.

Experience

The main product produced by the Fall River mills then was cotton print cloth, and the American Print Works was one of the largest such operations in the United States between 1870 and 1872.

The best results were obtained from pure white cloth. In 1872, Borden traveled to Europe after he became a trained chemist to study the process of bleaching and dyeing textiles.

Upon his return to Fall River in 1873, Borden gathered mill owners to explore the idea of establishing a large-scale bleachery. Sites were viewed in the area but eventually the site at the mouth of Sucker Brook near South Watuppa Pond was chosen for its pure spring-fed water and high flow rate.

Education

Local Fall River schools.

Skills

Borden's father, Jefferson, was selected as the first president of the firm, which still stands in part today on Jefferson Street in the city's Maplewood section. By 1906, the Fall River Bleachery had a capacity of 50 tons of cloth per day.

Interlachen

Also of Note

Borden built and lived in a grand home on the banks of the North Watuppa known as "Interlachen." Called the "Big House," it was considered the grandest of Fall River estates. The estate included riding stables for Borden's prize Arabian horses, hiking trails, tennis courts, a golf course and fishing in the North Watuppa Pond.

Information gathered from *Wikipedia, Parallel Lives* and *Victorian Vistas 1901-1911*
—photos courtesy of *Wikipedia* and *Victorian Vistas*

WILLIAM C. DAVOL
Inventor and Manufacturer

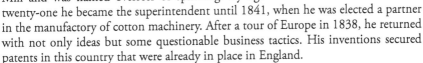

Profile
William C. Davol was born in Fall River in 1806 and
died in 1892. He was the son of Abner Davol and
Mary Durfee. He had four siblings.

Experience
At age thirteen, Davol joined the workers at the Troy
Mill and was named overseer of spinning. By age
twenty-one he became the superintendent until 1841, when he was elected a partner
in the manufactory of cotton machinery. After a tour of Europe in 1838, he returned
with not only ideas but some questionable business tactics. His inventions secured
patents in this country that were already in place in England.

Litigation by the English was costly for Davol but he was aided by Micah Ruggles
who was an agent for the Pocasset Company and won his legal battles eventually. His
patents produced 180,000 spindles. New patterns were developed nearly annually and
Davol found a productive field for his carders, speeders and drawing frames.

Education
Local Fall River schools.

Skills
In 1876 the famed Iron Works on the Taunton River erected the Metacomet Mill.
Plans for the mill came from England. The new construction replaced wooden parts
and girders with iron parts and girders that reduced friction and loss of power to the
mill. Such a move allowed the new factory to increase production over foreign competition and over others in the city that were constructed with wood. This also allowed
for a larger output for the rapidly increasing consumption of goods.

Also of Note
The Davol Mills were named after him and are still in place on the banks of the
Quequechan River near what was called Big Berry Stadium, where many a soccer
match was held. In the mill at the time, the manufacture of sheeting, shirtings and
sileias was produced.

Not only were mills named for the Fall River inventor and manufacturer, but also a
school and a street.

Although Davol was born before the established time frame for this book, he is
included because his inventions greatly influenced the landscape and economic
foundations of Fall River and other area communities.

Information gathered from and photo courtesy of *Our County and Its People-the City of Fall River*

LEONTINE LINCOLN
Businessperson and Community Leader

Profile
Leontine Lincoln was born in Fall River in 1846. His parents were Abby Luscomb and Jonathan Thayer Lincoln. Lincoln married Amelia Dioncone and they had two sons and two grandchildren. He died suddenly of appendicitis in 1923 and is buried in Oak Grove Cemetery.

Experience
Lincoln was a Fall River businessperson who became treasurer and the fourth president of a firm founded by his father, the Kilburn and Lincoln Company. The company produced machinery for the manufacture of silk and cotton. Lincoln was named by then-Governor Fredic Greenhalgh to the State Board of Lunacy and Charity in 1894. He was a member of the Fall River School Committee for 24 years between 1880 and 1904 and served as chair for 16 years. Lincoln was one of the organizers of the Bradford Durfee Textile School, elected president in 1903 and holding office until his death in 1923.

Lincoln served as secretary of the Board of Trustees of Durfee High School.

At the time of his death, he served as president of seven different textile firms in Fall River at the same time.

Education
Local Fall River schools and a private school in Providence. He received an honorary Masters of Arts from Brown University.

Skills
He was well known and highly respected for the time and talent he devoted to the public good and private charitable organizations. One of the best known and highly regarded men of his day, Lincoln was a member of the State Board of Lunacy and Charity and he addressed a panel on "Leprosy and Treatment in Massachusetts."

Also of Note
Lincoln was appointed to the Fall River Public Library Board of Trustees in 1878 and served as president of that body between 1896 and 1923. He oversaw the construction of the present library on North Main Street and brought the project in under budget by $3,000.

Lincoln served as a member of the Old Colony Historical Society and then as a founder of the Fall River Historical Society.

He refused nominations for mayor and congress and refused any payment for his community efforts.

An elementary school in Fall River was named in his honor.

Information gathered from and photo courtesy of *Our County and Its People-the City of Fall River*

WILLIAM LINDSEY
Cotton Broker

Profile
Son of William Lindsey, Sr., and Ariadne Maria Lovell, William Lindsey was born in 1858. He was married to Annie Sheen and they had three children. He died in 1922.

His daughter Leslie and her husband Stewart were honeymooning aboard the *Lusitania* when it was sunk by a U-boat during World War I. Her parents designed a memorial for them and built the Lady Chapel at Emmanuel Church in Boston. With the purchase of 27 Newbury Street in Boston, the Leslie Lindsey Chapel was constructed but not finished before her father died in 1922. It is today owned by Boston University.

Experience
After a brief stint working with his father in a Fall River mill, Lindsey moved to Boston in 1876 and became a cotton broker for the next twenty years. He moved to London in 1900 and developed and maintained the rights to a cotton belt that became in great demand by the British military during the Boer War. His company's success earned him a large fortune, permitting his early retirement at age forty-six.

Lindsay's Boston Tudor mansion

Education
Fall River schools. No higher education (his father did not permit him to go on to college).

Skills
Early retirement gave Lindsey the opportunity to pursue his interest in literature. From his Tudor manor in Boston's Back Bay, he wrote poems, plays and historical romances in his third floor study that he accessed through a secret door in his bedroom. He was also known for his theatrical designs and supported artists of his day.

Also of Note
In 1903, Lindsey donated $100,000 to create, build and furnish the William Lindsey School of Drafting and Designing. The school was an adjunct to the Bradford Durfee Textile School. The value of the gift in today's dollars would be more than $2.2 million. It was dedicated as a memorial to his father, a leading Fall River manufacturer. This was just one of many schools and universities that benefited from Lindsey's generosity as well as various Fall River institutions in his home town.

There is a Durfee High School Scholarship in the joint names of William Lindsey and William H. Lambert.

Information gathered from *Parallel Lives*—photos courtesy of the Fall River Historical collection

Bank Presidents Educated in Fall River 1850-1925

John S. Brayton	B.M.C. Durfee Trust Company
Henry H. Earl	Citizens Savings Bank
Joseph Healy**	Citizens Savings Bank
John C. Milne	Citizens Savings Bank
Joseph Osborn	Citizens Savings Bank
S. Angier Chace**	Fall River Five Cent Savings
George S. Davol	Fall River Five Cent Savings
Walter C. Durfee**	Fall River Five Cent Savings
Leontine Lincoln	Fall River Five Cent Savings
James Marshall	Fall River Five Cent Savings
David Anthony	Fall River National Bank
Richard Borden	Fall River National Bank
Ferdinand H. Durfee	Fall River National Bank
Guilford H. Hathaway	Fall River National Bank
Oliver S. Hawes	Fall River National Bank
Wendell E. Turner	Fall River National Bank
Abner B. Davol	Fall River Peoples Co-Operative Bank
Charles H. Durfee	Fall River Peoples Co-Operative Bank
John H. Estes	Fall River Peoples Co-Operative Bank
John C. Batchelder	Metacomet Bank
Jefferson Borden	Metacomet Bank
Thomas J. Borden	Metacomet Bank
Simeon B. Chace	Metacomet Bank
Walter C. Durfee**	Metacomet Bank
William Lindsey	Metacomet Bank
Frank B. Stevens	Metacomet Bank
Jesse Eddy	National Union Bank

Bank Presidents Educated in Fall River 1850-1925

Oliver Chace	Pocasset Bank
Samuel Hathaway	Pocasset Bank
Joseph Healy**	Pocasset Bank
Weaver Osborn	Pocasset Bank
George W. Slade	Pocasset Bank
Andrew J. Borden* **	Troy Co-Operative Bank
Jerome C. Borden**	Troy Co-Operative Bank
Spencer Borden	Troy Co-Operative Bank
George W. Eddy, Jr.	Troy Co-Operative Bank
Andrew J. Borden * **	Union Savings Bank
Jerome C. Borden**	Union Savings Bank
Augustus Chace	Union Savings Bank
Benjamin Covel	Union Savings Bank
Adam W. Gifford	Union Savings Bank
S. Angier Chace**	Wamsutta Bank

* There is a scholarship in his memory benefiting the graduates of Durfee High School
** Batchelder, Andrew and Jerome Borden, Walter Durfee and Healy served as president of more than one bank over the years.

1850-1925

Government

Recipe for Greatness

To bear up under loss;

To fight the bitterness of defeat and the weakness of grief;

To be victor over anger;

To smile when tears are close;

To resist disease and evil men and base instincts;

To hate hate and to love love;

To go on when it would seem good to die;

To look up with unquenchable faith in something ever more about to be;

That is what any man can do, and be great.

ZANE GREY

HONORABLE JAMES BUFFINGTON
First Mayor and Congressman

Profile
Born in 1817, the Honorable James Buffington died in Fall River in 1875 at age fifty-seven while serving in Congress and is buried in Oak Grove Cemetery.

Experience
Before being elected Fall River's first mayor, Buffington served as a member of the Board of Selectmen from 1851 to his election in 1854. He served in that capacity for one year under a new city government. He was then elected to the United States House of Representatives from Massachusetts 1st and 2nd District for a total of 14 years, first as a member of the American Party and then as a Republican. Buffington served as Chair of the Accounts Committee and as a member of the Military Affairs Committee.

In 1861, he was mustered into the military but discharged two months later. Deciding not to run again in 1862, he became a special agent of the United States Treasury and in 1867 served as the state director of the Internal Revenue Service until 1870 when the Republican was again elected to serve three consecutive terms in Congress.

Education
Fall River Common School and Friends College in Providence, Rhode Island.

Skills
Buffington was blessed and cursed. When he took over the leadership of a newly formed City of Fall River in 1854 from a small township, he was blessed with a flourishing and prosperous model of a city. When the mill machinery ceased each day, the hard working community could relax by their fires.

The city went from peace to turmoil when a feared cholera epidemic took over with a deadly grip. It was necessary to isolate family and friends from each other to prevent the illness from spreading, and still death took over the city for six long weeks. When the scourge ended, more than 100 citizens had been stricken. The first to contract the disease within a family died in a matter of hours of not feeling well. The disease was passed rapidly within families and even nationalities, which tended to be clannish.

This tragedy may have been one of the reasons Buffington did not seek reelection as mayor, having served during such a sad time. Instead he moved on to Congress, far removed from the individual tragedies of fellow neighbors.

Also of Note
Buffington studied medicine but never practiced. Later, he engaged in mercantile pursuits before his political career.

Information gathered from *Wikipedia* and *Victorian Vistas Fall River 1880-1890*—photo courtesy of *Wikipedia*

HONORABLE JOHN WILLIAM CUMMINGS
Mayor, State Senator and Representative

Profile
The son of John and Mary Rogers Cummings, John William Cummings was born in 1855 in Stockport, England. He died in Fall River in 1929 and is buried in St. Patrick's Cemetery. He had three brothers and married Mary C. Brennan; they had six children and six grandchildren.

Experience
As an infant, Cummings traveled across the ocean with his parents from England and was declared dead on shipboard, but his mother would not allow his body to be disposed of overboard. He began breathing again, to everyone's amazement and relief. Eventually the family settled in Providence, Rhode Island, but Cummings moved at an early age to Fall River, where he grew up in the then-Irish section of the city on Whipple Street. He graduated from Boston University and its Law School at the age of twenty, earning both an undergraduate and law degree in three years due to a near—photographic memory.

In 1884 at age twenty-nine, Cummings served as the first Irish and first Catholic mayor as well as youngest (he retains that distinction to this date) mayor in the city's history. In 1883 at age twenty-eight, he was elected to the Massachusetts Senate and after serving a second term as mayor in 1886, was voted to the Massachusetts House of Representatives in 1888. The young elected official was an Independent, neither a Republican nor Democrat.

Education
Local Fall River schools and Boston University. Cummings was admitted to the Massachusetts Bar at age twenty-one years and one month. His admission was deferred one month since he was not yet considered a man at age twenty when he passed the bar examination.

Skills
Cummings was a respected barrister and political leader. President of both the Fall River and Massachusetts Bar Associations, he was a member of the Judicature Commission as well as founder and president of the Fall River Clover Club and the organization which is now known as Family Service Association of Fall River. He declined numerous offers of high appointments, including a judgeship in the Superior Court and an ambassadorship to Austria from President Calvin Coolidge.

Also of Note
Not only was Cummings an elected official, he was a highly respected lawyer in Fall River and throughout the state. He very rarely resorted to notes when arguing a case in court, even in summation that sometimes lasted for hours. A member of the Massachusetts Constitutional Convention from 1917 to 1919, he wielded power in the drafting of laws into the Constitution of the Initiative and Referendum. He was a member of the Electoral College that informed Woodrow Wilson of his election as 28th President and was a close associate of the 30th President Calvin Coolidge, former Massachusetts Governor. His portrait in charcoal (above) was sketched by world famous artist, John Singer Sargent.

Information gathered from *Wikipedia*; *Victorian Vistas 1880-1890*, and personal family history—photos courtesy of the author

ROBERT DOLLARD, ESQ.
Attorney General of South Dakota

Profile
One of two children born in Fall River in 1842 to Mary Colyer and Mr. Dollard, Robert Dollard's ancestry was Scottish. He was married to Carrie Dunn in 1875 and died in Santa Monica, California, in 1912.

Experience
Dollard moved to the Dakota territory from Illinois after passing the bar in 1870. He was recorded as the first settler in Douglas County in South Dakota. As well as being elected to various local offices, the young lawyer participated in the state convention in 1883 and 1885. Before South Dakota achieved formal statehood, the former Fall Riverite served as its appointed Attorney General and was elected to that post in 1889 and reelected in 1890. He then served as a state senator in 1892 and a representative in 1896, both from the Republican party.

Education
Local Fall River schools.

Also of Note
Dollard was a member of the Fourth Regiment, Massachusetts Volunteer Militia, part of the Minutemen of Massachusetts. He was one of the first to respond to the call for Civil War volunteers and achieved the rank of major at age twnety-two—the youngest officer of his rank in either army.

Information gathered from *Wikipedia*, the South Dakota Historical Society and
Atty. General's Office—photo courtesy of the state of South Dakota

WILLIAM STEDMAN GREENE
Mayor and United States Congressman

Profile
Born in 1842 and died in Fall River in 1924, William Stedman Greene is interred in Oak Grove Cemetery.

Experience
An active city councilor, Greene was president of that body from 1877 to 1879 until he was elected mayor for the first time in 1880. Mayor Greene was reelected the following year but resigned soon after to become postmaster. He again served as mayor in 1886 and in a fourth term from 1895 to 1899. The highly regarded Republican first joined the Congress after the death of John Simpkins. Greene served from 1898 until his death in 1924.

Education
Local Fall River schools.

Skills
Representative Greene was chair of the Committee on Expenditures in the Department of the Navy and a member of the committee on Merchant Marine and Fisheries during his years in Congress.

Also of Note
Appointed Fall River Postmaster in 1881, Greene acted in that capacity until 1885. He became general superintendent of the state prison from 1888 to 1898. An elementary school in Fall River is named after him.

Mayors Who Were Educated in Fall River

James Buffington	1854-1855	Merchant
Edward P. Buffinton	1856-1857 1860-1867	Merchant
James F. Davenport	1874-1877	Textile Supervisor
Crawford C. Lindsey	1878-1879	Merchant
William S. Greene	1880-1881 1886 1895-1897	Real Estate/Insurance Broker
John W. Cummings, Esq.	1885 1887	Law
Amos M. Jackson, M.D.	1898-1899	Physician
John H. Abbott, M.D.	1900-1901	Physician
George Grime, Esq.	1902-1904	Law
Thomas F. Higgins, Esq.	1911-1913	Law
James H. Kay	1913-1923	Machinist
Edmond P. Talbot	1923-1926	Druggist

On the following pages, some mayors due to their significance in Fall River history like Buffington, Cummings and Greene warrant a full page.

Fire and Police Chiefs Educated in Fall River

Police Chiefs

Rufus B. Hilliard	1886-1909
John Fleet	1909-1915
William Medley	1915-1917
Martin Feeney	1917-1931

Fire Chiefs

Stephen Davol	1850-1852
James Buffington	1853
Asa Eames	1854
Jonathan E. Morrill	1855-1856
Chester W. Greene	1857
Jonathan E. Morrill	1858-1859
Southard Miller	1860-1869
Thomas J. Borden	1870-1872
Holder B. Durfee	1873-1874
Thomas Connell	1875
William C. Davol, Jr.	1876-1881
John C. McFarlane	1882-1883
William C. Davol, Jr.	1884-1897
James Langford	1889-1900
William C. Davol, Jr.	1901-1920
Joseph Bowers, Jr.	1920-1922

1850-1926
Media

———————

Efficiency

The right man in the right place at the right time

doing the right thing in the right way.

———————

CORNELIUS F. KELLY
Newspaper Publisher

Profile
Cornelius F. Kelly was one of five children of Margaret Harrington and Jeremiah Kelly. He was born in 1874. He married Elizabeth R. Kennedy and they had six daughters. He died in 1938 and is buried in Valhalla, New York.

Experience
At age 20, Kelly was named Business Manager of the *Fall River Globe*. He bought the *Fall River Herald* and the *Fall River News* in 1926 and merged them. Three years later, he acquired the *Globe*. In the newspaper field, he was believed to be one of the greatest publishers in the nation.

Although he moved out of the city to Westchester County, New York, Kelly maintained a close connection with Fall River and his paper, devoting time and resources to what he felt were in the best interests in his hometown.

Education
A graduate of B.M.C. Durfee High School in 1891 after attending local Fall River schools, the future publisher studied at Bryant and Stratton Colleges.

Skills
Kelly kept tight reins on his paper. Despite living in New York, he was not an absentee owner. He appointed his sister, Anna H.C. Kelly, as vice president and treasurer. She and his other sister, Julia T. Murphy, were permanent residents of Fall River.

Also of Note
One of his first jobs after college was as a bookkeeper and then money order clerk in the Fall River Post Office. In 1910, he formed Kelly Smith, a national advertising business. Kelly was the agent for dozens of the nation's newspapers and owner of two other papers besides the *Fall River Herald News*.

Information gathered from *Fall River Herald News Sesquicentennial Edition*:
September 19, 1953—photo courtesy of the *Fall River Herald News*

1850-1925
Military

The Soldier's Dream
or
Old Glory

On the field as I lay at the close of day,
When the heat of the sun and the smoke of the fray
Had lulled me to sleep on my cushion of clay,
I dreamed of my home and friends far away.
For dreamers may dream, and armies may fight,
And battles be won for the wrong or the right,
But the glory that's true and the flag that is best
Are the glory and flag that have right for their crest.
So here's to Old Glory, the Red, White, and Blue
The emblem of justice and liberty too!
Oh! The Stars and Stripes may they never be furled
Till Freedom and Right shall rule o'er the whole world.

And I dreamed of old England's red emblem of power,
Of Austria's Eagles where Alpine Clouds lower;
The flag of the Russias growled deep like their bear
And Germany's Ensign waved high in free air;
And France's Tri-Color was greeted with cheers;
And Erin's Green Standard was freshened with tears.
But of all nations' pennants, whatever their hue,
Far dearest to me is the Red, White and Blue!
So here's to Old Glory, the Red, White, and Blue
The emblem of justice and liberty too!
Oh! The Stars and Stripes may they never be furled
Till Freedom and Right shall rule o'er the whole world.

JUDGE JOHN J. McDONOUGH

JOHN J. DORAN
Medal of Honor Recipient

Profile

John J. Doran was the first born to Irish immigrant parents, Matthew G. and Elizabeth Watters Doran, in 1864. Born in Charlestown, Massachusetts, where his father worked at the Naval Shipyard, his playground was Bunker Hill. Before the births of any of six his siblings, the family moved to Fall River and lived near South Park in Saint Louis Parish after Lee surrendered in the Civil War. Doran's father went to work in Newport as an expert craftsperson while his mother stayed home tending to the growing Catholic family. After his death in the southern hemisphere in 1904, Doran's remains were returned to Fall River for burial beside his father in St. Patrick's Cemetery.

Experience

As a young man living in proximity to Newport and the visibility of Navy personnel, Doran felt the call of the sea and the urge to serve his country. He enlisted as a sailor in 1884 and trained on the ship New Hampshire for the first year. When that period was up, he reenlisted and served aboard the *Vandalla*, the Raleigh, and the *Kearsage*. He was promoted steadily and by 1892, at age twenty-eight, he volunteered for extremely dangerous duty that resulted in saving the lives of fellow sailors on the *Kearsage*.

Doran's real heroic act occurred in 1898. Off the shores of Cuba during the Spanish-American War, three warships were sent to dispatch boatloads of sailors to destroy an underwater cable back to Spain. Doran was the coxswain in the boat SS *Marblehead* and was one of six men wounded by heavy gunfire from Spaniards who were protecting the cable. Although his hip was shattered at the start of the mission, Doran hid his injury and continued to work at successfully cutting both cables. Following the encounter, Doran was given the rank of master-at-arms—the highest rank an enlisted man could achieve at the time. For his bravery, Doran was bestowed the Medal of Honor.

Education
Morgan Street School.

Skills

The raid on the Cuban port to cut the cable was anything but a surprise to the enemy, who were visibly preparing a defense. U.S. sailors could see the faces of the enemy in their rifle pits waiting for them. President Franklin D. Roosevelt and the Department of the Navy named a destroyer, the U.S.S. *Doran*, in his honor and memory.

Also of Note

Twenty years after his passing, the Fall River community honored Doran's service to his country by naming a school in his memory and honor. The John J. Doran School serves students in the Fountain and Columbia Street area as well as other elementary students from other parts of the city, as it has for nearly ninety years.

Reverend James Fogarty, pastor of the Church of Saint Louis, said during his funeral:
"The name of John J. Doran will be uttered by children of generations yet to come; yes, it will be spoken of forever."

Information gathered from *The Phillips History of Fall River* and the *Fall River Herald News*
—photo courtesy of *Wikipedia*

JAMES HOLEHOUSE
Medal of Honor Recipient

Profile
Born in Stockport, England, in 1839, James Holehouse died in 1915 in the Soldiers' Home in Chelsea, Massachusetts, and is buried in Oak Grove Cemetery.

Experience
Holehouse served in the Civil War as a Private in Company B, Seventh Massachusetts Volunteer Infantry, and was the recipient of the Congressional Medal of Honor for bravery in 1863 at the Battle of Chancellorsville at Mayre Heights in Virginia. At the time, Private Holehouse and another enlisted man advanced beyond their regiment to the crest of the hill. Colors were then advanced with the regime and the position held.

Education
Local Fall River schools.

Skills
After the Civil War, Holehouse was a loom fixer in the mills in Fall River where he lived before entering the Soldiers' Home.

Also of Note
His citation in part reads, "With conspicuous daring...the colors were brought to the summit, the regiment was advanced and the position held."

Information gathered from Find A Grave—photo courtesy of Find a Grave and *Wikipedia*

ALEXANDER MACK
Medal of Honor Recipient

Profile
Born in Rotterdam, Netherlands, in 1834 and died in New London, Connecticut, in 1907, Alexander Mack is buried in St. Patrick's Cemetery in Fall River. Mack married Margaret O'Neil and they had one son.

Experience
Mack was a sailor during the Civil War; as a Chief Boatswain while on board the U.S.S. *Brooklyn*, he was wounded by rebel gunboats in Mobile Bay on August 5, 1864, during the attack on Fort Morgan. After treatment for his wounds, he returned to his post and armed himself again. Despite heavy enemy fire Mack continued to fight, until again, wounded and totally disabled, he was finally forced to stop fighting.

Education
Attended local Fall River schools.

Skills
After his commendation, Mack was later promoted to Captain of his own ship, the U.S.S. *Top*.

Information gathered from *Wikipedia*—photo courtesy of *Wikipedia*

MICHAEL O'REGAN
Medal of Honor Recipient

Profile
Michael O'Regan was born in 1864 and died in 1933 in Fall River. He was buried in St. Patrick's Cemetery.

Experience
O'Regan fought in the Apache Wars as a member of the Eighth U.S. Cavalry and was charged with the assignment of protecting settlers in Arizona in 1868. He fought Apache raiding parties and faced sniper

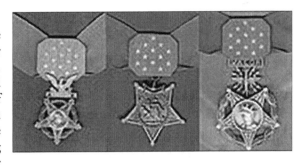

attacks and together with his small group of fifty soldiers met heavy fighting.

Although it was never determined and he probably did not realize it, most likely he fought Geronimo, the Apache chief and warrior.

Education
Local Fall River schools.

Skills
O'Regan's bravery and that of his colleagues earned thirty-four soldiers the Medal of Honor. It was the largest presentation of the medal then for "bravery in scouts and action against Indians." He was only twenty-three years old at the time.

Also of Note
In 1886, the war drew to a conclusion with the surrender of Geronimo. According to the chief, the terms of the surrender were not met and he was never allowed to return to his homeland.

Information gathered from *Wikipedia* and World Press—images courtesy of *Wikipedia*

FRANK ALLEN WILCOX
Colonel United States Army

Profile
Frank Allen Wilcox was born in 1869 and died in France in 1918 and is buried in Oak Grove Cemetery in Fall River. He was the son of Benjamin Wilcox and Lydia Howland Allen Wilcox.

Experience
Wilcox was a career military man. After graduating from West Point, he was commissioned as a first lieutenant and was stationed in Cuba during the Spanish-American War. He was promoted to the rank of major during his Philippine tour of duty. When he returned to the States he was named second in command at West Point.

The United States entered World War I in 1914 and Wilcox was again promoted and was sent to France as a lieutenant colonel to serve with General "Black Jack" Pershing and was quickly promoted to full colonel in Pershing's staff. Wilcox had previously served with Pershing and George S. Patton as they pursued Pancho Villa in Mexico.

While in France, not having fully recovered from poor health he had contracted in Mexico, Wilcox died of virulent pneumonia at the young age of forty-nine years.

Education
Local Fall River schools, B.M.C. Durfee High School in 1887, U.S. Military Academy at West Point. Wilcox was the first person from the Fall River area to graduate from the Academy.

Also of Note
Until the turn of this century, local veterans gathered periodically at the American Legion Frank Allen Wilcox Post 126 on Bedford Street in Fall River. In 1934, a monument was dedicated in his honor on Plymouth Avenue, a main north-south thoroughfare in the city.

Information gathered from *Parallel Lives*—photo courtesy of *Parallel Lives*

Heroes Who Died in the Civil War

Albro, Thomas
Alden, Frederick D.
Ashton, Thomas
Avery, James
Barnett, John
Beers, Hiram S.
Borden, Theodore F.
Borden, Wanton W.
Bowen, Samuel C.
Brightman, Abram S.
Brightman, James L.
Broadbent, Charles
Broadbent, James W.
Bullock, Jesse D.
Candey, William B.
Cantwell, Patrick
Carroll, Henry
Caswell, Elijah C.
Cockett, John
Connell, Charles
Connor, Dennis
Curran, Francis
Denny, Obediah
Donavan, Edward M.
Donovan, John
Eddy, Henry B.
Emerson, William
Evans, James
Fish, Joseph H.
Ford, John W.
French, Asa B.

Garvey, John
Gerry, Nathaniel S.
Gordon, Charles H.
Gray, Elery
Grush, Frederick A.
Grush, John C.
Haggerty, Thomas
Harding, Christopher
Harding, Christopher C.
Harding, Lawrence
Hardy, John
Harrington, Jeremiah
Haseltine, William
Hathaway, Alvin P.
Hathaway, Charles W.
Hayes, John
Hesketh, Joseph
Higgenbottom, John
Kay, Thomas
Keith, Charles B.
Kenyon, John
Lawton, Abner M.
Lawton, Andrew S.
Lawton, David
Leary, James
Lee, Thomas
Lever, John
Lewin, William H.
Lynch, James
Marlor, Kinder
Mars, Matthew

McCartan, James
McCarty, Daniel
McClusky, Thomas
McDermott, Thomas
McFarland, Thomas
McGee, John
Mitchell, Peleg
Monks, Major
Moore, John S.
Murphy, Jeremiah
Nichols, Henry W.
O'Connor, Bernard
O'Neil, James
O'Sullivan, James
Patterson, Harley W.
Peckham, Daniel H.
Peckham, William W.
Peters, John
Powers, Edward
Powers, James
Purcell, Patrick
Read, John F.
Read, Thomas

Heroes Who Died in the Civil War

Rippon, William

Rockett, George

Rooney, Hugh

Rouke, Patrick

Rowcroft, Thomas

Ryan, James

Ryan, Patrick

Sanford, Abram

Shaw, Benjamin A.

Shay, Cornelius

Shay, Timothy

Shepard, Joseph

Shirce, Joseph

Shurtleff, John W.

Smith, Thomas

Smith, William H.

Snow, George E.

Storm, Louis

Sullivan, Timothy

Tolley, Peleg N.

Uncles, William

Wallace, Martin

Wallace, Thomas

Wardell, George

Warhurst, William

Weedon, Welcome

Welch, Frank

West, Edward P.

Weysser, Charles W.

Williamson, Joseph

Willman, John A.

Wordell, Henry H.

Wright, Ellington L.

Wynn, Hugh

Information gathered from Historical Data Systems-images courtesy of *Wikipedia*

Heroes Who Died in the Spanish American War

Bannister, William

Borden, Charles

Carbory, Philip

Coffey, Jeremiah

Cook, Alvin

Corcoran, Stephen

Daley, Joseph

Doran, John J.

Durand, Phillip

French, Lynward

Garvins, Frank

Gavigan, Thomas

Hart, Charles A.

Higgins, James

Lavoie, Alex

Neilan, Michael J.

O'Brien, Charles W.

O'Hearne, Richard

Ploude, Edward

Reed, Ally

Reynolds, Charles

Robeson, John F.

Shea, Dennis

Smith, Frederick

Information gathered from City of Fall River Veterans Affairs: Ray Hague—images courtesy of *Wikipedia*

Heroes Who Died in World War I

Ainsworth, Herbert E

Aitken, Herbert L.

Albro, Arthur Raymond

Allison, James
(British Forces)

Alves, Andrew

Amaral, Mariano J.

Anderson, Peter Francis

Augustus, Joseph

Bastile, Henry Aloysius

Bearsdell, Herbert
(Canadian Infantry)

Bernier, Ovila

Blair, Andrew C.

Bolton, Harrry

Borden, Robert R.

Botelho, John

Botelho, Joseph M.

Bouchard, Alfred

Bowden, James A.

Briggs, Thomas
(Canadian Infantry)

Byron, Walter A.

Campbell, Robert
(British Army)

Canuel, Fred D.

Carabine, Thomas Francis

Caya, Alfred S.

Chefetz, Harry

Conn, George Irving

Connelly, John T.

Cook, Chester Hall

Cournoyer, Alphonse

Crowley, Jeremiah Francis

Cullen, John Patrick

Culligan, Patrick W.

Darcy, Thomas, Jr.
(Canadian Infantry)

Daudelin, Omer

Davis, Andrew L.

Davis, Frederick Joseph

Delisle, Fred

Deschenes, R. (Canadian
Overseas Forces)

Desmarias, Joseph N.

Desrochers, Rodolph

Devine, John Thomas, Jr.

Donabedian, Krikos S.

Donald, Alexander

Dooley, Henry

Duck, Henry

Dumont, Alphonse

Earle, Amos Everett

Elzear, Joseph A.

Farland, Alfred

Farrar, Joseph

Ferland, Alfred

Ferry, John J.

Ferry, Robert
(British Ex. Force)

Fitzpatrick, William

France, Louis

Francis, Joseph

Franklin, Irving

Furtado, Henry Perry

Gagnon, Alexander George

Gagnon, Joseph Fred

Galvin, Ella May-Yeomanette
(Naval Reserve Forces *)

Garon, Henry P.

Gettings, Carroll G.

Giblin, George

Gierman, Arthur

Gifford, Frederick O.

Gignac, Aime

Goodwin, Frank (Canadian)

Griffin, Martin G.

Hagensen, Carl Hans Christian

Hall, John
(British Ex. Forces)

Halpen, Charles E.

Information gathered from City of Fall River Veteran Affairs Office-Ray Hague
—photos courtesy of *Wikipedia* and Bernard A.G. Taradash

Heroes Who Died in World War I

Hanley, John W.

Harrington, Michael Matthews

Higgins, James Patrick

Hinchcliffe, Joseph E.
(Canadian Overseas Force)

Hockenbull, Harold
(Canadian "Black Watch")

Hornby, William Henry

Horsfall, George Harold

Johnson, James
(British Army)

Jokeem, Manuel

Jones, H.
(Canadian Ex. Forces)

Jones, Percy
(Canadian Infantry)

Kelly, Christopher Cantwell

Kelly, Ignatius John, Jr.

Krasnow, Samuel

Laliberte, Edmond J.

Leary, Timothy J.

LePage, Jean B.
(Canadian Army)

LePou, Harry

Levesque, Arthur

Levesque, Joseph

Loxley, Edward
(British Ex. Forces)

Mailloux, Simeon

Malone, (Milim) Antone

Manchester, Russell Brace

Marsden, Arthur Osborn

May, James Charles

Maynard, Albert C.

McArthur, Richard Grey

McCann, Charles Anthony

McCarville, John

McCoy, John

McCreery, William Henry

McGrath, Francis J.

McMahon, John M.
(note: see James Moore)

McNamara, Thomas F.

Merrill, Edward Stoddard

Milotte, Theodore

Monahan, James Raymond

Moore, James
(see John M. McMahon)

Moreau, William

Morris, William Sarsfield

Morris, James

Mosa, Adib

Mullins, Peter

Mullins, William M.

Nadeau, Etienne, Jr.

Nadeau, Joseph
(Canadian Ex. Forces)

Newman, Harold

Noonan, Henry Lee

O'Grady, John Percy

Olivera, Manuel

Orr, William
(Canadian Infantry)

O'Rourke, Simon Anthony

Petterson, Henry M.

Pecheca, Joseph

Pelletier, Florian

Perry, George H.

Perry, Manuel

Pollan, John

Reardon, Timothy Patrick

Regean, Robert F. (Regan)

Renaud, Pierre

Reuss, Louis Joseph

Reynolds, Patrick James

Richmond, Arthur D.

Roberts, George
(British Ex. Forces)

Robinson, Alfred, Jr.

Robinson, Arthur
(Canadian Infantry)

Rockett, Edward Francis

Rockett, Patrick Lewis, Jr.

Rodrigues, Aliva

Rodrigues, John

Rosa, Louis

Rosenberg, Jacob

Ruthman, Orville H.

Ryder, Herman Kenneth

St. Amand, Napoleon J.

Shallow, Jeremiah Charles

Information gathered from City of Fall River Veteran Affairs Office-Ray Hague
—photos courtesy of *Wikipedia* and Bernard A.G. Taradash

Heroes Who Died in World War I

Shaw, Chester A.

Shay, Charles Francis Joseph

Shea, Timothy Joseph

Shea, William F.

Sheldon, John H.

Shelmerdine, Albert

Slup, Morris

Smeaton, William

Smith, Luger Eugene

Smithies, Robert
(British Ex. Forces)

Souza, Antone

Stafford, James F.

Stafford, John F.
(Lt. Royal Air Force)

Stefanik, Albert

Storey, Daniel Dewey

Stinziano, James

Stratton, William A.

Sunderland, Samuel

Sylvia, Anthony Francis, Jr.

Synnott, Terrance

Tallant, John Francis

Tanguay, Armory A.

Tattersall, Herny Earl

Tavares, John Botelho

Taylor, Thomas H.

Thivierge, John

Thornley, George Henry

Tobin, Thomas Aloysius

Tremblay, Joseph Auguste

Trembley, Wilfred

Turcott, George L.

Turner, William George

Wadington, Elmer H.

Wall, William Thomas

Walsh, Earle G.

Walsh, Martin Anthony

Ward, Herbert Victor

Waring, Fred

Weinstein, George

Wheeler, Warren F.

Whittaker, Fred
(British Ex. Forces)

Whittaker, Samuel J.

White, George Ellis
(British Ex. Forces)

Whittle, Ernest Clifford

Wilcox, Frank A.

Wilkinson, Martin A.
(Welsh Infantry)

Williams, Ellis E.

Williams, William

Wiseman, Edward Jerome

* Galvin-Only Woman Listed

Information gathered from City of Fall River Veteran Affairs Office-Ray Hague
—photos courtesy of *Wikipedia* and Bernard A.G. Taradash

1850-1925

Others with Ties*

———•◆•———

Retirement at sixty-five is ridiculous.

When I was sixty-five I still had pimples.

———•◆•———

GEORGE BURNS

* Despite not having attended school in Fall River,
the following individuals in the category are so
closely associated with Fall River that they
deserve inclusion in this book.

NAP LAJOIE
Hall of Fame/Professional Baseball Player

Profile
Nap Lajoie was born in Woonsocket, Rhode Island, in 1893 to Jean Baptiste and Celina Guertin Lajoie and died in Daytona Beach, Florida, in 1959. He was one of eight children.

Experience
Lajoie played a season for the Fall River Indians before beginning his 21-year major league career with the Philadelphia Nationals. He was often favorably compared to Ty Cobb.

In 1902, Lajoie and several other National League players jumped ship to the startup American League. Lajoie played for Connie Mack's Athletics and set the all-time single-season mark of .426 for the highest batting average. He moved to Cleveland and joined the Broncos. His career statistics included a .338 batting average, 3,252 hits, 1,504 runs scored, and 83 home runs. Lajoie managed 700 games with a 377-309 won-loss record. He led the majors with a batting average of .376 for his second consecutive batting title.

Lajoie retired in 1916 from the Philadelphia Athletics as a player but joined the International League as a manager and player and at age forty-two led the league in batting. He retired completely from baseball in 1918.

Education
He received little formal education.

Skills
As a child, Lajoie was forced to support the family upon the premature death of his father. He worked in a textile mill and became a horse and buggy taxi driver.

He also served as the team manager of the Broncos after being the team Captain and Field Manager and the team name was changed to the "Naps." In 1904, he received a suspension after he spat chewing tobacco juice in the eye of an umpire.

Also of Note
Lajoie was elected a member of the Baseball Hall of Fame in 1937.

Information gathered from *Wikipedia* and the *Fall River Herald News*—photo courtesy of *Greater Fall River Baseball*

LEO LARRIVEE
1924 Paris Olympic Track Star

Profile
Born in Fall River in 1903 to Cyril and Anna B. Larrivee, he died in an auto accident in 1928.

Experience
Although Larrivee did not attend school in Fall River, he was born here and was considered one of our own. The little man from New Bedford was a middle distance runner for both College of the Holy Cross and the Boston Athletic Association. The speed merchant from the North End of the Whaling City was hailed by most as he reached the pinnacle of the track world. Although he failed to qualify for the Olympic team in the 1,500 meters (the mile), he came back to earn a spot on the team in the 3,000 meters. His fastest mile was a record-breaking 4:21.8 at the intercollegiate championship at the Manhattan Games in New York; his fastest two-mile was 8:47 in 1924.

Education
Larrivee attended Sacred Heart School in New Bedford and graduated from New Bedford High School before graduating cum laude from College of the Holy Cross after attending Assumption College. Larrivee was studying medicine at Loyola in Chicago when he was killed before receiving his degree.

Also of Note
He was posthumously inducted into the Holy Cross Sports Hall of Fame in 1985. Larrivee was heralded as the best middle distance runner in the college world in 1924. The Leo Larrivee Two-Mile Race at the annual Knights of Columbus Track Meet was held yearly in the old Boston Garden.

Information gathered from College of the Holy Cross—photo courtesy of College of the Holy Cross

DANIEL FRANCIS MURPHY
Professional Baseball Player

Profile
Born in Philadelphia in 1876, Daniel Francis Murphy and his family moved to New England. He joined the Fall River team in the New England League at age twenty. He died in Jersey City, New Jersey, in 1955, and is buried in Norwich, Connecticut.

Experience
Murphy knew how to impress his boss on the first day of work, although he showed up late and with no uniform or shoes. He was playing at Fenway and his manager was none other than the legendary Connie Mack. Mack found him equipment, albeit the shoes were way too big. That did not affect his hitting performance as he went six for six with a grand slam home run off the great Cy Young of the Red Sox. Murphy played for fifteen years, starting in 1900 with the New York Giants and then eleven years with the Philadelphia Phillies and his final two years with Tip-Tops.

Education
There is no record of Murphy attending any schools.

Skills
His batting average was .289 with over 700 runs-batted-in. His fielding percentage over his career was 955. He played in more than 1,450 games, primarily in the out-field.

Also of Note
Although not born or educated in Fall River, Murphy played sandlot baseball in the city after his parents had moved from Philadelphia. He was considered one of the best and most powerful hitters in baseball at the time.

Information gathered from *Greater Fall River Baseball*—photo courtesy of *Greater Fall River Baseball*

1850-1925
Professional

———◆◆◆———

The measure of success is not whether

you have a tough problem to deal with,

but whether it is the same problem

you had last year.

———◆◆◆———

John Foster Dulles

HONORABLE EDWARD F. HANIFY
Youngest Massachusetts Justice Ever Appointed

Profile
Edward F. Hanify was born in Fall River in 1881 to Michael and Elizabeth Brennan Hanify. He married Mary Elizabeth Brodkord and they had three children. (Edward B. Hanify, his oldest child and first of three sons, is also highlighted in this book.) Hanify died in 1954 at age seventy-three at New England Baptist Hospital, after surgery for a stomach ailment.

Experience
After attending Harvard Law School, Hanify returned to Fall River and practiced law with Thomas F. Higgins in the firm of Higgins and Hanify. The partnership was dissolved after Higgins was elected Mayor of Fall River and Hanify joined his administration as city solicitor for one year. He was appointed as a Second District Court Judge in 1912 at age thirty-one, named by Governor Foss to replace Judge John J. McDonough (also cited herein) as one of the youngest judges ever named to a judgeship in Massachusetts.

The Judge spent forty-two years on the bench, the last twenty-five as a Massachusetts Superior Court justice.

Education
Fall River schools, B.M.C. Durfee High School, College of the Holy Cross (1904) and Harvard Law. An Honorary Doctorate of Laws from Holy Cross was bestowed on him in 1919.

Skills
Considered a true humanitarian by fellow officers of the court as much as a learned jurist, on one occasion while hearing an eviction case in Fall River, he said: "If certain members of the local bar continue to assist heartless landlords in doing their dirty work in the eviction of poor families, I shall tender my resignation and leave to a cold-blooded judge the task of assisting these lawyers and landlords."

Also of Note
Judge Hanify was a trustee for over a decade of the Fall River Public Library.

Information gathered from College of the Holy Cross—photo courtesy of College of the Holy Cross

JUDGE JOHN J. McDONOUGH
First Irish Catholic Judge in District Court

Profile
John J. McDonough was born in Fall River in 1857 to Ellen Hays and Michael McDonough. He had two brothers, both of whom were priests and a sister who became a nun. He married Elizabeth McCarthy and they had five children and six grandchildren. In 1912, he died after a bout with pneumonia and is buried in St. Patrick's Cemetery in Fall River.

Experience
Judge McDonough was the presiding justice in the District Court from 1893 until his death in 1912.

On May 22, 1905, the first Catholic judge in Fall River District Court began his campaign against "Jew-Baiting." McDonough pronounced from the bench that no Jews living in Fall River should be persecuted and he imposed heavy sentences on those brought before him. One such person was found guilty of assault and battery and sentenced to six months in jail.

Another incident occurred "out the Globe" where a Jewish peddler and rag man was harassed by a group of young thugs. "I am going to stop the persecution of this much persecuted race if I can. These boys are fined $25 each," ordered the judge. The judge ordered their parents to "take those boys home, get a good strap and give them a good thrashing."

Education
McDonough attended local Fall River schools and Canadian Seminary of St. Sulpice, where he studied for the priesthood. However, he became a lawyer, graduating from the College of the Holy Cross and Boston University Law School. He was awarded an Honorary Law Degree from College of the Holy Cross—a rare instance of an undergraduate degree recipient being awarded an honorary doctorate.

Skills
Not only did McDonough practice law and sit on the bench as a distinguished jurist, he also was a member of the Massachusetts House of Representatives for two terms and a newspaper editor for the *Fall River Herald* and the *Catholic Advocate*.

Also of Note
Fall River honored "the fearless and upright" Judge McDonough by naming an elementary school after him. The McDonough School, dedicated in 1911, was located on Williams Street in the section of the city called "Below the Hill," but is now closed.

A vocal advocate for the "old sod", McDonough was called upon often as a speaker and never failed to rail against the British and to sympathize with Ireland and the Irish. Ironically, he had never laid foot on his ancestors' native Ireland.

Information gathered from *Victorian Vistas 1901-1911* and his grandson, John A. McDonough
—photo courtesy of his family and image courtesy of *Victorian Vistas*

JUDGE JAMES MADISON MORTON
Supreme Judicial Court of Massachusetts

Profile
Born in Fairhaven in 1837, James Madison Morton was the son of James M. and Sarah (Tobey) Morton. He died in Fall River in 1923 and is buried in Oak Grove Cemetery. He was the brother of Anne Morton Smith.

Experience
Morton joined John S. Brayton in the practice of law until Brayton moved on to banking and industrial activities. Morton was joined by Andrew J. Jennings, an attorney who played a significant role in the Borden murder trial. He was the city solicitor from 1864 to 1867.

Morton had practiced law in Fall River for nearly thirty years when he was appointed Associate Justice of the Supreme Judicial Court by Governor Brackett. From age fifty-three to seventy-six he served as Associate, then Senior Associate. In 1913, Judge Morton retired from the bench and spent his remaining decade in Fall River. At the Massachusetts Constitution Convention in 1919 he was elected to debate with fellow conventioneers the fundamental law. Judge Morton was eighty years old at the time.

Education
Fall River High School, Brown University and Harvard Law School.

Skills
As well as being highly regarded as both an attorney and jurist, Judge Morton was an active member of the local Unitarian Society and an avid outdoorsman. He made frequent trips to fish for trout and salmon and met fellow anglers on the banks of the North Watuppa Pond before it was closed to recreational activity.

Also of Note
To honor Judge Morton, Fall River named a junior high school after him—James Madison Morton Junior High. (The school, now a middle school, is where Judge Morton's great-great granddaughter Anne Dawson Brown recently taught math and reclaimed the portrait of her great-great grandfather. It was on its way to the Fall River landfill during demolition of the old school.) It is also where many listed in this book were educated. A new, modern school has been constructed on President Avenue and North Main Street (see above from North Main Street side) where his portrait (restored by his family) again hangs.

Information gathered from *The Philips History of Fall River* and W. Hugh M. Morton
—photo courtesy of Atty. W. Hugh M. Morton

JUDGE JAMES MADISON MORTON, JR.
Circuit Judge of the United States Court of Appeals

Profile
James Madison Morton, Jr. was born in 1869, died in 1940 in Fall River and is buried with his parents in Oak Grove Cemetery. Son of Judge James Madison Morton and Nancy Brayton Morton, he was the father of four children: James, Sally, Brayton and Special Justice Hugh Morton of the Fall River Second District Court.

Experience
Morton practiced law in Fall River from 1894 to 1912. He was in partnership with both Andrew J. Jennings and John S. Brayton.

Judge Morton, like his father, was a Federal Judge on the United States District Court for the District of Massachusetts and confirmed by the United States Senate only three days after he was appointed by President William H. Taft, who was a City of Fall River guest during the Cotton Centennial in 1911. Judge Morton and his father may have been the first and only father and son federal judges sitting on the bench then.

President Herbert Hoover nominated Morton for elevation to a seat on the United States Court of Appeals for the First Circuit. Within a month he had been confirmed again by the Senate. He achieved senior status in 1939, serving in that capacity until his death in 1940 in Fall River.

Education
Fall River schools, Harvard College 1891 and Harvard Law School 1894.

Information gathered from *Wikipedia* and Atty. W. Hugh M. Morton—photo courtesy of Atty. W. Hugh M. Morton

JUDGE FRANK M. SILVIA
First Portuguese-American Judge
District Court

Profile
Born in 1882 in Fall River, Frank M. Silvia died in his home in 1948 and was buried in St. Patrick's Cemetery. Son of Frank M. and Maria Dutra Silvia, Silvia was the spouse of Eda A. Clorite, brother to seven siblings including Catherine, the city's first Portuguese-American School principal and Monsignor John Silvia. Father to three sons and a daughter, he was brought up "Below the Hill" on Division Street. His father was the acknowledged lay leader of Fall River's first generation Portuguese ethnics and was the essential contributor in the development of Santo Christo Parish.

Experience
After dropping out of high school due to the untimely passing of his father, Silvia's first job was at the Globe Street Railway as an office assistant. He was a top trial lawyer and Vice Consul for Portugal before being named a Second District Court Judge by then-Governor Calvin Coolidge in 1920.

Education
Local Fall River schools, B.M.C. Durfee High School, Fall River Law School and admitted to the Massachusetts Bar in 1911.

Skills
Judge Silvia served as President of the Fall River Bar Association and the local Chamber of Commerce. He was a founder of the Fall River Trust Company and the Portuguese-American Civic League. He was also chair of the Fall River Draft Board during World War I and World War II.

Also of Note
An elementary school in Fall River located on Meridian Street in the North End is named in honor of Judge Silvia. He was the first Portuguese-American to earn that distinction. Judge Silvia was probably the first Portuguese-American Judge in Massachusetts and perhaps in the United States.

Information gathered from Dr. Philip T. Silvia, Jr., who is also highlighted herein—photo courtesy of *Victorian Vistas*

DR. PHILEMON EDWARDS TRUESDALE
Physician/Pioneer Surgeon

Profile
Born in Quebec, Canada, in 1874, Philemon Edwards Trues-
dale was one of five children. At age five, his family settled in the
French-speaking Flint section of Fall River. Truesdale was married to
Minna Dickinson and they had three sons and four daugh-
ters and twenty-nine grandchildren. He died in 1945.

Experience
After graduating from medical school, the young physician
concentrated his interest in surgery and founded a private
surgical hospital in Fall River at the corner of Winter and
Pine Streets in 1905. In 1910, he built Highland Hospital
and less than four years later established Truesdale Clinic (a first of its kind group practice
in Fall River) on Rock Street. In 1915, Highland Hospital became public and was renamed
Truesdale Hospital. The hospital merged with Union Hospital and later the joint facility was
named Charlton Hospital. Today, the building shown above is used as an apartment complex.

Truesdale was fortunate to have his name affiliated with the names of Charlton (also highlighted in this book) and McHenry. Woolworth cofounder and Fall River and Westport resident,
Earle Perry Charlton was a successful merchant who single-handedly contributed $500,000 in
1927 to create the Charlton Surgical Wing at the hospital in appreciation for the treatment
Dr. Truesdale and his staff gave to his son, Perry, who was saved after the youngster's appendix
ruptured and peritonitis set in.

Perhaps Truesdale's most well-known surgery involved Alyce Jane McHenry, a ten-year-old
from Omaha who was born with diaphragmatic hernia (an upside down stomach). During her
1,500-mile train trip to Fall River, she was accorded celebrity status and called "Sunshine" by
the national press who descended upon Truesdale Hospital in 1935. More than forty medical
professionals observed Truesdale operate in the Charlton operating room. Two hours later, the
successful surgery gave the little girl a new life and *Time* Magazine put Alyce on its March 11
cover. The event caused angst for Truesdale, as numerous peers viewed the attendant publicity
as a violation of his oath.

Education
Local Fall River schools, B.M.C. Durfee High School 1894, Harvard Medical School 1898.
He was one of the founding members of the American College of Surgeons.

Skills
Dr. Truesdale's surgical expertise with hernias developed in World War I when he discovered
the new surgical technique while serving in France. During the war, he spent the majority of
the time as a battlefield surgeon and rose to the rank of major.

Not only was he a great surgeon, Dr. Truesdale was also a pioneer of animated film depicting
surgery for a diaphragmatic hernia. This led to motion pictures being used as medical teaching
aids and Truesdale being awarded a gold medal from the American Medical Association.

Information gathered from Truesdale Clinic, *Charlton Health System: Our Story* and Coulter Press/The Item
—photos courtesy of *SouthCoast Health Systems: Our Story*

1850-1925

Sports

———◆———

God's Country

Who shares his life's pure pleasures,

And walks the honest road,

Who trades with heaping measures,

And lifts his brother's load,

Who turns the wrong down bluntly,

And lends the right a hand,

He dwells in God's own country,

He tills the Holy Land.

———◆———

Louis F. Benson

BEN BOWCOCK
Professional Baseball Player

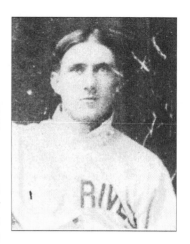

Profile
Ben Bowcock was born in Fall River in 1879 and died in 1961. He married Helen Drislan and they had four children, two boys and two girls.

Experience
Scouting reports at the time called Bowcock an excellent fielder, accomplished hitter and speedy base runner. Those accolades were enough for the St. Louis Browns to acquire him in 1903. The right-handed hitter's game faltered during his first major league season. He played 14 games on the road and hit a more than respectable .320 average with one home run, but he became homesick for Fall River.

While his batting was more than proficient, his fielding was insufficient—he made seven errors in 61 games as a second baseman. The infielder preferred being at home, blasting the throwing of the New England League pitchers. He tried another stint, this time with Seattle in the Pacific Coast League (where years later another Fall River favorite son, Russ Gibson, would play). The second attempt for Bowcock ended like the first and he was back home in Fall River.

Education
Local Fall River schools and B.M.C. Durfee High School.

Also of Note
Being homesick seemed common among professional players of the era. See Art Butler.

Information gathered from *Wikipedia*, Baseball Almanac and *Greater Fall River Baseball*
—photo courtesy of *Greater Fall River Baseball*

CHARLES BUFFINTON
Professional Baseball Player

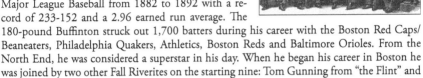

Profile
Born in Fall River in 1861, Charles Buffinton died suddenly at the young age of forty-six in 1907 from heart disease while serving as an executive at Bowenville Coal Company on the Taunton River at the base of President Avenue. He is buried in Oak Grove Cemetery in Fall River.

Experience
Buffinton batted and threw right-handed in American Major League Baseball from 1882 to 1892 with a record of 233-152 and a 2.96 earned run average. The 180-pound Buffinton struck out 1,700 batters during his career with the Boston Red Caps/Beaneaters, Philadelphia Quakers, Athletics, Boston Reds and Baltimore Orioles. From the North End, he was considered a superstar in his day. When he began his career in Boston he was joined by two other Fall Riverites on the starting nine: Tom Gunning from "the Flint" and Jim Manning from "up the Globe." Both are also highlighted in this book.

Buffinton recorded more career victories (231) than Hall of Fame pitchers Sandy Koufax, Bob Lemon and Dizzy Dean among others, yet he has never been inducted into the Baseball Hall of Fame by the Veterans Committee. The speedy right-hander with the exploding curve ball won 20 or more games in 7 of 11 seasons in the big leagues. In 1884, with his pal Tom Gunning behind the plate, he won 47 games. He pitched a total of 3,404 innings over eleven years and one year with Philadelphia he recorded a 1.91 ERA.

Considered by many as the first "impossible dream" year, 1883 provided Boston with its first title thanks in part to Buffinton's 24-game win season. After his stint in Maryland and in the City of Brotherly Love, Buffinton regained his skills in Boston and finished 1891 with a 28-9 record.

Rather than take a mid-season pay cut, Buffinton retired in 1892. In 1893, the distance between the mound and plate increased from 50 to 60 feet, 6 inches, and ended his chances of returning.

Education
Local Fall River schools. Despite his lack of higher education, he was one of the most highly paid players in the early days of professional baseball.

Skills
His records include: ERA, top 5 three times; wins, top 5 four times; winning percentage, led league once (1891) and top 5 four times; shutout, top 5 four times; strike outs, top 5 six times and strike outs to walk ratio, top 5 five times.

Also of Note
He was also the playing manager of the Athletics in 1890.

How does one city at one time produce three major league ball players on the same team? The *Boston Herald* had the answer: **"There must be something in the air in Fall River."**

Information gathered from *Wikipedia* and *Greater Fall River Baseball*—photo courtesy of *Greater Fall River Baseball*

ARTIE BUTLER
Professional Baseball Player

Profile

Artie Butler was a lifelong Fall River resident except for his stint in the major leagues. Butler was born in Fall River in 1897, the son of William and Olympe Bouthillier. He changed his name for his baseball career after playing for Border City in the North End League in North Park (on the lower field near the fire station). He married Laura Dumas. He died in 1984 and is buried in the Notre Dame Cemetery in Fall River.

Experience

Butler played six seasons in the majors in a total of 454 games and a lifetime batting average of .241. Butler played every infield position except first, pitcher and catcher. He was also used in the outfield and had 54 stolen bases.

Butler began his career with the Fall River team and was sold to the Boston Braves in 1911 in what then was a controversial trade. Fall River wanted the return of Butler or more money for his services by the Braves. The appeal failed and Butler remained with Boston in the National League until he was traded to the Pittsburgh Pirates. He remained with them until 1914 when he joined the St. Louis Cardinals. There, Butler became friendly with as well as the roommate of the great Rogers Hornsby. Butler was not a great hitter, but three of his most memorable moments are when he broke up a no-hitter by Grover Cleveland Alexander; his five-hit day against the Braves, and finally, driving home Wagner with the winning run against the Cardinals. After that, he returned to the hometown he loved and remained there until his long life ended at age ninety-six.

Education

Local Fall River schools.

Also of Note

When asked what town he liked the best, Butler answered, "I liked Milwaukee. I liked Albany, but I liked Fall River the most. That was my weakness in baseball: homesickness. When I used to come up from Providence, the smell of the Taunton River was like cologne to me."

A major thrill, according to Butler, was receiving a note from President Ronald W. Reagan on his 94th birthday, congratulating him on being the oldest living baseball player.

Information gathered from *Greater Fall River Baseball*—photo courtesy of *Greater Fall River Baseball*

TOM CAHILL
Professional Baseball Player

Profile
Tom Cahill was born in 1868 and died at age twenty-six and is buried in St. John's Cemetery in Fall River. He was the son of Irish immigrants. His father, Thomas, was a laborer.

Experience
Cahill began his baseball career at nineteen, playing in Worcester while attending College of the Holy Cross. He graduated to the majors in 1891 and played only one season for the Louisville Colonels. His batting average that season was .253 with 44 runs batted in and 38 stolen bases. Primarily a catcher, the rugged former Corky Row resident played multiple positions in the infield and outfield and recorded a fielding percentage of .930. He was tied for first in the majors for stolen bases and second in the league in doubles.

Education
Local Fall River schools, Fall River High School, College of the Holy Cross and the University of Pennsylvania School of Medicine. He was one of the first college players ever to play in the majors.

Also of Note
Cahill continued his interest in baseball while attending medical school and played and managed the Scranton Indians. The same year he signed on as a football coach at University of Pennsylvania. He died on Christmas Day at the young age of twenty-six, never to practice medicine.

ANTHONY "TONY" CUSICK
Professional Baseball Player

Profile
Born in Fall River in 1860, Anthony "Tony" Cusick died in 1929 serving as a police officer in the windy city of Chicago.

Experience
Cusick played professional ball for four years with the Phillies. The 190-pound utility player threw and batted right and signed on at age 24. Tony played in 95 games, most behind the plate over four years and had a .220 lifetime batting average and an .849 fielding average.

Education
Local Fall River schools.

Also of Note
Cusick was a baseball protege of police officer Bart Shea, who sent five of his Fall River players to the big leagues. Cusick's baseball card is considered to be very rare.

Information gathered from *Wikipedia, Baseball Almanac* and *Greater Fall River Baseball*
—photo courtesy of *Greater Fall River Baseball*

TOM DROHAN
Professional Baseball Player

Profile
Tom Drohan was born in 1887 in Fall River and died in 1926 in Kewanee, Illinois. He worked as a firefighter in Illinois.

Experience
Drohan's major league baseball career was perhaps the briefest of any of the many from the Spindle City. He pitched one season for the Washington Senators in 1913 after a five-year stint in the minors. Drohan hit and threw right-handed. He only pitched in two big league games and suffered with a 9.00 ERA as a result of the two runs he gave up in his two innings pitched. During his early days in the minors, especially in 1911 and the following season with Kewanee in the Central Division, he combined for a 43-16 record.

Education
Local Fall River schools.

Also of Note
Drohan returned to the minor leagues and ended his professional days in 1917. He lived out his life in Kewanee, the site of his glory days.

JEAN DUBUC
Professional Baseball Player

Profile
Born in Vermont in 1888, Jean Dubuc died in Fort Myers, Florida, in 1958.

Experience
"Chauncey" Dubuc began his major league career with Cincinnati in 1908 after an outstanding pitching experience at South Bend, Indiana, where he suffered only one defeat in three varsity seasons. He threw 1,441 innings over nine years with a 3.04 ERA and 428 strikeouts. His won-loss record was 85-75 over his career with Detroit, Boston (for its 1918 Pennant drive), the New York Giants and Cincy.

Dubuc spent his youth in Fall River playing ball in South Park while his dad helped build St. Anne's Church. After his playing days, Ty Cobb's roommate was hailed for his selection of young talent as a baseball scout. His picks included Hank Greenberg and Bernie Tebbetts. After some time as a minor league manager, he went to Detroit as a coach and then returned to coach the men at Brown University in Providence, Rhode Island.

Education
Local Fall River schools, B.M.C. Durfee High School and the University of Notre Dame.

Also of Note
At the conclusion of his scouting days, Dubuc took his talents to another sport and became one of the fathers of hockey in southern New England. He managed the Providence Reds for twelve successful playoff years in the American Hockey League.

Information gathered from *Wikipedia* and *Greater Fall River Baseball*—photo courtesy of *Greater Fall River Baseball*

FRANCIS J. FENNELLY
Professional Baseball Player

Profile
Francis J. Fennelly was born in Fall River in 1860 and died at his home there in 1920 of a heart attack. Fennelly was married to Julia and lived in Sacred Heart Parish his entire life. They had a son, Daniel Fennelly, who became a physician.

Experience
Fennelly played seven years in the majors starting in 1884. He was a shortstop when he joined Washington in his rookie year, but the team disbanded before the season ended and he was bought by Cincinnati for $3,500. Fennelly's value was in no doubt—he became the field captain for the team in 1885. His future leadership qualities were evident at an early age.

Education
Local Fall River schools.

Skills
Fennelly's lifetime batting average was .257 over 786 games and 3042 at bats. He threw and hit right-handed.

Also of Note
After his brilliant playing days were cut short by a leg injury, Fennelly chose politics as his next career. He was elected to the Massachusetts House of Representatives from Fall River for 4 terms, where he became most identified with the pro-labor movement.

TOM GUNNING, MD
Professional Baseball Player

Profile
Tom Gunning was born in 1862, the son of Mary Reynolds and Robert Gunning and he had a sister. He was the spouse of Ida Corcoran and they had a son, Father Thomas, and daughter. He died in 1931 on St. Patrick's Day.

Experience
While in Fall River, Gunning was the battery mate for hard-throwing Charlie Buffinton. He played for the Flints and professionally for the Red Sox from 1884 to 1886 before moving to the Philly's for his final 3 years.

Education
Fall River High School, College of the Holy Cross, Boston College and Pennsylvania State Medical School.

Skills
His lifetime batting average was .205 over 146 games and 537 at bats. He threw and batted right-handed.

Also of Note
He was a coach of the College of the Holy Cross baseball team after his final year in 1889 with Philadelphia. After his baseball career, Gunning returned to his native city as so many young athletes did and served as a physician and Bristol County Medical Examiner.

Information gathered from *Baseball Almanac* and *Greater Fall River Baseball*
—photo courtesy of *Greater Fall River Baseball*

JOE HARRINGTON
Professional Baseball Player

Profile
Joe Harrington was born in 1889 and died in Fall River in 1933.

Experience
Harrington only played two years (72 games) of professional ball for the Boston Beaneaters.

Education
Local Fall River schools.

Skills
His lifetime average was .220 with 38 runs batted in (RBI's) and 3 home runs. His first HR came during his first major league at-bat on September 10, 1895. He was the first player to accomplish the feat. Harrington possessed a strong arm and was acknowledged as a speedy base runner. After his playing days were over, he did some local umpiring.

JIM MANNING
Professional Baseball Player

Profile
Jim Manning was born in Fall River in 1862 and died in Texas in 1929. His body lies in the North End Burial Ground in Fall River.

Experience
Manning played for Boston, Detroit and Kansas City over his five year career. An infielder, he moved from the field to the managerial ranks and front office with little difficulty. He was part of a world baseball tour and he participated in exhibition games in Asia, Australia, Egypt (next to the pyramids), Rome (in the Colosseum), and London.

Education
Local Fall River schools.

Skills
Manning threw right-handed but batted from both sides of the plate for a lifetime average of .215. As a manager he compiled a 61-73 record for Kansas City.

Also of Note
After his playing days ended in 1891, Manning's baseball career was just beginning. In 1894, he took over as field general and owner at Kansas City. He was also the architect and builder for the first major league stadium in the nation's capital. The breadth of his baseball accomplishments during his career may make him, perhaps, the only such baseball standout ever.

Information gathered from *Baseball Almanac, Wikipedia* and *Greater Fall River Baseball*
—photo courtesy of *Greater Fall River Baseball*

MIKE McDERMOTT
Professional Baseball Player

Profile
Mike McDermott was born in Fall River in 1864 and died in 1947 and is buried in St. Patrick's Cemetery. He lived in the North End of Fall River his entire life and owned McDermott's Diner with his wife, Mary. He was a member of Sacred Heart Parish.

Experience
McDermott had one of the shortest major league careers of anyone from Fall River, second only to Chris McFarland (see below). He played in only nine games in September 1889. The right-handed pitcher was a member of the Louisville Colonels.

Education
Local Fall River schools.

Skills
McDermott won only one game for the Colonels and lost eight. He suffered a 4.11 earned run average (ERA) over the 84 innings pitched. He struck out 22 and walked 34 before calling it quits and heading back to Fall River to operate the diner.

CHRIS McFARLAND
Professional Baseball Player

Profile
Born in Fall River in 1861, Chris McFarland died in New Bedford in 1918.

Experience
McFarland was twenty-two when the big leagues came calling. He pitched briefly for the Baltimore Monumentals. In 1884, McFarland saw action in only four games. He pitched in one and lost with an ERA of 15 during the three innings he threw. McFarland followed that weak performance with three games in center field and a .214 batting average.

Education
Local Fall River schools.

Information gathered from *Baseball Almanac*

ED O'NEIL
Professional Baseball Player

Profile
Ed O'Neal was born in Fall River in 1859 and died there at the young age of thirty-three from an asthma attack in 1892.

Experience
O'Neal reached the major leagues as a right-handed pitcher in 1890 with the Toledo Maumees at age thirty-one.

Education
Local Fall River schools.

Skills
O'Neal pitched right-handed in eight games, six with the Philadelphia Athletics, and played in four other games at third base and center field. He lost all eight games on the mound and finished with an ERA of 9.26 and 19 strike outs. His short-lived career also resulted in a .125 batting average.

Information gathered from Baseball Almanac, Wikipedia and Greater Fall River Baseball

WALTER "RED" TORPHY
Professional Baseball Player

Profile
Walter "Red" Torphy was born in 1891 and died in Fall River in 1980. He was married to Helen Waldron; they had no children.

Experience
After a stint as a "jack-of-all-trades" in the minor leagues, Torphy was signed with the Boston Braves in 1920 and played for one year.

Education
Local Fall River schools, B.M.C. Durfee High School.

Skills
Torphy only played in three games, the fewest of any of his Fall River fellow pros. He was the only local to play first base where he hit .200 in his 15 at bats while he had only one error.

Also of Note
North Park was his home field, where he honed his skills before seventeen years on the road. He returned home to work as a mechanic for the Eastern Massachusetts Railway Company.

Information gathered from Baseball Almanac, Wikipedia and Greater Fall River Baseball
—illustration courtesy of Greater Fall River Baseball

MARTIN CANOLE
Boxer

Profile
Martin Canole was born in 1883 in Ireland and died at age eighty-two in Fall River in 1965. He was the son of Thomas and Catherine McQueeney Canole. He is buried in St. Patrick's Cemetery.

Experience
Canole was a 5-foot, 7-inch, scrappy 130-pound Fall River teenager when he began his boxing career. He had 33 total fights, winning 19 and losing nine with five draws. He hung up his gloves in 1914 after twelve years at age thirty-one. In more than 35 percent of his fights, he scored a knockout. He fought up and down the East Coast but primarily in New England. Canole's biggest fight came in 1903 when he lost in a decision to World Lightweight Champion Jimmy Britt in only his second year in the ring.

Education
Local Fall River schools.

Skills
Not only was Canole a boxer, he also devoted time to training, managing, coaching and serving as a boxing referee over the years.

Also of Note
Canole was the business agent for the local Bartenders Union for many years.

Information gathered from St. Patrick's Cemetery, the *Fall River Herald News* and FightsRec.com
—photo courtesy of *Wikipedia*

MARTIN RILEY
Boxer

Profile
Martin Riley was the son of Michael and Catherine Cotter Riley and spouse of Margaret Frazier Fregault. Father of four sons and two daughters, he was born in 1874 and died in Fall River in 1929 and is buried in St. Patrick's Cemetery. He lived on Division Street his entire life.

Experience
Riley was an accomplished prize fighter around the turn of the century, winning 9 fights with 2 knockouts and lost 16 fights and had 1 draw. He was only knocked out once. Riley became the New England Welterweight Champion, which earned him a fight with Spike Sullivan for the World Championship.

Education
Local Fall River schools.

Skills
The 5-foot 7-1/2-inch, muscular Riley weighed in at 135 pounds for most of his pugilistic events.

After his boxing career ended, he worked for the City of Fall River until he passed away at the young age of fifty-six. He was the grandfather of the Black brothers (who also appear in this book).

Also of Note
Riley fought in New England and in Australia and was classified as a super feather-weight.

Information gathered from Michael Black and the Riley family—photo courtesy of the Black family

PETER SULLIVAN
Boxer

Profile
Peter Sullivan was born in 1885 in Ireland to Catherine Shea and Mr. Sullivan. Peter's father died at a young age, leaving his wife to raise Peter and his two sisters in Fall River.

Experience
Before his boxing career, Sullivan worked in the city mills as a doffer, a worker who removes empty spindles or bobbins from machines in a cotton or textile factory and replaces them with new ones.

Sullivan's first fight in 1901 was against another Fall River boxing legend, Martin Canole, at the Casino on Morgan Street in Fall River. He lost on points in 12 rounds but he was not one to give up quickly. His next fight was a rematch against Canole in the spring of 1902, and in this event he only lasted six rounds before Canole knocked him out.

Sullivan fought consistently over the next few years and by 1906 he was ready again to take on his Fall River nemesis in Providence, Rhode Island. On this night, Sullivan was awarded a technical knockout in round 11 of the scheduled 15 rounds. His last fight was victory number 19 in Park City, Utah, where he knocked out Nig James in round six of the 20-round bout.

Education
Local Fall River schools.

Skills
Sullivan won 19, 9 by knockout, and lost 12 with 8 classified as a draw.

Also of Note
The Fall River welterweight had the biggest fight of his twelve-year career in February, 1904, in New Bedford. He lost on points to the retired heavyweight champion John L. Sullivan in an exhibition match.

Information gathered from FightsRec.com and Box Red—photo courtesy of seamheads.com

SANFORD B. "SAMMY" WHITE
All-American Football Player
Athlete Extraordinaire

Profile
Sanford "Sammy" White was born in Fall River in 1888 to Mr. and Mrs. Charles F. H.White, who died at young ages. He married Jeanette McAusland and they had two sons and two daughters. White died of a heart attack in 1964.

Experience
While baseball was his true sports love, it was football where White made his name as an All-American. Although White did not like football, he was persuaded to try out for the Princeton Tigers football squad in 1910. He played as a substitute before becoming the starting left end on the 1911 team, leading them to an 8-0-2 record and the Big Three Championship. He was named a consensus First Team All-American in 1911. He scored every point in Princeton's 1911 victories over both Harvard and Yale.

Education
Local Fall River Schools, B.M.C. Durfee High School, Phillips Exeter Academy and graduated from Princeton University in 1912.

Skills
At Durfee he scored the most points ever in a basketball game with 90 points in 1906 over Providence English.

A fine baseball and outstanding basketball player, White was elected captain of the Princeton baseball team as a junior and led the team to a championship. While at Princeton the Fall Riverite played football, basketball, baseball and track. He even tried out for the ice hockey team.

Following his college years, White served a stint with the Aviation section, U.S. Signal Corps then began his career with International Harvester Corporation in the Midwest. He retired as secretary of the corporation in 1947.

Also of Note
A born leader, White was also president of his Princeton class and the Senior Student Council at the Ivy League school. He was voted most popular, most respected, best all-around man and the man who did the most for his class.

The *Boston Globe* led its story of the Yale game with a front page headline: "Tigers' Football Hero For President."

The New York Times reported: "He can run, White can. He followed the ball like a hound follows a fox. Ever ready to scoop it up and run all the speed in his long, lithe limbs." One sports writer opined, "football has never known a player with a 'nose for the ball' like Sammy White." Another scribe wrote that he is the "greatest athlete the institution (Princeton) has ever produced."

White is a member of the Durfee Sports Hall Of Fame.

Information gathered from *Wikipedia*—photo courtesy of Princeton University

KATHERINE HARLEY
United States Women's Open Golf Champion

Profile
Katherine Harley was the daughter of Mary and James Harley. She had a brother James and married H. Arnold Jackson. Her father was a superintendent at the American Printing Company in Fall River where her brother also worked.

Experience
Harley won her first title in 1908 representing the Fall River Country Club. She qualified 14th in a field of 32 in medal play but went on in match play to win the championship at the Chevy Chase Country Club with an impressive 6 & 5 victory over Mrs. T.H. Polhemus.

After she married Jackson, they lived in Greater Boston. In 1914, playing out of the Oakley Country Club of Watertown (the first U.S. course designed by the internationally famous Donald Ross in 1899), Harley-Jackson beat Elaine Rosenthal, one up, at the Nassau Country Club for her second title.

Education
Local Fall River schools.

Skills
Harley-Jackson won the U.S. Women's Open twice in less than ten years; only nine women have won more than two titles in the 120 years that the event has been played.

Also of Note

Boston town is famed for beans,
For literature and art;
And also in the realms of sport.
She always does her part.

The Red Sox won the pennant,
They were world champions too;
And now the Braves are in that fight
To see what they can do.

Our Ouimet is the titleist,
And Mrs. Jackson-say!
In golf and baseball also
Does Boston lead the way?

The Minute Man

Information gathered from the Fall River Country Club, U.S.G.A. and Fall River City Directory, *American Golfer* and *Golf USGA Bulletin* October 1914—photos courtesy of the USGA

JOHN "CHICK" ALBION
Professional Soccer Player

Profile
John "Chick" Albion was born in Fall River in 1890, but where and when he died remains unknown.

Experience
By 1915, Albion was playing professional soccer in his hometown for the Fall River Rovers of the New England League. In 1916, the goalie helped take the Rovers to the National Challenge Cup Finals against Bethlehem Steel F.C. The next two years saw the same two teams in the Cup finals again, each winning one, but the Steelers took the best two out of three.

From 1921 to 1922, Albion took over as the back stopper for the newly created Fall River United and maintained a 2.38 goals against average (gaa).

Education
Local Fall River schools.

Also of Note
In 1922, Sam Mark (also highlighted in this book) acquired the Fall River United team with Albion as a member and the team was renamed the Marksmen.

Information gathered from Wikipedia

FRANK BOOTH
Professional Soccer Player

Profile
Frank Booth was born in 1887 and died in 1955 in Fall River.

Experience
Playing with his pal Chick Albion, Frank Booth was a member of both the Rovers and United/Marksmen from 1910 to 1922. He participated in the three Challenge Cup matches against Bethlehem Steel as a right full back for the Rovers.

Education
Local Fall River schools.

Also of Note
Booth retired from the Senior League at age 35 with 20 games played at that level.

Information gathered from Wikipedia—photo courtesy of Wikipedia

THOMAS SWORDS
Professional Soccer Player

Profile
Born in 1886, Thomas Swords died in Fall River in 1953 and is buried in St. Patrick's Cemetery. Son of Thomas and Jane Swords, he was married to Ann Worden.

Experience
Swords dominated the local soccer scene in the early part of the century. He began his professional career in 1903, playing with Whittenton Athletic Club of Taunton. The following season he came home and joined the Fall River Rovers through 1909 when they won the league title. In 1910, he played for two years with Philadelphia Hibernian before coming back to the area for a season with the New Bedford Whalers in 1913.

Swords jumped ship again in 1914 and for the final time until retirement in 1920. During this interval, he was the star forward with the Rovers and was a standout during the national Challenge Cup from 1916 to 1918. As has been noted in the previous Booth and Albion stories, the team lost two of three to Bethlehem Steel, FC.

Education
Local Fall River schools.

Skills
During the international contests against Norway and Sweden, controversy arose over who scored the first goal for the U.S. It was credited to another player but many said it was unassisted by Swords. That was his last time playing for the U.S.

Also of Note
He is a member of the National Soccer Hall of Fame and was the team captain on a U.S. tour of Scandinavian countries in 1916.

Information gathered from *Wikipedia*—photos courtesy of *Wikipedia*

JOHN B. CUMMINGS, ESQUIRE
Track Star/Olympic Trials

Profile
Born in Fall River in 1889 and buried in St. Patrick's Cemetery in 1978, John B. Cummings was the son of the Honorable John W. Cummings, Mayor of Fall River (included in the government section) and Mary Brennan. Cummings was one of six children who were brought up on Locust Street near Ruggles Park. He married Angela King after the death of his first wife. They had one son, the author of this book, two grandsons, and four great-grandchildren.

Experience
Cummings could be one of those acknowledged in more than one category, but in this instance he is being cited as a nationally recognized track star. His athletic prowess was first seen at Durfee High School as a member of the track team; at the school's field day in 1908 he took four first-place awards, including the 100 and 220-yard dash, broad jump and 220-yard low hurdles.

Cummings excelled in the 110-meter high hurdles in college. A member of the Harvard varsity track team from 1911 to 1913 and captain of the 1913 team, he was invited to participate in the 1912 Olympic Track and Field Trials. He ran in the I.C.A.A.A.A. track meet in 1911, finishing third in the low hurdles, and in 1913, he finished third in the high hurdles after becoming the New England Indoor Champion in the 45-yard high hurdles. Cummings represented his country in the Harvard and Yale versus Oxford and Cambridge track meet in England in 1911, finishing in second place and helping the American team to a victory. He frequently earned points for Harvard in the many dual meets in which he participated.

Education
Local Fall River schools, B.M.C. Durfee High School 1908, Stone School 1909, Harvard College 1913 and Harvard Law School 1916.

Skills
Recognized in Who's Who in American Sports, in later years, Cummings was acknowledged as a top area tennis and squash player, as well as a champion bowler.

Also of Note
Cummings was a first lieutenant, 163rd Infantry and 302nd Infantry during WWI and Chair of the Fall River Draft Board during WWII. He tried to serve again in WWII but was rejected due to age and health issues. Among his many community commitments, he served as chair of the Fall River Chapter of the American Red Cross and President of Truesdale Hospital. Cummings received the Durfee High School Distinguished Alumni Award in 1971.

Information gathered from family and the *Fall River Herald News*—photos courtesy of his family

1850-1925

Suburbs*

———◆———

When people agree with me
I always feel I must be wrong.

———◆———

OSCAR WILDE

* Despite not having attended school in Fall River,
the following individuals in the category are so
closely associated with Fall River that they
deserve inclusion in this book.

JOHN M. DEANE
Military Medal of Honor Recipient
Businessperson

Profile
Son of John and Lydia (Andros) Deane, John Deane was born in 1840 and died in 1914. He married Mary Gray Pearce. They had five children and he was the great-grandfather of Bob Deane, also cited herein.

Experience
Deane enlisted in the military in 1858 and was named sergeant and company clerk in 1860, a position that would serve as excellent training for his future occupation. Deane was promoted to third lieutenant in 1860 and upon the call in 1861 by President Abraham Lincoln for troops, he was assigned to Fort Monroe in Virginia. He was promoted twice in 1862, to captain in 1864 and major in 1865. Deane was awarded the Medal of Honor after the battle of Fort Steadman in Virginia, where he captured and disarmed a captain of the Fourth North Carolina regiment and later the same day did the same to a major of the Fourth Georgia regiment. He had duty in the campaign, in siege and service as a line, staff and field officer. Deane fought under General Sumner among other notables in the Civil War.

Education
Local Assonet/Freetown/Myricks Schools and Foxboro English and Classical School.

Skills
He began his career as an educator at age nineteen at Berkley Common School. After his final muster in 1865, Dean resumed his teaching career until he joined with Alonzo Hathaway in the general merchandise business in Fall River. The firm was known as Hathaway and Deane and sold groceries and general merchandise. His product list took up an entire newspaper page then.

Also of Note
Deane served as the Commander of Richard Borden Post No. 46 in Fall River from 1897 to 1902.

Information gathered from *History of the Town of Freetown*—photo courtesy of the town of Freetown

CLIFFORD MILBURN HOLLAND
Civil Engineer

Profile
Clifford Holland was the only child of John and Lydia F. Hood Holland. He was born in 1883, married Anna C. Davenport and they had four daughters. He died in 1924 at age forty-one while on the operating room table undergoing a tonsillectomy in Battle Creek, Michigan.

Experience
He began his career in New York City as an assistant engineer on the Joralemon Street Tunnel. Holland then became the engineer-in-charge of the construction of tunnels on Clark, Montague, and 14th Streets before he became the first chief engineer on the Hudson River Vehicular Tunnel Project.

Education
Somerset schools, Harvard in 1905 and a B.S. in Civil Engineering in 1906.

Also of Note
The tunnel between New York City and New Jersey was named in his honor, The Holland Tunnel.

Information gathered from *Wikipedia*—photo courtesy of Findagrave.com

Achievement

———·+·———

That man is a success who has lived well,

laughed often and loved much;

who has gained the respect of intelligent men and the love of children;

who has filled his niche and accomplished his task;

who leaves the world better than he found it,

whether by an improved poppy, a perfect poem or a rescued soul;

who never lacked appreciation of earth's beauty or failed to express it;

who looked for the best in others and gave the best he had.

———·+·———

ROBERT LOUIS STEVENSON

1926-Present

Arts

———•+•+•———

The Dream

Ah, great it is to believe the dream

As we stand in youth by starry stream;

But a greater thing is to fight life through

And say at the end, "The dream is true."

———•+•+•———

EDWIN MARKHAM

ALICE BRAYTON
Author

Profile

Alice Brayton was born in 1878 in Fall River to Thomas Edward and Martha Ireson Brayton. She had two sisters and a brother and grew up on Prospect Street in the Lower Highland section of Fall River. She never married and often said, "My father gave me permission not to marry."

Experience

Brayton became an author and is responsible to writing four books, now called vanity books.

They are:

George Berkley in Apulia (1946)

Scrabbletown (1952)

The Burying Place of Governor Arnold (1960)

Life on the Stream (1962)

Education

Home schooled while living in Fall River. She did not attend college.

Skills

Brayton was an extraordinary host and was known far and wide in Newport County for her parties.

Also of Note

Her parents bought a summer place in Portsmouth, Rhode Island and they traveled there by train from Fall River. The train stopped near their home on Cory's Lane. It was there that the family created "Green Animals Topiary Gardens." California privet, yew and English boxwoods were pruned by gardeners over many years into the shapes of animals, birds and other ornamental designs. The site became and still is a tourist destination.

Information gathered from family and *Parallel Lives*—photo courtesy of the Fall River Historical Society

FRED BUDA
Boston Pops Percussionist

Profile
Fred Buda was born in Fall River in 1935 and grew up on County Street around Columbus and Lafayette Parks. He has an older sister and they are the children of Carl and Julia Croatia Buda. He married Miriam Juda, a Holocaust survivor, and they have two sons.

Experience
Buda's first job was as a percussionist for a wedding band called Rhythm Makers. His idol was Gene Krupa but his motivational force, beside his parents, was Durfee High School teacher Faust Fiore. He played in the Durfee Jazz Band and upon reaching age sixteen was able to drive to various locations to sit in and listen to "a lot of great jazz players."

Buda applied for and was selected to be a member of The Boston Pops (America's Orchestra) in 1967 and played with the Pops at Boston's Symphony Hall for thirty-six years, fourteen with conductor John Williams who recently said of Fred: "You all sound great!" when referencing "The Fred Buda Quintet: The 2 Brass Hit: It's About Time." Buda's son David is also featured as part of the group and other members have played for Josh Groban, Aaron Neville, Tony Bennett and Frank Sinatra. He was a member of and set drummer for the Boston Pops and timpanist for the Boston Ballet Orchestra until retiring about ten years ago only to become busier than ever.

Education
Watson School, B.M.C. Durfee High School and Boston University.

Skills
Called a drumming legend, he has performed under most major conductors. He played with the Herb Pomeroy Big Band among others. Buda was Chair of Percussion at Berklee College of Music and a member of the faculty of University of Massachusetts Lowell.

Also of Note
Buda honed his skills while serving in the Navy where he had extra time to practice. There is a music room named for Buda and fellow graduate, Joe Raposo (also included herein) at Durfee High School.

Information gathered from Fred Buda, *Salem News* and the *Boston Globe*—photos courtesy of Mr. Buda

JAMES CHACE
Author and Historian

Profile
Born in Fall River in 1931, James Chace died of a heart attack in Paris in 2004 while doing research for a new book. He is buried in the family plot in Swansea, Massachusetts. He was the son of Hollister R. Chace and Mildred Clarke Chace and he had an older brother. Chace was married twice. He lived in New York City at the time of his death with his longtime companion, Joan Bingham. He was the father of three daughters.

Experience
After a military tour in France, Chace returned home where his interest in foreign policy grew. He served as managing editor for *East Europe*, a political review of Soviet Bloc affairs, from 1959 to 1969. His book, *Conflict in the Middle East*, was also written during this period. During that time he also served as a founder and managing editor of magazines *Interplay* and then *Foreign Affairs* from 1970 to 1983. He joined the *New York Times* staff as a book reviewer for international affairs in 1983 but soon left to go to the Carnegie Endowment for International Peace to write on foreign policy. He was editor of the *World Policy Journal* from 1993 to 2000.

Chace's photo from the Durfee 1949 yearbook.

Chace was a professor of American Foreign Policy at Bard College and one of the founders of the Bard Globalization and International Affairs Program.

Chace's work focused on American statesmanship. He was highly critical of both the Vietnam and the Iraq Wars. He felt there was not a proper balance between interests and resources to engage in battle in either war.

Education
B.M.C. Durfee High School and Harvard with a degree in Classics. He joined his good friend, Peter Collias, now a Fall River attorney, as a scholarship recipient in 1949 from Durfee High School to Harvard.

Skills
Chace went to France in 1954 to study but after returning home the military sent him back to be an Army translator of French newspapers for the CIA. His memoir about growing up in Fall River is entitled, *What We Had: A Memoir*.

Also of Note
He was a professor of government at Bard College in 1990. He was a recipient of the Durfee Distinguished Alumni Award in 2001.

Information gathered from *Wikipedia* and *What We Had: A Memoir*—photos courtesy of the Chace family and Durfee High yearbooks

MAUDE DARLING-PARLIN
Architect

Profile
Born in 1885, Maude Darling-Parlin died in 1979 at age ninety-three and is buried in Oak Grove Cemetery. She married her M.I.T. classmate Ray Parlin and they had three daughters. Ray died in 1924.

Experience
At a time when women architects were confined to designing only residential buildings, Darling stood out. Married to Ray Parlin, she joined her father's firm and soon after founded a firm with her brother to create Darling-Parlin.

She designed the Buffington Building, an imposing five-story structure located on Purchase Street at Bedford Street, in 1916. Next door on Bedford Street, the firm designed a limestone building in Art Deco style for the Fall River Cooperative Bank, which today also still stands. Around the corner, on Main Street, the Classical Revival-style three-story Fall River Trust Company Bank building was erected.

The Women's Club on Walnut Street in Fall River

Other organizations sought out Darling's talents, including the Women's Union Building on Rock Street (formerly the United Way and now the Family Service Association) as well as the YMCA on North Main Street.

Darling retired in 1976 at age ninety-one, leaving a legacy of impressive buildings, theaters, churches and more than 100 Fall River homes.

Education
Local Fall River schools, B.M.C. Durfee High School, M.I.T. and the Pratt Institute.

Skills
A pioneer female architect, Darling joined the family's architecture firm in 1921 and designed many buildings in Fall River, Massachusetts, including more than 100 homes.

Also of Note
Around 1925, the Women's Club of Fall River on Walnut Street hired Darling to remodel both the interior and exterior of the building. She added a Colonial Revival facade with a pedimented entrance and interior ornamentation.

Information gathered from the National Park Service, *The First American Women Architects* and the Fall River Historical Society—photos courtesy of the Fall River Historical Society collection

LAURA DIAS/MAYA DAYS
Actor and Singer

Profile
Born in Fall River, Maya Days is the only child of Nancy Dias and Joseph Thomas. Her grandparents, Albert and Laura Rogers, also live in Fall River. She is married to Keith, a New York City homicide detective, and is the mother of a son, Boston.

Experience
Days is a recognized leading actor and songstress. After watching plays at Kennedy Park in Fall River as a youngster, she knew singing and performing were in her blood. At Kuss Middle School her music teacher, Charlene Khoury, inspired her. At Durfee, theater director Jimmy Tavares nurtured her love of the stage while Vice Principal Tom "Skip" Karam (also highlighted herein) kept her on the straight and narrow.

In 1998, Days hit it big with her song, "Feel It", topping European pop charts. During the same period she garnered the leading role in the international production of *Rent* from 1996 to 1998. She also performed the leading role on Broadway in the Elton John-Tim Rice production of *Aida* at the Palace Theatre from 2000 to 2004. Days played the leading role of Mary Magdalene in *Jesus Christ Superstar* in 2000.

Education
St. Louis Annex, Lincoln School, Kuss Middle School, B.M.C. Durfee High School and Bristol Community College.

Skills
More recently Days has starred in her biggest role, mother to her son. She has, however, been able to appear on *Damages* and *Law and Order* in her spare time.

Days credits living in Fall River, as many in this book do also, with making it possible to survive every situation and interact with people from all backgrounds.

Also of Note
While in Los Angeles she worked for another Fall Riverite, Arina Cabral, who owned a food delivery service, "Why Cook?"

One of her first jobs was as a medical and office assistant for Dr. Richard H. Fitton at Truesdale Clinic.

She is a former Miss Fall River.

Information gathered from Maya Days and the *Fall River Herald News*

JAMES DEAN
Watercolor Artist and Smithsonian Art Curator

Profile
Born in Fall River in 1931 to John and Sadie M. Griffin Dean, James Dean is one of six children who grew up in the East End of the city. He married his high school sweetheart, Rita Williams, and they have three sons.

Experience
Dean began painting more than sixty-five years ago. He always wanted to be a visual artist and was motivated by his parents, friend Art Caroselli and art teacher Frank McCoy. Being a "carbonated engineer" at Duffy's Drug on Pleasant Street did not influence his lifetime work but if it was not for the Flash Gordon Serial films at the Strand Theater in the Flint, he may never have pursued NASA art later in life.

Fall River Carousel

Dean paints watercolors of American scenes from changing New England coastal landscapes to Florida space launches, shuttle landings in California and churches in Santa Fe, New Mexico. He is a former Curator of Art at the Smithsonian Institution's National Air and Space Museum. Dean is also the former director of the Fine Arts Program, NASA Headquarters, in Washington, D.C.

Presently, he paints at The "Other" James Dean Studio at the Torpedo Factory Art Center in Alexandria, Virginia, and travels to various museums with his sketchbook making inspirational notes. He travels yearly in the summer to Maine to paint and visit his friends Jamie, and in former times with his late father, Andrew Wyeth.

Education
Local Fall River schools, B.M.C. Durfee High School and Swain School of Design (now part of UMass Dartmouth).

Skills
Not only did Dean become a famous artist, he also wrote periodicals and *NASA/ART: 50 Years of Exploration; Journey into Space* and has illustrated *LIFTOFF, Story of America's Adventure in Space*.

Also of Note
Dean received the Durfee High School Distinguished Alumni Award in 1989. He received awards from the Art Directors Club in New York, the American Institute of Graphic Arts, and Communication Arts Magazine. He has designed two Christmas stamps and his Space Shuttle paintings were shown on ABC and NBC News. He is also listed in *Who's Who in American Art*.

"At the core, both art and aerospace exploration search for a meaning to life."
—JAMES DEAN, FOUNDING DIRECTOR, NASA ART PROGRAM, 1962 TO 1974

Information gathered from Mr. Dean and The "Other" James Dean Studio—photos courtesy of Mr. Dean

JOHN MICHAEL DIAS
Actor and Singer

Profile
Born in Fall River in 1980 but growing up in Tiverton, Rhode Island, John Michael Dias is the only child of Susan Mary Petisca, a nurse, and Peter Dias, a law enforcement officer.

Experience
His first job was as a clerk in a toy store, but rehearsals at Fall River Little Theater interrupted his work schedule and resulted in a joint parting of the ways. Before that, the faculty at Saints Peter and Paul School and its principal, Kathleen Burt, were all encouraging and provided great motivation for Dias.

He always wanted to be an actor and his parents provided him with the motivation he needed to succeed.

Auditioning for and then being tapped as the lead in the *Jersey Boys* National Tour as Frankie Valli from the Four Seasons in 2010 took Dias to fifty cities in twenty-eight states as well as Canada. His Broadway debut in *Jersey Boys* came in 2013. He has also performed in musicals *Grease*, *Oklahoma* and *Oliver*.

Education
St. Joseph's Montessori, Saints Peter and Paul's School, Bishop Connolly High School and Boston Conservatory of Music.

Skills
Performing with friends in a local group called "Broadway Babies" at First Night in Fall River set the stage for his future. Dias is also a talented fashion designer who will always have a job in the theater—his true love.

Also of Note
The New Bedford Festival Theater presented him with a theater achievement award in December 2012. The musical, *Jersey Boys*, received a 2006 Tony Award for Best Musical.

Information gathered from John Michael Dias and About The Artists—photos courtesy of Mr. Dias

LEONARD DUFRESNE
Artist

Profile
Leonard Dufresne was born in Fall River in 1941. He is the younger of two sons of Albert and Bernice Dufresne. His first marriage produced two daughters. He has since remarried and has another daughter by his second wife, sculptor Lee Stoliar. He has five grandchildren.

Experience
It was Dufresne's grandfather, Emile, who had the greatest influence on him. Grandfather owned a variety store "up the Globe" where Dufresne spent many hours reading all the books for sale, then he would accompany the elder Dufresne (Papere) to the Park Theater (Show) to watch everything that appeared on the screen in the 1950s. Looking back, it was those afternoons in the theater that provided the foundation for his artistic talents. Perhaps, even time as a Fall River Country Club caddy or a Quequechan

The artist in a fatigue hat, left, as a Quequechan Club pin-boy the night Cuba fell to Fidel Castro.

Club pin-boy in the bowling lanes played a role in his eventual decision to become an independent creative artist. Despite being attentive to his Durfee art teachers, Marion Torphy and Ruth Newkirk, school was not for him. He dropped out to enter the army and spent more than two years in Western Europe. Dufresne's time after military service was spent at school and finding himself as an artist. He felt he had no one to imitate in his hometown but visiting museums and art galleries in New York with his aunt fed his interests in the arts while military service in Europe taught Dufresne to speak another language and experience the broader world. Dufresne enjoyed all aspects of art while studying under David Loeffler Smith at Swain School. He draws every morning to create images from his own thoughts. He believes that out of ordinary events of one's own experience something "permanent and beautiful can be created."

Education
St. Patrick's School, B.M.C. Durfee High School, Swain School of Design in New Bedford, the Skohegan School of Painting and Sculpture in Maine and the Maryland Institute College of Art, where he received both bachelor and master degrees.

Skills
Dufresne has taught art at the Maryland Institute, Bennington College, New York University, The Art Students League and in Fall River at Bristol Community College.

Also of Note
Dufresne served his country in the U.S. Army from 1960 to 1963 before furthering his education.

Information gathered by and illustrations courtesy of Mr. Dufresne

C. HAZARD DURFEE
Artist

Profile
Carder Hazard Durfee was born in 1917 and spent most of his life in Tiverton, Rhode Island, specifically at Homelands, his family's historic farm estate overlooking the Sakonnet River and Nanaquaket Pond. He died in 2003 at age eighty-eight as a result of an automobile accident in Newport, Rhode Island. He and his two sisters were the children of Charles Hazard Durfee and Amy Ward Freeman Durfee.

Experience
After military service, Durfee began to pursue his dream of being an artist. He traveled throughout the world to find inspiration: Mexico, the West Indies, Italy, North Africa and across this country.

His early work in New York was cubism. He advanced to calligraphic watercolor and ink studies set in Italy and Morocco, then on to lush expressionistic landscapes and florals as his style matured.

Education
Local Fall River schools, Choate Preparatory School and Yale University School of Fine Arts, where he received a Fellowship in 1940.

Skills
Durfee was featured in *Life* Magazine in 1950 as one of the "country's best artists under 36." He exhibited in the Whitney Museum, The Denver Art Museum, the Metropolitan Museum of Art and the Newport Art Museum among others.

Also of Note
Durfee served as part of the Greatest Generation in World War 11 from 1941 to 1945 as a camouflage engineer. His works have been featured in many art publications and journals and found in private, public and corporate collections. Awards include: Audubon Artist Award in 1954 and Jane Peterson Award also in 1954, the American Academy of Arts and Letters in 1954 along with e.e. cummings and Ernest Hemingway.

Information gathered from The Newport Art Museum, *Ask the Artist* and *The Artist Bluebook*, The National Institute of Arts and Letters and close personal friends—photos courtesy of close friends

ARTHUR FARIA
Musical Staging and Choreography

Profile
Arthur Faria was born in 1942 and brought up in Fall River on O'Grady Street near Ruggles Park. He and his sister, Noella, were the children of Arthur and Dorothea Faria. Arthur Sr. was a foreperson at a local hat making company.

Experience
Faria's enduring claim to fame has been the musical staging and choreography for the 1978 Tony-Award-winning *Ain't Misbehavin'*. Faria earned nominations for both the Tony and Drama Desk Awards and shared the Obie for the original production at the Manhattan Theatre Club. He then recreated the work in 1988 for the tenth anniversary Broadway revival starring the original cast. Since that time he has also directed major productions of the show starring The Pointer Sisters, Della Reese, and Martha Reeves and the Vandellas.

In 1981, Faria was honored to be selected by Lena Horne to create and direct her return to Broadway in *Lena Horne: The Lady and Her Music*, for which he was nominated for a second Tony and Drama Desk awards. The show won a Tony Award.

Education
Sacred Heart School, B.M.C. Durfee High School and an Honorary Doctorate from UMass Dartmouth in Fine and Performing Arts.

Skills
Faria has earned two Emmy nominations for his work on PBS Great Performances production of *Duke Ellington: The Music Lives On*. Faria also staged the American Idol National Tour with Ruben Studdard. He continues to stage and direct performances of *Ain't Misbehavin'* in various parts of the country.

Also of Note
Stars who have called upon Faria's talents include Bette Midler, Bette Davis, Richard Gere, Bobby Short, The Fifth Dimension, The Village People, Liv Ulman, Alice Faye and members of the Bolshoi Ballet. Faria has also performed in many musical shows, including *The Boy Friend, Sugar* and *Gregory*.

Information gathered from *Internet Broadway Database* and Soul View Studios—photo courtesy of Mr. Faria

JOHN/PAUL GEARY
Actor

Profile
John/Paul Geary was a son of George and Anita LeBlanc Geary. Born in Fall River in 1940, he died in Fall River in 1987 and is buried in St. Patrick's Cemetery. He was the second oldest of five boys and lived on Seabury Street across from Ruggles Park. Paul never married and did not have any children.

Experience
Geary later changed his first name from John to Paul for professional reasons, but he was always John at his first job as a "soda jerk" at Taylor's Pharmacy around the corner from his home on Seabury Street.

When William Faulkner wrote *The Long Hot Summer*, he certainly did not imagine that Fall Riverite Paul Geary would play the role of Jody Varner in the television version. Jody was the fun-loving, girl chasing son of patriarch Will Varner, played by Edmond O'Brien.

This was not Geary's first performance. After participating in the Durfee Dramatic Club with Barbara Wellington, he played summer stock in New England and progressed to minor roles in theater and eventually landed a role in the Broadway hit, *Take Her, She's Mine*.

Geary was featured in the December 1964 issue of *Movie Stars Magazine* in a section entitled, "TV's Hottest New Men" along with Bill Bixby, Robert Vaughan, David Mc-Callum, Ed Nelson and Anthony Franciosa.

Geary admitted at times things could get tough. He did not work for 6 months and "survived on chocolate fudge day in and day out," he said. Then the big day came and he was awarded a 5 year contract with Bing Crosby and Pendick Productions.

Education
Sacred Heart School, B.M.C. Durfee High School and Dramatic School of Fine Arts in New York.

Skills
Geary always felt he might have a second career as a recording artist but it was not meant to be. He did, however, write some television scripts that were accepted by various show producers.

Also of Note
He arrived in Hollywood in 1962 and found television roles in *Laramie, Checkmate, My Three Sons* and *The Great Adventure*. He was regularly featured in the daytime series, *Ben Jarred-Attorney*.

Information gathered from Mike Geary, *Movie Stars Magazine*—photo courtesy of the Geary family

KELLY ANN ALBANESE HATOSY
Actress

Profile
Kelly Ann Albanese was born in Fall River in 1977. She is the daughter of Susan Carlino and Michael Albanese and is married to fellow actor Shawn Hatosy. They have a son.

Experience
Albanese's first acting role came in fifth grade at the urging of her voice coach Jane Dufault, when she landed the part of Alice in *Alice in Wonderland*. Her stage-fright was overcome when she got the part and Albanese was thrilled by the entire process: costumes, sets, rehearsals. She caught the bug and was hooked for life. But her self-confidence waned in high school and college and drama was abandoned for sports. Albanese always knew after college graduation, she had to give it another try, it was in her blood.

Off to L.A, Albanese took acting classes, got an agent and occasionally booked a role. Her most significant influence has been her husband. Also an actor, he is imparting his talents as she continues to grow in the acting profession.

Albanese has been a Hollywood actor for more than 10 years. Some of her credits include *Stuck on You* (2003), *Monk* (2004), *Dear Jimmy* (2005), *Desire* (2006), *Playing with Fire* (2008), *The Tab* (2009) and *Street Boss* (2009). Albanese also starred as the voice of Buffy Summers in *Buffy the Vampire Slayer Season Eight* motion comic in 2010. Her most recent performances occurred on *Southland* and *Reckless*.

Education
Notre Dame School, Westport High School and Bridgewater State University.

Also of Note
Albanese was a competitive gymnast as a youngster and at age nine was invited to train with the world-famous coach, Bela Karolyi, in Texas. Being a mother is now a top priority for the local girl making it big.

Information gathered from Ms. Albanese—photo courtesy of Ms. Albanese

HOWARD EARL KANOVITZ
Photo Realist

Profile
Born in Fall River in 1929 to Dora Reims and Meyer Kanovitz, Howard Earl Kanovitz lived in Southampton, New York, at the time of his death in 2008 at age seventy-nine. His first marriage to Mary Rattray ended in divorce and at the time of his death he was married to Carolyn Oldenbusch who is also the director of the Howard Kanovitz Foundation. He had one child, a daughter, Cleo, and two grandsons.

Experience
As a student of Franz Kline, Kanovitz's early works in the 1950's were in the Abstract Expressionist mode in the style of Kline and Jackson Pollock. He broke away from that style in the early 1960's. His first solo show in 1962 was at the Stable Art Gallery in New York City.

"The Opening, 1967."

Kanovitz's signature work at right is titled "The Opening, 1967." His technique was to project photographic images onto a canvas and paint over them. "The Opening" is a photo painting of artists and critics in the New York art scene looking at and being looked at simultaneously. His solo show in 1966 at the Jewish Museum in New York City put him in the forefront of a movement.

Education
Local Fall River schools, B.M.C. Durfee High School, Providence College, Rhode Island School of Design and New York University.

Skills
Kanovitz's first career was that of a musician. Gene Krupa included Kanovitz as his trombone player. He and fellow artist and saxophonist, Larry Rivers, were part of a group known as the East 13th Street Band. He was among a group of artists, musicians and writers who lived in Greenwich Village and the East End of Long Island during the '50s and '60s.

Also of Note
Kanovitz maintained studios in Greenwich Village in New York City and Nice, France. His website is howardkanovitz .com

Information gathered from the *New York Times*—photo and image courtesy of Carolyn Oldenbusch

JAMES KEARNS
Screenwriter and Producer

Profile
James Kearns was born in 1947 in Newport, Rhode Island to Aloysius J. and "Kay" A. McGinnis Kearns. They lived in the Highland section of Fall River. He was one of four siblings. Kearns lives in California and has two daughters.

Experience
Kearns wrote and co-produced the feature film JOHN Q which was directed by Nick Casavettes. It was released by New Line Cinema and starred Denzel Washington, Robert Duvall, James Woods, Anne Heche, Ray Liotta. The movie opened number one at the box office, earning nearly 24 million dollars.

The success of the film prompted the Kaiser Family Foundation to sponsor a debate at the National Press Club in Washington, D.C. entitled "John Q Goes To Washington". The event was widely attended by members of Congress, insurance executives, HMO organizations, health advocacy groups, academia and the media. The discussion centered on "the responsibilities and impact of the media when reporting on health issues to the public."

JOHN Q was his second straight screenplay sale after his first script, DEAD OF SUMMER, was bought by Universal Studios. He has adapted "Slightly Out Of Focus," based on the life of renowned World War II photographer ROBERT CAPA for Walt Disney Pictures. He spent two years researching and writing ABOUT FACE, the true story of an American soldier wrongly accused of cowardice and sentenced to death while serving in Iraq. His most recent film project is THE LAST RIDGE, a true story about the formation of the U.S. Mountain Division that fought in the mountains of Italy towards the end of WWII.

Before writing for film, Kearns worked extensively as a freelance writer for a number of dramatic and comedy series, most notably the Emmy award winning series A YEAR IN THE LIFE. He was the executive story editor for the acclaimed CBS series WISEGUY and has written numerous television movies for CBS, ABC, NBC, TNT and LIFETIME.

Kearns began his writing career as a playwright in New York City. His first play, DAYS IN THE DARK LIGHT, was produced by American Theater Arts in Los Angeles. His second full length play, FAVORITE SONS was a Selection Committee Finalist at the Eugene O'Neill Theater Center in Waterford, CT and was subsequently produced by the Actors Producing Company in New York City.

He is currently completing his first novel, excerpts of which were published in the San Francisco literary magazine ZYZZYVA. The story was nominated for the prestigious Pushcart Prize, honoring poetry, short stories, essays published by small presses over the previous year.

Education
Sacred Heart School, DeLaSalle Academy, Manhattan College. Rhode Island College and Hunter College Graduate Playwriting Program.

Skills
From 2005 to 2008, he was a member of the National Institutes of Health's Council Of Public Representatives (COPR), advising then NIH director Dr. Elias Zerhouni on a variety of health issues from the public perspective. His work with COPR educated him to the challenges facing our nation as it struggles to deliver quality medical care to all Americans.

Also of Note
He is a spokesperson, and public speaker on behalf of those suffering from mental health issues, and has appeared on CNN, CBS, FOX, NBC television and radio affiliates as a spokesperson for BRIDGE FOR TOMORROW, a national campaign dedicated to increasing awareness for depression, bipolar disorder and other psychiatric conditions.

He was a guest speaker and panelist at "Investing In Media That Matters" Conference, sponsored by Robert Redford at the Sundance Film Festival, and is a long-standing member of the Writers Guild of America West and PEN international.

Information gathered from and photo courtesy of Mr. Kearns

J. MICHAEL LENNON, PH.D.
Author and Educator

Profile
J. Michael Lennon was born and grew up in the Corky Row section of Fall River with his three siblings. He is the son of John and Mary Mitchell Lennon. The family moved to Somerset when he was a youngster. He married Donna Pedro and they have three sons and four grandchildren.

J. Michael Lennon, right, is the archivist and authorized biographer for the late Norman Mailer, left.

Experience
After military service and while in graduate school, Lennon became interested in the prolific novelist Norman Mailer. He and Mailer became friends in 1972, the year Lennon began teaching at the University of Illinois-Springfield. He edited Mailer's *Pieces and Pontifications* while he was publisher of *Illinois Issues* magazine and director of its radio and public television stations. Those posts led to the creation of the University's Institute of Public Affairs, where Lennon became first executive director in 1988. All during this period, Lennon and his family grew closer to Mailer and his multiple family members during summer months on Cape Cod and in Maine.

Mailer's authorized biographer at the time was a University of Pennsylvania professor who became Lennon's mentor. By 2006, the professor passed on and left the uncompleted work to his protegé to finish. Lennon spent the next six years doing just that. At the time he was teaching at Wilkes University but he realized it would take a full time effort to research and write a biography more than 340,000 words. The result—*Norman Mailer: A Double Life* which has received wide acclaim.

Lennon's writing life has not been exclusively devoted to Mailer. He wrote about James Jones, helped found the Jones Society and edited a collection of Jones' war writings, among other efforts. He also co-produced a 1985 PBS documentary on Jones.

In 1992, Lennon was appointed Vice President for Academic Affairs at Wilkes University, a position he held until 2000 when he moved to the English Department, he remained there until retirement in 2005. Lennon is currently editing the 25 million words of Mailer's 50,000 letters for another book to be published in the fall of 2014.

Education
St. Mary's School, Somerset schools and Somerset High School. He graduated from Stonehill College and received graduate degrees from the University of Rhode Island.

Skills
Lennon was a U.S. Naval Officer during the Vietnam War and served five years of active duty. After sea duty on the U.S.S. *Uvalde* for thirty months, he returned to Officers Candidate School in Newport, Rhode Island where he met his wife and began teaching military law and history. He concluded his military career as a lieutenant commander.

Also of Note
Lennon is the founder and current President of The Norman Mailer Society and past president of The James Jones Literary Society. He is also the Chair of the Editorial Board of *The Mailer Review*.

His work has appeared in *The New Yorker, Paris Review, Mailer Review, James Jones Literary Society, Playboy* and *Creative Nonfiction* among others. Most recently he edited *Moonfire: The Epic Journey of Apollo 11* and *Norman Mailer/ Bert Stern: Marilyn Monroe*.

Lennon is currently editing Mailer's letters and serves on the advisory board of both the Wilkes M.F.A. Program and The Mailer Colony. He and his wife, Donna, received the *Choice Magazine* award for outstanding scholarly title in 2001 for their work, *Norman Mailer: Works and Days*. It is considered the standard Mailer bibliography.

Information gathered from Mr. Lennon, his website, the *Boston Globe*, the *Fall River Herald News*
—photo courtesy of Christina Pabst

VICTORIA LINCOLN
Author

Profile
Victoria Lincoln was born in Fall River and died in Baltimore in 1981 at age seventy-six. Married to Professor Victor A. Lowe, she had two daughters, a son and eight grandchildren.

Experience
Lincoln was an author of a dozen books, primarily fiction and biographies. She was best known for *February Hill* published in 1934. It was later adapted for both stage and film under the title of *Primrose Path*.

Two of her well-known novels are *Out of Eden* and *Celia Amberly*. She also published *A Private Disgrace: Lizzie Borden by Daylight*.

Education
Local Fall River schools and B.M.C. Durfee High School. She majored in English at Radcliffe.

Skills
Lincoln completed a biography of St. Theresa of Avila before her death.

Information gathered from *Wikipedia* and Fall River Historical Society—photo courtesy of *Wikipedia*

JOHN MORIARTY
Musician and Conductor

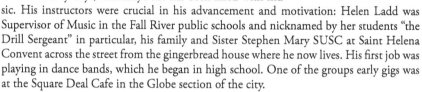

Profile
John Moriarty grew up on Bedford Street with his two younger sisters. He was born in 1930 to John J. and Bella Moriarty and today lives on Rock Street in Fall River when not serving as artistic director emeritus of the Central City Opera in Colorado.

Experience
From his early days, Moriarty's life has been filled with music. His instructors were crucial in his advancement and motivation: Helen Ladd was Supervisor of Music in the Fall River public schools and nicknamed by her students "the Drill Sergeant" in particular, his family and Sister Stephen Mary SUSC at Saint Helena Convent across the street from the gingerbread house where he now lives. His first job was playing in dance bands, which he began in high school. One of the groups early gigs was at the Square Deal Cafe in the Globe section of the city.

After graduating with highest honors from New England Conservatory of Music in 1952, Moriarty studied piano in Italy and vocal repertoire in France with great masters. He expected to tour the world playing concertos but it was not to be.

Moriarty's love turned to opera and he joined many opera companies across the country until he landed back in Boston as a teacher of opera performance as well as piano. Teaching became his passion and he traveled between Boston and the Central City Opera in Colorado giving lessons. For sixteen years, Moriarty served as artistic director of the Opera Company in Central City until 1998. Today a street next to the opera house is named "Moriarty Lane" in honor of the man who is legendary in his field.

Education
Sacred Heart School, B.M.C. Durfee High School and New England Conservatory of Music. He also studied at Brandeis, Mills College, and throughout Europe. He received an Honorary Doctorate of Music from the New England Conservatory of Music in 1992.

Skills
Moriarty helped found the South Coast Opera Club in 2002. He was a piano soloist with the Boston Pops and served as Chair of the Opera Department of both the Boston Conservatory of Music and New England Conservatory of Music.

Also of Note
Moriarty was a recipient of the Durfee Distinguished Alumni Award in 2006. He is also listed in Who's Who in America and the International Who's Who in Music among other similar groups. He has created a generous scholarship through the Durfee High School Alumni Association for graduating Durfee High students in memory of his parents.

Information gathered from *Wikipedia*, the *Fall River Herald News* and Mr. Moriarty—photo courtesy of Mr. Moriarty

CHARLIE QUINTAL
Recording Artist and Musician

Profile
Charlie Quintal is the son of Charles and Hilda Quintal. He has one brother and two sisters. He presently lives in the Flint section of Fall River in the home where he grew up. Previously married, he has five children and nine grandchildren.

Experience
Quintal's career began not as a singer or musician as he wished, but as a grocery delivery boy like many others in this book.

His teachers, especially Miss Fitton at Henry Lord, as well as entertainer Buddy Holly, provided the most motivation to Quintal. He signed a contract with Columbia Records in 1975 and performed with rock legends around the country.

In 1969, Quintal formed his own band, "Talk of the Town," after performing with the Spi-Dells. He was a regular for a dozen summers at the famed Warwick Musical Tent.

Quintal scored national hits including "Take Me As I Am" and "Baby" and recorded regional favorites "Georgia on My Mind" and "Lovely Lies."

Education
Letourneau School, Henry Lord Junior High School and B.M.C. Durfee High School.

Skills
Quintal stays in contact with many of his contemporaries, including Gerry Granaham, who enjoyed hits in the 1950s under his own name and as Dicky Doo and the Don'ts and the Fireflies.

Also of Note
Quintal has shared the stage with such music legends as Jerry Lee Lewis, Ricky Nelson, Fats Domino, Roy Orbison, Neil Sedaka, The Supremes and Aerosmith.

Information gathered from Mr. Quintal and *East Bay Publications*—photo courtesy of Mr. Quintal

JOSEPH G. RAPOSO
Composer and Musician

Profile
Joseph G. Raposo was the only child of Jose Soares Raposo and Maria A. Victorinho Raposo. Born in Fall River in 1937, he was raised in the North End of the city. He died in 1989 and is buried in Chatham, Massachusetts. He married his first wife, Sue Nordland, soon after graduating from Harvard and they had two sons. He had two more children with his second wife, Pat Collins, whom he married in 1976.

Experience
Raposo's first reported job, after performing side music in piano bars in Boston to make ends meet, was at the Music Theater at Lincoln Center in New York for Richard Rodgers (who became his mentor). He was classically trained in Paris but also enjoyed funk and jazz.

Raposo's greatest professional accomplishment was co-creating *Sesame Street* with Jim Henson. He served as the first and longtime musical director for the show and composed such classics as "It's Not Easy Bein' Green" and "Sing." He did voice overs for *Sesame Street* characters as well.

Raposo also wrote music for other television show such as *The Electric Company* and sitcoms *Three's Company* and *The Ropers*, including their theme songs.

Education
Local Fall River schools, B.M.C. Durfee High School, Harvard University in 1958, New York University and was bestowed an honorary doctorate from the University of Massachusetts Dartmouth.

Skills
At an early age Raposo's parents encouraged him to play piano and compose music. They saw the same musical talent that Richard Rodgers saw and that, combined with Jim Henson's comedy skits on the *Ed Sullivan Show*, made for a magical combination.

Raposo was also the musical supervisor and arranger for the off-Broadway run of *You're a Good Man, Charlie Brown*.

Also of Note
Raposo won five Grammy Awards, was nominated for an Oscar and wrote and co-produced many gold and platinum records for Frank Sinatra (a close friend who called Raposo a genius), Barbra Streisand and Kermit the Frog among others. In the 1970s, Raposo wrote original music for *Raggedy Ann and Andy: A Musical Adventure*. Raposo also narrated a slide show for the United Way of Greater Fall River in the early 1980s.

Information gathered from Pat Collins, the *New York Times* and *Wikipedia*—photo courtesy of his family

DAVID REITZAS
Grammy and Emmy Award Winning
Audio Recording and Mixing Engineer

David with Barbra Streisand

Profile
Born in Fall River, David Reitzas is the third of four children of Gary and Atty. Lois Reitzas of the FR Knitting Mills family. He and his family lived north of St. Patrick's Cemetery in the Highland section of Fall River. He currently lives in California with his wife, Aya, and their two sons.

Experience
Reitzas began his musical career doing the lights for local disc jockey, Steve Yoken. As a young teen, he worked nearly every weekend for three years with Yoken (whose older brother is also highlighted in this book). He was introduced to the latest hit songs and dance crazes. His first job in California was as a studio runner/assistant.

David with Stevie Wonder

David with Celine Dion

Reitzas raves about his Fall River school teachers who joined his parents as his biggest influences, including Tansey School Principal Sam Swidey (whose son is also highlighted in the book). At Morton Junior High he connected well with Mr. Woodward in Band; at Durfee High School it was Edmund Machado, his music teacher, and Mr. Tavares who taught English, among others.

Reitzas was mentored by the famed producer, songwriter and musician David Foster. His inspiration allowed Reitzas to share time with many of the great performers in the country, including those pictured with him on this page. He has had the opportunity to work with some of the greatest in the recording industry.

Education
Tansey School, Morton Junior High and B.M.C. Durfee High School. He attended the University of Rhode Island, Berklee College of Music and the Institute of Audio/Video Engineering in Hollywood.

Skills
Reitzas participated in both Marching and Stage Band from his days at Morton through his days at URI. During Stage Band at Durfee High, he would mimic Led Zeppelin drummer, John Bonham, even to the extreme of throwing his drum sticks into the audience after a solo.

Also of Note
Uncle Jim Reitzas provided him with musical instruments for practice and predicted a Grammy in the youngster's future. He did win his first Grammy as an engineer for the Natalie Cole and Nat King Cole duet, "Unforgettable," less than nine years out of Durfee High School.

Information gathered from Mr. Reitzas—photos courtesy of Mr. Reitza

MINDY ROBINSON
Actor and Model

Profile
Born in Fall River, Mindy Robinson now lives in Hollywood. She grew up in the Maplewood section of the city. Robinson is the daughter of William Robinson of Tiverton, Rhode Island and Jane Robinson of Fall River. She is the youngest child of four in her family.

Experience
Robinson is a Los Angeles-based performer, model, comedian and reality star. Robinson has appeared in numerous comedies, horror films, music videos and as a TV personality on major network shows, most notably and recently the FOX show *Take Me Out* with comedian George Lopez. The local actor and model also appeared on *The Haunting of Whaley House*, *King of Nerds* and most recently *Casting Couch*. Robinson has appeared in more than 100 TV shows, movies and music videos since 2011.

Robinson's first job was as a bagger at Stop and Shop in Somerset. The cross country runner and student government leader wanted to own a pet store, never thinking that she would end up in Hollywood. She credits her East Coast work ethic for making her dreams possible.

Education
Fall River schools, Henry Lord Junior High, Bristol Agricultural School in Dighton, Massachusetts, and California State University San Bernardino.

Information gathered from Miss Robinson and IMDB—photo courtesy of Ms. Robinson

LORI "CHICK" SARDINHA
Model and Plumber

Profile
Born in 1972, Lori Sardinha and her brother were raised in Fall River, the children of Tiberio and Diane Sardinha. She has a daughter.

Experience
Most young girls dream of winning beauty contests but even Sardinha, whose family owns and operates Sardinha Plumbing and Heating in Fall River, never imagined herself as being named America's Sexiest Plumber in 2005.

Sardinha competed in the American Standard-sponsored event and appeared on the Sexiest Plumber Calendar, winning a trip to Super Bowl XXXIX in 2005. She beat out a dozen men for the top honor in the national competition to find plumbers with great looks, personality and dedication to the business. In an online vote, American Standard vendors and customers voted Sardinha the winner and presented her with a tiara and toilet-brush scepter.

Education
Local Fall River schools and Diman Regional Vocational High School.

Information gathered from Miss Sardinha and UPI.com—photo courtesy of Miss Sardinha

JOHN SCANLON
Classical Musician: Violist and Violinist

Profile
John Scanlon is the adopted only child of Olga and John T. Scanlon, Jr. He was born in 1964 and lived in Somerset, Medford and Fall River. Scanlon is not married but has been with his same partner, Richard, for twenty-five years. When not working in Tacoma, Washington, he visits his mother Olga, who still lives in Fall River.

Experience
Scanlon was interested in the viola from his youth. He began playing in eighth grade under the direction of Ann Danis. By the time he was at Durfee High School, Scanlon was playing with the Cape Cod and Fall River Symphonies and was a regular at St. Mary's Cathedral for special masses. It was Danis and Ruth Trexler who built the Fall River public school string program into a real powerhouse, besting schools from all over the state in competitions.

After a year with the Florida Philharmonic, Scanlon moved to Los Angeles, where he performed with many classical musicians. Scanlon has played on hundreds of pop albums for everyone from Mel Torme to Ashlee Simpson.

Scanlon played a solo in front of 18,000 people at the Hollywood Bowl and has performed with John Williams. He also played on the sound track of *Titanic* and 400 other movies as well as in Philharmonic, Opera and Chamber Orchestras. Scanlon estimates his music has been heard by over a billion people.

Education
Westall School, Morton Junior High, B.M.C. Durfee High School, University of Michigan and U.C. Santa Barbara.

Skills
Not only did Scanlon become proficient with a musical instrument, he worked at the Fall River Public Library and during summers as a tour guide at Hammersmith Farm, the family home of Jackie Kennedy.

Before eighth grade, Scanlon's interest was science. He wanted to become an astronomer or an Egyptologist.

Also of Note
Scanlon credits his teachers, not his city, with his success. Although, like others in this book, growing up in the Lower Highlands between North and Ruggles Parks brought back fond memories of street hockey and backyard baseball, he felt Fall River did not provide the environment for success as a classical musician.

Information gathered from Mr. Scanlon and the Max Aronoff Viola Institute—photo courtesy of Mr. Scanlon

HYMAN J. SOBILOFF
Poet and Filmmaker

Profile

Hyman J. Sobiloff was born in Fall River in 1912 and was the son of Israel and Fannie Gollub Sobiloff. He had a brother and two sisters. He was married to Adelaide Goldstein and they had a son. Sobiloff died in New York in 1970 of a heart attack.

Experience

Sobiloff was a filmmaker, industrialist, philanthropist and poet. He began writing poetry as a diversion to his busy business life but soon his avocation became much more. Constantly writing and associating himself with other poets, he contributed to *Poetry* and various anthologies. His first poem, "When Children Played as Kings and Queens", was privately printed in 1948. Six years later his second poem, "Dinosaurs and Violins", was printed and another 5 years passed before "In The Deepest Aquarium" was published in 1959. He had two more published poems—in 1963 and again in 1971.

Education

Local Fall River schools and B.M.C. Durfee High School. Sobiloff attended the University of Arizona, Boston University and New York University. Sobiloff funded Albert Einstein College of Medicine in New York.

Skills

Sobiloff not only enjoyed the creative aspect of writing poetry, he also engaged in the creative art of short filmmaking, including *Montauk, Central Park* and *Speak To Me Child*.

Also of Note

He received an Academy Award nomination for his short film, *Montauk*, narrated by Sobiloff and Ed Begley in 1959 and was named an Honorary Chancellor and received an honorary law degree from Florida Southern College.

Information gathered from *Book Rags*, HighBeam Research and Fall River Historical Society
—photo courtesy of the Fall River Historical Society collection

NANCY SOREL WEGLOWSKI
Actress

Profile
Born in 1964, Nancy Sorel Weglowski lived on Harding Street with her parents, Al and Diane Weglowski, and her older brother and sister. She lives in Canada with her husband, Paul Magel, also an actor, and their two children.

Experience
Family played a large role in Sorel's youth. Influences include her dad Al, brother Marc and sister Carole Fiola, teachers Pat Dillon and Durfee dramatics teacher James Tavares along with Jane Fiore and Janice MacDonald. Her time in ReCreation Summer Street Theater as well as the Fall River Little Theater helped mold her into a bona fide thespian.

Then came the casting call for the long-running television soap opera, *All My Children*, where she was cast as Taffy, a teenage prostitute. This role gave her a start in the business but she was highly critical of her own performance; she retained a teacher to help improve her craft. Subsequently, she moved on to *One Life To Live*, another daytime drama.

On to Canada and a Canadian Television series entitled *Less Than Kind*, where she starred as Clara, a complex, funny and bold character that has given Sorel great satisfaction to play. She has also had roles in *Murder, She Wrote*, *The X-Files*, *Crow's Nest* and *I Love You, Don't Touch Me*.

Her next film to be released in April 2014 is the Sony Pictures film, *Heaven Is for Real* in which she plays Dr. Charlotte Slater.

Education
Spencer Borden School, B.M.C. Durfee High School and University of Massachusetts.

Skills
Sorel has also performed with Rob Estes, William Devane and Laurie Holden in the television movie *The Man Who Used To Be Me*.

Also of Note
Sorel has won two Canadian Comedy Awards and her goal is to be nominated for and to win an Emmy.

MADLYN-ANN C. WOOLWICH
Artist and Author

Profile
Madlyn-Ann Crawford was born in Fall River in 1937, moved to Somerset at age eleven and then lived in New Jersey with her retired physician husband Joseph Woolwich.

Experience
Woolwich was one of many recognized artists from Fall River. Not only is she a recognized pastel artist, she is also a writer.

Woolwich has written articles for *The Artist Magazine* and *Pastel Journal*. She has published two books, *Pastel Interpretations* (published in France as well as the USA) and *The Art of Pastel Portraiture* (also published in China).

Education
Local Fall River schools, Bridgewater State College (B.S. and M.Ed), Parsons School of Design, The American Academy of Design, UMassDartmouth and Brookdale Community College.

Also of Note
She is a Master Pastelist and former vice president of the Knickerbocker Artists.

Information gathered from *Wikipedia*

HOLDEN DURFEE WETHERBEE
Artist

Profile
Born in 1902 in Lowell, Massachusetts, Holden Durfee Wetherbee was a true Yankee whose ancestors emigrated from England around 1625. H.D., as he was called, died in Greenwich Village in 1976 at the age of seventy-three.

Experience
Wetherbee began his career in Manhattan cutting silhouettes freehand for newspapers as well as in department stores and at state fairs. He painted murals, seascapes and portraits. It was during his years on Block Island in the late 1940s that he produced more than forty paintings and murals and published his book, *Wetherbee's Block Island.*

Education
Wetherbee graduated from B.M.C. Durfee High School in 1920 and then attended Williams College and Harvard.

Also of Note
Wetherbee was a member of the Arts Club of Gramercy Park, and The Newport and Provincetown Art Associations, where he exhibited his silhouettes and paintings.

Information gathered from *Wikipedia* and *Wetherbee's Block Island*

1926-Present

Business

───◆·◆───

Nothing is really work

unless you would rather be doing something else.

───◆·◆───

JAMES M. BARRIE

MALCOM "MAC" ALDRICH
Commonwealth Fund Chair
All-American Football Player

Profile
Malcom Aldrich was born in Fall River in 1900. The son
of Stanley A. and Jane Pratt Aldrich, he had two brothers.
He married Ella Buffington and they had three children
and six grandsons. Aldrich died of pneumonia in 1986 in
South Hampton, New York.

Experience
After graduating from Yale in 1922, Aldrich joined the
staff of philanthropist Edward S. Harkness. Upon Harkness's death in 1940, Aldrich became president of the
Commonwealth Fund, a charitable foundation dedicated
primarily to the support of medical research and education. Aldrich became chair of the board of the foundation
from 1953 until his retirement.

His counsel was sought by many for profit and not-for-
profit groups alike. He served on the board of directors of
The American Museum of Natural History, The Metropolitan Museum of Art, the Columbia-Presbyterian Med-
ical Center, The New York Trust Company, the American Electric Power Co. and the
New York Central Railroad, among other entities.

Education
Local Fall River schools, B.M.C. Durfee High School, Pomfret Preparatory School and
Yale University. He was also honored by University of Massachusetts Dartmouth, Boston
University and Columbia University with honorary doctorates.

Skills
A member of the Greatest Generation, Aldrich achieved the rank of captain in the Naval
Reserves after serving as special assistant to the Assistant Secretary of the Navy for Air
during World War II.

Also of Note
Aldrich received the very first Durfee Distinguished Alumni Award in 1961 and in 1979
the football field at the high school was dedicated in his honor. He was also a member
of the Durfee Sports Hall of Fame for his performance as captain of both the baseball
and football teams. Likewise, he was an All-American football and baseball player at
Yale, where he also served as captain of both sports. He was inducted into the National
Collegiate Football Foundation Hall of Fame and received the Yale Medal.

Information gathered from the Football Hall of Fame, the *Fall River Herald News* and Fall River Historical Society
—photos courtesy of the Fall River Historical Society collection

THE BLACK BROTHERS—BOB, BILL, MIKE AND JIM
Largest Independently Owned Shipping Agency

Profile

The four sons of Irene Riley (her father is also highlighted in the book) and Francis R. Black have all played key leadership roles in advancing the Moran Shipping Agencies into national prominence. The Black brothers—Bob, Bill, Mike and Jim—were all born in Fall River and lived "below the hill" in the row houses on Broad-

From left: Bill, Bob, Mike and Jim Black

way with their three sisters. Bill married Fall River girl Elaine Dempsey and they have two daughters and four grandchildren. Mike married Fall Riverite Sally Manning and they have six children and six grandchildren. Jim married Beth Abbey Black and they have two sons while Bob, the oldest, is now married to Marrita Black and he has three sons.

Experience

Moran Shipping Agencies was founded in 1937, but the expansion did not occur until the Black brothers became involved in the early '70s. Bob Black acquired ownership in 1974 and was joined by his youngest sibling, Jim. Shortly thereafter Mike came on board in 1982 and provided another level of expertise to the growing firm. It was during that time the shipping firm opened offices in the Gulf of Mexico in Texas and Florida but has always maintained corporate headquarters in Providence, Rhode Island. There are twenty full-service offices in nearly 100 ports in North America with 150 full time employees working at the ISO 9001:2000 certified company. The firm provides support to all types of vessels on the East and West Coasts and in the Gulf. It is the largest independently owned shipping agent in the country.

Education

The brothers all attended St. Louis School. Bob Black graduated from Monsignor Coyle High School, Bryant College and took advanced classes at University of Rhode Island, University of Houston and Nanzan University in Japan. He also received his Ph.D. from Bryant. Bill Black graduated from Monsignor Coyle High School and University of Rhode Island; Mike Black graduated from Durfee High School after a time at Coyle High School and then graduated from Durfee College of Technology and University of Rhode Island. Jim Black graduated from Bishop Stang High School and Southeastern Massachusetts University.

Skills

J.F. Moran, which is owned by brother Bill Black, is a worldwide leader in full service customs brokerage, supply chain management, worldwide logistics, compliance, port security insurance, foreign freight forwarding, international trade, importing, exporting and trucking.

Also of Note

Both firms are now employing the next generation of Black family members as they continue to provide international leadership in ports of call all over the world.

Information gathered from the Black family and *Wikipedia*—photo courtesy of the Black family

THOMAS J. BROWN
Diversity and Job Placement Activist

Profile
Thomas J. Brown was born in Fall River in 1925 and died in 2013. He was one of five children of William and Bessie Brown. His wife was Inez (Bev) Brown and they were married for sixty years.

Experience
After graduating from college, Brown took a position as an account executive with an advertising agency. In 1965 he became a special assistant to Edwin H. Land at Polaroid Corp. There he created a "bully pulpit" to assist and place unemployed African-Americans with positions in the Boston area.

Brown founded the Jobs Clearing House and teamed with the owner of a local jobs paper, *The Bay State Banner*, to place more than 10,000 Boston area residents in jobs throughout New England and the nation. No job seeker ever paid a fee and Brown never took a salary as he administered the nonprofit entity for more than thirty years.

"Brownie" photo from 1942 Durfee yearbook.

Education
Local Fall River schools, B.M.C. Durfee High School and Brown University.

Skills
Melvin Miller, founder and publisher of the Bay State Banner, said of Brown, "He was one of the people who did more for the welfare of black people than everybody will ever know."

Also of Note
Brown was the first African-American student accepted into the regional DeMolay International (also known as the Order of DeMolay), an international organization for young men ages twelve to twenty-one dedicated to teaching young men to be better persons and leaders. He entered the service after high school, serving three years in the Army before returning to Fall River and entering Brown University on the GI Bill.

He was the 1987 recipient of the Durfee Distinguished Alumni Award. He was also elected to the board of trustees of both Brown University and Suffolk University. Brown also received the John S. Hope Award in 1997 for outstanding commitment to volunteer public service.

Information gathered from the *Fall River Herald News*, ehe *Boston Globe* and Mrs. Brown—photos courtesy of Mrs. Brown and Durfee High School yearbooks

BLAIR BROWN
Cofounder Architectural Design Firm

Profile
Blair Brown, born in 1941, was the son of Dr. Samuel Brown and Kathryn Borden Brown. He and his brother lived on Rock Street while growing up in Fall River. Brown and his wife, Carol Hedstrom, have four children.

Experience
Although he aspired to be a physician like his father, Brown turned to architecture while in college. While attending graduate school, he and his college friend and fellow Fall Riverite Lionel Spiro found a need in the business end of the profession and filled it. Jointly they started the Charrette* Company, an architectural office supply firm. His experience as a gas station attendant in Fall River as one of his first jobs or writing and producing a play in his senior year of college did not influence his choice of occupations. His sixth grade teacher, Josephine Chase, may have been a motivating factor, however.

Charette expanded and over thirty-three years provided supplies to engineers, government agencies and industrial firms. More than 800 employees worked for the firm at 26 locations when the business was sold in 1997.

Education
Local Fall River schools, Morton Junior High, Phillips Exeter Academy, Harvard University and Harvard graduate school.

Skills
Brown and his brother's college roommate, Lionel Spiro (also include herein), conceived the idea for the supply store while they were both studying at Harvard University.

Also of Note
* The name of the firm, Charette, is a well known term used in the business. When students and professionals in architecture stay up all night to meet a deadline they say they are "charretting." The term came from the leading French school, *Ecole de Beaux Arts*, which would allow students to place their works in a wagon, a charrette, at midnight for teacher consideration.

Information gathered from Mr. Brown and Examiner.com

CHARLES W. CAREY
Banker

Profile
Charley Carey was born in Fall River in 1941 to Mary M. and Charles P. Carey. He is the oldest of seven children and grew up on Seabury Street in the Ruggles Park area. Carey married his college sweetheart, Pamela Plumb and they have two sons and five grandchildren.

Experience
Carey's first job was close to home working for the city of Fall River as a summer counselor at nearby Ruggles Park. The most influential person in his life was Coach Luke Urban, who is also highlighted in this book. In high school Carey played three sports, not uncommon at the time, and spent nearly three hours daily with Urban who taught him discipline, hard work and team work. He was the Most Valuable Player in football and baseball his senior year and named to the All-Bristol County team in both sports.

Carey wanted to play baseball for the Boston Red Sox but that was not to be. (His sons, however, played in the minor leagues for the Red Sox.) He moved into the corporate world after his service in the military and graduate school. Becoming a successful banker and corporate leader at Fleet Bank, working his way through the ranks, Carey was named President of the Fleet equipment leasing company and then vice chair of the Fleet Financial Group, one of the largest financial institutions in the country. As vice chair, he was responsible for commercial banking, real estate activities, the investment banking subsidiary and asset-based lending.

Education
Sacred Heart School, B.M.C. Durfee High School, Colby College and a masters degree in Economics from the University of Maine.

Skills
Carey's pre-business life revolved around the sports he played and learned in Fall River. He was captain of the Colby College football team in his senior year and was named to the All- New England baseball team in his senior year in college.

Also of Note
Carey served in the Air Force and fought in the Vietnam Conflict in 1966 and received the Bronze Star. He was a member of the National Honor Society while at Durfee High School. Carey, like his father, is a member of the Durfee High Sports Hall of Fame. He was named Student Athlete of the Year at graduation from Colby in 1963.

Information gathered from Mr. & Mrs. Carey and Fleet Bank—photo courtesy of the Carey family

RICHARD F. COTTRELL
Rocket Scientist

Profile
Richard Frederic Cottrell was born in 1920 and brought up in the Highland section of Fall River with his brother, Tom. He was the son of James T. and Louise Thompson Cottrell. Married to Jean for sixty-six years, he was the father of seven children, fourteen grandchildren and eight great-grandchildren.

Experience
Cottrell enjoyed a twenty-year career with Aerojet, a rocket and missile propulsion manufacturer based in California from 1956 to 1976. In 1956, Cottrell became chief rocket project engineer for Polaris, the U.S. Navy's submarine-launched missiles. He was also the Chief Engineer, Minuteman in 1961. He was principally responsible for the conversion from liquid-fueled design to the new solid-fuel design rockets. The firm was the primary supplier on a number of ICBM projects, including the Titan and Minuteman missiles.

From 1976 when he left Aerojet until retirement, Cottrell served as founder and president of Imotek, a cogeneration company. While at Imotek, he demonstrated the effectiveness of alternative fuels sources, such as garbage and other forms of waste, to various industries.

Education
Highland School, Morton Junior High, Worcester Academy and Massachusetts Institute of Technology.

Skills
A member of the Greatest Generation, Cottrell served in the U.S. Navy from 1941 to 1946 on board the aircraft carrier *Altamaha* in the South Pacific. During the Korean Conflict, he attained the rank of Commander.

Also of Note
Cottrell received an award from NASA for his pioneering work in the sector of propellant fuel, the large solid propellant rocket motor-the "260." Aerojet was selected to develop and build the main engine for the Appollo Command/Service Module. Cottrell had predicted problems with the o rings as part of the propulsion system of the Space Shuttle, Challenger before its 1986 the launch and tragic results.

Information gathered from the *Fall River Herald News* and the Cottrell family—photo courtesy of the Cottrell family

ROBERT A. DEANE
Inventor and Industrial Instrumentation Manufacturer

Profile
Robert Deane was born in 1928 and grew up with his older brother in Assonet, Massachusetts. He was the son of Ruth Arnold and John A. Deane. He is the great-grandson of Major John M. Deane, who is also highlighted in this book. Deane married Clarisse "Claire" Dupont, also from Fall River; they have three children, five grandchildren and a great-grandchild.

Experience
Deane's scientific career began as a youth in Assonet, where after school jobs included work on a small truck, on dairy farms and as an usher at the Durfee Theater in Fall River. In 1944 and 1945 he worked for the Massachusetts Department of Entomology and Plant Quarantine to try to control the gypsy moth problem. After moving to California in 1954 with his wife, he worked in the aircraft and missile industry for five years and then as a manufacturers representative until 1964.

In 1964 he formed a partnership and started Fluid Components International (FCI), an industrial instrumentation manufacturer of flow and level switches. The business began in his garage and the first year was anything but profitable.

Still a family owned business today, but no longer operating out of his garage, there are now more than 250 employees and the products are used all around the world including at the damaged nuclear energy reactor site in Japan.

After seeing the world with the Navy, Deane relocated to Southern California for the opportunity and lifestyle it presented, but he returns to New England yearly.

Education
Assonet elementary schools, Morton Junior High School, B.M.C. Durfee High School and the Allen School of Aeronautics.

Skills
Deane obtained U.S. patents for his fundamental technology and in 2003 the company added the AS9000 certification to its list of accomplishments. The company maintains a world-class flow and level calibration facility in California and has offices in Europe, Japan and China.

Also of Note
Deane joined the Navy after graduating from Durfee. He was accepted into submarine service and became a "Qualified Submariner" in 1947. It was there that he learned how to operate the many systems of a diesel submarine.

Information gathered from Mr. Deane and Fluid Components International—photo courtesy of Mr. Deane

C. NORMAN DION
Instrumental in Developing 5.25" Floppy Disc

Profile
Camille Norman Dion was born in Fall River in 1931. He is the son of Camille and Beatrice (Demers) Dion and lived in the Maplewood section with his five siblings. He married Genevieve Galego, also of Fall River, in St. Louis Church next to South Park in 1950. They have two children.

Experience
With a degree in electrical engineering from Durfee College of Technology, Dion set out on a career path. He spent eight years at IBM before moving on to Memorex, which had just entered the computer disc pack field in 1970. He oversaw product development there from 1970 to 1973.

In 1973, he was joined by two other engineers and started Dysan Corp in California. The business plan for the firm was to grow and diversify as a manufacturer of information storage devices for the data processing industry. The firm concentrated on developing magnetic products. By 1983, *Forbes* Magazine reported Dysan sales were $161 million with profits of $41 million annually.

Dysan employed more than 1,200 people and was ranked among the top ten private sector employers in the Silicon Valley. The headquarters and manufacturing facility in Santa Clara was an architectural wonder at the time, with lush indoor landscaping, waterfalls and ponds. In 1985, Dion sold his interest in the firm and Dysan merged with Xidex Corporation.

Education
Local Fall River schools, graduated from the Bradford Durfee College of Technology.

Skills
A year after selling his interest to Xidex for $250 million, Dion donated $1 million to the University of Massachusetts Dartmouth to help create the C. Norman Dion Science and Engineering Building on the North Dartmouth campus. The gift at the time was thought to be the largest unrestricted sum ever donated to a public entity of higher learning in Massachusetts.

Also of Note
In 1980, Dion received the Lifetime Achievement Award from his alma mater.

Information gathered from the *Fall River Herald News*
—photo courtesy of *SMU Notes 1989*

WILLIAM H. GAUDREAU
Men's Clothing Manufacturer/Retailer

Profile

Bill Gaudreau was born in Fall River, the only child of Agnes Griffin and William H. Gaudreau, Sr., both born in Fall River. After meeting a college girl at the Lincoln Park Ballroom, he married Fall Riverite Lorraine Houle while in college. They had two sons and two daughters. Lorraine died at aged forty-nine and Bill married another Fall River woman, Therese Chouinard Gibney, eighteen years ago.

Experience

Like many others in this book, Gaudreau's first job was as a newspaper carrier, but it was working his way up the Anderson-Little ladder that provided him with the insight of manufacturing, advertising, distribution, real estate buys and leasing to eventually serve as president of the four-factory, 360-retail-store business.

He felt his greatest business achievement was the merger of Anderson Little and Richman Brothers into the Woolworth Company. Upgrading fabrics and quality control while maintaining low prices was an objective of the firm, which was further bolstered by free alterations for both men's and women's suits for the life of the garments.

Education

Local Fall River schools, B.M.C. Durfee High School and Bryant College.

Skills

Gaudreau served his country in the Navy on a light cruiser and saw duty at sea in Europe and the Mediterranean.

Also of Note

He received the Durfee Distinguished Alumni Award in 1990.

Information gathered from Mr. Gaudreau—photo courtesy of Mr. Gaudreau

BENJAMIN C. GIFFORD
Textile Executive

Profile
Benjamin Gifford was born in Fall River in 1916 to Florence Chase and Paul Gifford. He and his sister were brought up in the Highland section of the city. He married Adelaide Winsor and they had three children and eight grandchildren.
He married Katharine Eddy, who had three children from a previous marriage. He died in Westport in 2011 at age ninety-five.

Experience
Gifford spent his working life in the textile trade, first working for Pepperell Mills in Fall River. After serving in various capacities at textile plants, he became president of Erwin Mills in Durham, North Carolina, which at the time was the largest producer of denim cloth in the country.

When Burlington Industries bought Erwin, he went to work for Burlington Industries in 1960; he concluded his career at Burlington as its executive vice president.

Education
Highland School, Pomfret School and Harvard College 1939.

Skills
Gifford spent time in the Navy as part of the Greatest Generation in WW II as a lieutenant commander of a mine sweeper in the Panama Canal Zone.

Also of Note
After his 1976 retirement, Gifford moved back to the area from New York and was an active volunteer participant in community activities. He served for many years as board chair of Stanley Treatment and Rehabilitation (SSTAR) in Fall River and as a member of the Lloyd Center Board of Directors in South Dartmouth.

Information gathered from the *Fall River Herald News*—photo courtesy of the Gifford family

RONALD A. GOLZ
Bank Executive

Profile
Ronald Golz was born in Fall River in 1934 to Irene F. and Alfred E. Golz. The oldest of three children, Golz lived with his family on Lincoln Avenue near North Park. He has three children and eight grandchildren.

Experience
Golz did not know what he wanted to become as a young-ster, but his father taught him values and to be the best you can be. Luke Urban, also highlighted herewith, taught him how to win. Growing up in Fall River allowed Golz to form many lasting friendships, including Skippy Karam, John Freeman and Morton Dean, some of whom are all highlighted herein as well.

Golz, like many others in this book, was fortunate to have family support as he moved up the ladder in his business life.

His career began at IBM, but his greatest accomplishment occurred while working at State Street Bank in Boston. Starting in 1974, Golz developed a new product for institutional investors that created more than 3,000 new jobs and made the company the largest custodian for pension funds, endowments and foundations worldwide. He became a State Street legend during his career at the banking institution, retiring as an executive vice president.

Education
Local Fall River schools, Morton Junior High, and B.M.C. Durfee High School, where he was the 14th-highest scoring basketball player in the 1950s at nearly 11 points per game. He graduated from Bowdoin College then Villanova University for advanced studies.

Skills
Serving in the U.S. Army for three years, Golz received a Commendation Ribbon with Medal Pendant and achieved the rank of captain.

Also of Note
Golz is a member of the Securities Services Hall of Fame. He is also a senior consul-tant for Rhumbline Adviser with more than $15 billion under management.

Information gathered from Mr. Golz and Manny Papoula—photo courtesy of Mr. Golz

GEORGE GRABOYS, ESQUIRE
Bank Executive

Profile
George Graboys was born in Fall River in 1932. His parents were Rebecca Sobiloff and Lewis Graboys. There were four children and the family lived in the Highlands. He married Lois Wolpert, also a Durfee graduate from Fall River, and they had three children. His brother, Dr. Tom Graboys, is also highlighted herein.

Experience
The left-handed Graboys wanted to become a dentist but with instruments designed for right-handed people he sought another occupation. He was steered toward finance by Durfee teacher and Vice Principal Dan Kelly. It was family, his wife of fifty-four years and his parents who have had the greatest influence on him.

Shortly after graduating from law school, Graboys came to Rhode Island to practice law in 1958 and was named executive vice president at U.S. Finance Corporation. Ten years later Citizens Bank, headquartered in Providence, Rhode Island, bought the finance company and acquired the services of its future president, chair and CEO. After seventeen years of providing vision and unprecedented growth to the institution, including building a new fourteen-story building in downtown Providence and an operations center on forty acres in East Providence, Grayboys spearheaded the acquisition of the bank by the Royal Bank of Scotland Group, the second largest bank in Europe in 1988. He retired four years later in 1992.

Education
Local Fall River schools, Morton Junior High, B.M.C. Durfee High School, Tabor Academy, Dartmouth College and University of Pennsylvania Law School. He received honorary doctorates from Bryant University, Johnson and Wales University and the University of Rhode Island, Rhode Island College as well as the New England Institute of Technology.

Skills
Grayboys served in the military as a member of the Reserves with one year of active duty. He served 12 years on the State of Rhode Island Board of Governors for Higher Education, the final three years as chair and served for a time as an adjunct professor at Rhode Island College of Business. He was elected chair of the board of the Rhode Island Foundation.

Also of Note
Graboys was named Businessperson of the Year by *Ocean State Magazine* and *New England Business Magazine* in the same year, awarded the Torch of Liberty from the Anti-Defamation League and the Rotary Club Citizen of the Year Award. Graboys also received the Dartmouth Supportive Class of 1954 Award.

Information gathered from Mr. Graboys—photo courtesy of Mr. Graboys

FRANCIS C. GRAGNANI
Japanese Coca-Cola Franchisee, Investment Banker and Real Estate Executive

Gragnani's Providence College graduation photo.

Profile
Frank Gragnani was born in Fall River in 1917 to Dora Caruso and Joseph Gragnani, a shoemaker. He and his brother and two sisters grew up in the Columbus Park area. He married Charlotte Baldwin in Japan, and had no children. He died of cancer in 1991 at age seventy-four and is buried in St. Patrick's Cemetery.

Experience
Gragnani was a go-getter. Not only did he work summers and after school hours at the local Coca-Cola plant as a member of the carton sampling crew, he sold neckties at Paul Woltman Men's Store and was an usher at the Durfee Theater. It was his interest in Coke products that led him to such a successful career.

From working as a Coke salesperson after college graduation, then serving his country, the youngster from Fall River moved to Japan and represented the Coca-Cola Company as a plant manager, then as a sales manager, and eventually as a regional vice president. While Coke products could only be sold to American military personnel during the Korean Conflict, the end of the conflict gave Gragnani another opportunity. In 1962 his application to the company for a bottler's franchise was approved. He was the only Caucasian to be granted a franchise in Japan. His franchise employed 400 employees with 120 route trucks delivering to more than 17,000 retail outlets from two bottling plants.

By 1983, it was time for Gragnani to return to the States. Inflation was on the rise and the cost of ingredients for the product was also escalating. He returned to the U.S. and began a more active role with First Winthrop Corporation, a Boston-based real estate company that he founded in 1975.

Education
Local Fall River schools, B.M.C. Durfee High School and Providence College. He was awarded an honorary doctorate of Law from Providence College in 1976.

Skills
A member of the Greatest Generation, Gragnani entered the Army Air Corps in 1942 and served for four years, retiring with the rank of captain.

Also of Note
Gragnani received the Durfee Distinguished Alumni Award in 1978 and there is a scholarship in the names of Charlotte G. and Francis L. Gragnani at Durfee High School. He was a major benefactor of many Fall River charitable organizations but especially to Providence College, where a scholarship benefits graduates of Durfee High School. In 1997, Gragnani's widow donated $3 million towards the construction of a new chapel at the college. In 1989 he was called the most generous benefactor in the history of the college.

There is also a scholarship in his memory at Durfee High School to benefit graduates.

Information gathered from Providence College and the *Fall River Herald News*—photos courtesy of Providence College

MELVIN HOWARD
Corporate Executive

Profile
Melvin Howard was born in 1935 and was raised in Fall River with his sister on 16th Street. They are the children of Mollie Sager and John Horvitz. He married a Fall River girl, Beverly Kahan, and they had two children. After Beverly passed away, he married his current wife, Vivien Kantor.

Experience
Howard had an impressive business career. He has provided leadership to some of this country's top business firms including Ford Motor Company in the 1960s, chief financial officer at Xerox during the 1970s and vice chair and chief executive officer of Xerox Financial Services in the 1980s.

In 1985 he became chair and chief executive officer of Crum and Foster, a Xerox subsidiary.

Howard was vice chair and headed Xerox's $5 billion financial services operations when he retired at age fifty-five in 1990.

Education
Local Fall River schools, B.M.C. Durfee High School, University of Massachusetts Amherst and a master's degree in business from Columbia University.

Skills
Howard has served on the University of Massachusetts Amherst Foundation board of directors and the board of the University's elite Commonwealth College. He also created the Melvin Howard Scholarship Endowment at the University.

Also of Note
Howard served as a member of President Ronald W. Reagan's Disarmament Commission. He was also a recipient of the University of Massachusetts Distinguished Service Alumni Award and received the Chancellor's Medal in 1999.

Information gathered from UMass Amherst and the *New York Times*, Mr. Howard—photo courtesy of UMass Amherst

MARCEL JOSEPH
Telecommunications Executive

Profile
Marcel Joseph was born in 1935 in Fall River, one of four children of F. Joseph Joseph and Maria Joseph. They lived on the border of the Flint and Maplewood sections of the city. He married Linda Neto and they have two sons, a daughter and two grandchildren.

Experience
Joseph not only made news over the years, he also delivered the news as a paper carrier for the *Fall River Herald News* when he was a youngster. His brother Carmel, a jet pilot who fought in WWII, as well as educators Bob Nagle, Harry Jackson and Helen Donovan were motivating forces for a young person who did not benefit from extracurricular activities because he needed to work.

Becoming a vice president and general manager at General Electric, and working along with executive Jack Welch, was one of his career achievements. After twenty-five years at GE, Joseph's career continued at the Communications Satellite Corporation, Comsat, where Joseph became president.

Serving as president, CEO and eventually chair of Augat, Inc. was Joseph's crown jewel. Augat was one of the largest manufacturers of connector products in the world. It designed and manufactured a wide range of electromechanical components for the electronics industry and produced integrated circuit sockets, coaxial cable networks as well as fiber optic products.

Education
Brayton Avenue School, Henry Lord Junior High, B.M.C. Durfee High School, Bradford Durfee College of Technology and a master's at Rensselaer Polytechnic Institute.

Skills
In 1996 after eight years at the helm, Joseph retired from Augat, Inc. at age fifty-nine. He stayed on with the company as chair of the board.

Also of Note
He received the Durfee Distinguished Alumni Award in 1991.

Information gathered from Mr. Joseph and the *New York Times*—photo courtesy of Mr. Joseph

WILLIAM A. KALIFF
International Business Executive

Profile
William Kaliff was born in Fall River in 1913, the oldest of two sons to Rose Chlala and Ibrahim Kaliff. They lived in the Flint section of the city. He married Laurette Mautouk and they had six children. He died in 2004 and is buried in Fairfield, Connecticut.

Experience
Setting up duck pins on the bowling alley in Fall River was Kaliff's first of many jobs he held as he worked to help out the family. His objective had always been to provide a comfortable life for his family. This desire to help provide for his mother and younger brother naturally evolved into his role as spouse and father.

Kailiff set out for New York after the Great Depression to be part of a growing business, and Morton Salt first benefited from his talent and determination. He headed up West India sales for Morton and became a vice president for Morton International.

Education
Local Fall River schools, B.M.C. Durfee High School and Bradford Durfee College of Technology.

Skills
Kaliff was a great negotiator. That was evidenced by his negations with King Faisal for a land lease in Egypt and with the West India sales on behalf of Morton International.

Also of Note
Kaliff was part of the Greatest Generation. As a Major in the army and fluent in Arabic, he served as an interpreter for General Dwight D. Eisenhower. As an interpreter he took part in meetings with the famous King of Saudi Arabia, 'Abd al-'Aziz.

Information gathered from the Kaliff family and Saudi Aramco World—photo courtesy of the Kaliff family

EMERIL J. LAGASSE, III
Celebrity Chef, Author, Television Personality, Businessperson and Musician

Profile
Emeril Lagasse was born in Fall River in 1959 to Hilda and Emeril Lagasse, Jr. He and his brother and sister lived on the border of the Flint and Maplewood sections near the famed St. John's Club. His first wife was Elizabeth Kief, whom he met while they both worked at the Venus De Milo Restaurant in Swansea. He had two daughters with Kief. He is presently married to Alden Lovelace and they have a son and daughter.

Experience
BAM! Lagasse began his food career by working in a Portuguese bakery as a teen, then worked in kitchens at Whites of Westport and Venus de Milo Restaurants (the owners of both are included in this book) and the Quequechan Club in Fall River to help pay his way through school.

Sensing it was time to "Kick it up a notch!", Lagasse became the Executive Chef at Commander's Palace in New Orleans in 1982. He opened his own restaurant, Emeril's, in 1990. It was television, though, that really launched Lagasse's career. After appearances on various Food Network programs he hosted his own show, *The Essence of Emeril*. With a personality bigger than life, he was perfect for television and developed a string of shows— *Emeril Live, From Emeril's Kitchen, The Emeril Lagasse Show, Emeril's Table* and *Emeril Green*. Lagasse has developed a broad line of products and spice blends that he sells under his own label as well as at least 18 cook books and 13 restaurants that he owns in four states. He has appeared on the Shop at Home Network and more recently on the Home Shopping Network.

Education
Local Fall River schools, Diman Regional Vocational Regional High School and Johnson and Wales University. He received an honorary doctorate from Johnson and Wales.

Skills
Lagasse is also a talented percussionist and earned a scholarship to the New England Conservatory of Music, but his true love has always been cooking.

Also of Note
Lagasse is presently the owner of thirteen restaurants including Emeril's, which was named Best New Restaurant of the Year by *Esquire* magazine in 1990, *Time* magazine named *Essence of Emeril* one of the 10 best shows on television in 1991. Lagasse was the Grand Marshall of the 2008 Tournament of Roses Parade. He is a member of the Diman Regional Vocational Technical High School Hall of Fame.

Information gathered from *Wikipedia*—photo courtesy of Steven Freeman

LOUIS E. LATAIF
Automotive Executive and Educator

Profile
Louis Lataif was born in Fall River in 1939. He is the son of Linda Salwan and Louis Lataif and grew up in the Flint with his brother and sister. Lataif is married to Najla Lataif and they have four children and nineteen grandchildren.

Experience
His working career began in his father's rug business, where the entire family worked. His father's emphasis on faith, personal integrity and reputation impressed Lataif and he brought those values to his management training program in marketing at Ford Motor Company in 1964. From that experience, it was hands-on in the showroom in Dearborn, Michigan, at a dealership selling cars and trucks. His career at the international auto giant took him and his family from the East Coast to the West Coast and everywhere in between.

Lataif had a twenty-seven-year distinguished career with the Ford Motor Company. During the 1980s his career at Ford catapulted forward. In 1981 he was elected a corporate vice president and general manager of Ford Division, the youngest Ford officer then. In 1985 he was named Vice President, North American Sales Operations, and three years later he was named President, Ford of Europe, until 1991 when he moved on to Boston University to become Dean of the School of Management.

Education
Local Fall River schools, B.M.C. Durfee High School, Boston University and an MBA from Harvard. He holds honorary degrees from University of Massachusetts Dartmouth, Boston University and Lycoming College.

Skills
Named Dean of the Boston University School of Management in 1991, he served in that capacity for more than eighteen years. During that time, applications from undergraduates to the School of Management soared from just 2,000 to 4,300. Lataif also oversaw the construction of a new, modern building to house the expanding School of Management. He has served on the board of directors of Abiomed, Inc., Intier Automotive, Inc., Group 1 Automotive and Magna International.

Also of Note
Lataif is the recipient of the Ellis Island Medal of Honor and is a trustee of the Iacocca Foundation. In 1961 he was chosen as the Boston University Man of the Year. Today, he holds the title of Dean Emeritus of Boston University School of Management.

Information gathered from Mr. Lataif and Boston University—photo courtesy of Mr. Lataif

ROBERT F. LEDUC
Space System Executive

Profile
Robert Leduc was born in Fall River to Omer and Ruth Leduc. He has an older sister and they lived in the South End section of the city near Kennedy Park. He married Jeanne Roy and they have two daughters.

Experience
Leduc began his employment at St. Anne's Hospital in the housekeeping and maintenance departments when he was not going to school. He aspired to become an automotive engineer and entered Pratt and Whitney in 1978 as an entry level engineer.

He served as executive vice president and chief operating officer of Pratt & Whitney and then was named president, Flight Systems and U.S. Classified Programs at Hamilton Sundstrand in 2004. Leduc is currently president of Boeing Programs and Space Systems for United Technologies Aerospace Systems.

Education
Fowler and St. Anne's Schools, Bishop Connolly High School and University of Massachusetts Dartmouth.

Skills
Giving back is a big part of the Leduc family lifestyle, coming from family values of both the Roy and Leduc families. It is not unique to those families but characteristic of people from Fall River of all backgrounds.

Also of Note
Leduc is a trustee of the UMass Dartmouth Foundation. He and his wife, Jeanne, have created the Robert and Jeanne Leduc Center for Civic Engagement in the School of Education, Public Policy and Civic Engagement at University of Massachusetts Dartmouth. He is also chair of the board of Hamilton Sundstrand Space Systems International.

Information gathered from Mr. Leduc and UMass Dartmouth—photo courtesy of Mr. and Mrs. Leduc

ALBERT A. "ABE" LIST
Industrialist and Philanthropist

Profile
Born in Fall River in 1901, Abe List died in New York in 1987 of heart failure at age eighty-six. List was the youngest of four children of Ethel Haimovich and Alter List. He married Vera Glaser from Boston and they had four daughters, twelve grandchildren and twenty-three great-grandchildren. He is buried in the Jewish Cemetery in Fall River.

Experience
List learned about business and had his first of many major successes in Fall River. His father was a major influence in learning business and he went to work at age fourteen in his father's grocery business when his two older brothers entered World War I. When they returned from the war in 1918, List and his brothers expanded the grocery business and acted as a distributor for the Frigidaire division of General Motors Corporation. Subsequent to that he began his own company, Crescent Corporation, which bought defunct firms and revitalized them. A tireless businessperson, List was known for working eighteen hour days. By age thirty-six, List had made over $1 million and retired.

His retirement was short-lived, though, and he reentered the business world in 1942. List acquired control of several companies and in 1957 he gained control of Glen Alden and later the Hudson Coal Company, the country's major hard coal producers. He turned both entities into a conglomerate that included the 47-theater RKO chain. One of his final business ventures was ownership of Strahl & Pitsch, a refiner of natural waxes.

Education
Local Fall River elementary schools and night school. He was forced to leave school at age fourteen to work in his father's store.

Skills
List had two great skills: making money and giving it away. His philanthropic interests include medical research, arts, education and social justice. Major beneficiaries of his generosity, later continued by his wife, Vera, were Mount Sinai Hospital and the New School for Social Research, now New School University. He believed strongly that one was put on earth to be productive and share with humanity. He donated funds for art centers at M.I.T., Brown University, Swarthmore and Kirkland Colleges. His support of Jewish charities and studies was also well-known. He also did not forget his hometown with donations to the United Way and Boys and Girls Club among other groups.

Also of Note
Vera List received the National Medal of the Arts from President Clinton in 1996.

Information gathered from Lauren Small, a granddaughter and the *New York Times*—photo courtesy of Ms. Small

ALAN "MICK" MANNING
*Consulting Engineer
and Business Founder*

Profile

Alan Manning is the son of longtime Fall River Department of Public Works Director, Franklin B. Manning and Katherine Kelly. Manning and his brother and two sisters were all born in Fall River and lived near Maplewood Park. He married a Fall River and Sacred Heart Academy girl, Mary Owen. They have three daughters and seven grandchildren.

Experience

A few years after college, Manning formed Environmental Management Associates in Minnesota in 1975. He served as CEO until 2000 and then moved up to chair of the board for a decade.

The employee-owned corporation, EMA, Inc. changed its name to EMA after realizing that its scope of work offered far exceeded Environmental Management. The company focus now includes work practices and technologies for its customers to become and remain competitive.

Manning and his associates served as consulting engineers for municipalities, utilities and manufacturers by providing practical, sustainable technology and management solutions in water and waste water.

Education

Local Fall River schools, B.M.C. Durfee High School and University of Massachusetts Amherst.

Skills

Manning had the skill and saw the need to automate public utilities in 1975, which resulted in the formation of the firm.

Information gathered from Mr. Manning and EMA, Inc.—photo courtesy of Mrs. Manning

JOHN P. "JACK" MANNING
Real Estate Executive

Profile
Jack Manning and his younger brother, Mike, were born in Fall River to Dr. John E. Manning, a well-known pediatrician and Lily Manning, who contracted polio when her children were very young and remained confined to an iron lung for her entire life. Manning, born in 1948, has been married twice. His present wife is Lyle Howland and he has two children.

Experience
Manning held two positions in the investment advisory field before co-founding Boston Capital Corporation. He structured investments in real estate for the Private Wealth Management division of Fleet Financial until 1972. From 1972 to 1974, Manning was a vice president for Beverly Hills Bancorp and was responsible for structuring new real estate development in the Los Angeles metropolitan area.

Boston Capital Corporation's goal since its inception in 1974 has been to provide equity investment capital for the development of apartment properties across the country.

The corporation is now the largest owner/investor in apartment properties, approximately 2,400, in 49 states in the nation and the Virgin Islands.

Manning's current role as CEO is to oversee the firm's business development goals, including expansion of investment capital for renewable energy developments. His friendship with various political figures including President Clinton led to the creation of tax-credit legislation for low-income housing.

Education
Sacred Heart School, Monsignor Coyle High School and Boston College.

Skills
Manning has served on the boards of a number of national housing organizations and governmental commissions. President Clinton appointed him in 1997 to the President's Export Council and he was also an appointee to the President's Advisory Committee on the Arts.

Also of Note
Manning serves on the board of Beth Israel Deaconess Medical Center, The American Ireland Fund, the John F. Kennedy Presidential Library Foundation and the Liberty Mutual Group. The *Boston Globe* has reported that Manning is a billionaire as a result of his real estate empire.

Information gathered from Mr. Manning and EMA, Inc.—photo courtesy of Mrs. Manning

DOUGLAS J. MELLO
Telecommunications Executive

Profile
Doug Mello was born in Fall River in 1942 to Alice D'Ponte and John C. Mello. He and his sister grew up in the South End of Fall River, later living on President Avenue. He married a Fall River girl, Ellen Mooney, whose brother Dan is also highlighted herein. They had two children and two grandchildren.

Their twenty-five-year-old son, Christopher, was one of the victims in the 9/11 tragedy. He was a passenger on one of the planes that hit the Twin Towers.

Experience
Mello worked for NYNEX for 35 years after beginning his career with New York Telephone after graduating from college. He held a variety of senior management positions with the communications giant, serving as chair, president and CEO of NYNEX Business Information Services. Mello led a sales force of more than 10,000 and doubled revenues to $1 billion. He was group vice president, Manhattan, at NYNEX before being named president of Large Business Sales, North, for Bell Atlantic in 1996. He served in that capacity for three years.

Education
Local Fall River schools, B.M.C. Durfee High School, Boston College and Duke University.

Skills
He started his own firm, DJM Advisory Services, Inc. in 1999.

Also of Note
Mello serves on the board of directors of Warwick Telephone Company, Xstream Solutions, USA Datanet and Straitshot Communications. He is also a member of the advisory board of Marcum Cronus Partners, LLC.

DANIEL L. MOONEY, PH.D.
Physicist

Profile
Daniel L. Mooney, born in Fall River in 1943, is the first child of eight of Dr. Daniel L. and Mary Mullery Mooney. Mooney married fellow Fall Riverite and Durfee graduate, Madeleine Yvonne Dufresne. They have three children and ten grandchildren.

Experience
Mooney always wanted to be a physicist and his dream was encouraged by his father. However, it was a single high school teacher who doubted his ability to get an advanced degree that really motivated him. A friend helped him get a job at Lincoln Laboratory at M.I.T. in 1970 and he has been there ever since, most recently mentoring young physicists.

Lincoln Labs has provided technology for national security and Mooney was part of many development teams. The most recent team of seven developed an infrared imaging processor on low power. It brings high sensitivity, high resolution, large field of view and a fast data rate to IR imaging. It is a digital-pixel focal plane array.

Education
Sacred Heart School, DeLaSalle Academy, College of the Holy Cross and University of Connecticut.

Skills
Over 700 patents have been granted to Lincoln Lab for technologies, many developed by Mooney and his teams over the years.

Also of Note
Mooney and his other team members were recognized in 2010 with a Research and Development 100 Award that recognizes the year's 100 most technologically significant innovations.

Information gathered from Lincoln Labs and Dr. Mooney—photo courtesy of Dr. and Mrs. Mooney

JOSEPH E. MULLANEY, JR., ESQUIRE
International Consumer Products Executive

Profile
Joseph E. Mullaney, Jr., was born in Fall River in 1933 and is the fourth of five children of Judge Beatrice Hancock Mullaney (also highlighted herein) and Joseph E. Mullaney, Sr. He married the late Rosemary Woodman and they are the parents of five children and have eight grandchildren.

Experience
After his military service, Mullaney began his career as an associate attorney with the Cleveland law firm of Jones, Day, Reavis and Pogue where he became a partner specializing in business and corporate law.

Mullaney joined the Gillette Company as associate general counsel in 1972. His career at Gillette included time as general counsel, corporate vice president, senior vice president and then as a director and vice chair in 1990. He remained in that capacity until he retired in 1998.

Mullaney's Durfee yearbook photo.

Education
Local Fall River schools, B.M.C. Durfee High School, College of the Holy Cross and Harvard Law School, all with the high honors.

Skills
Mullaney served as a lieutenant in the Judge Advocate General's Corps of the U.S. Air Force from 1958 to 1960.

In 1971, Mullaney was appointed general counsel to the Office of Special Trade Representative in Washington. That office coordinated and supervised trade policies of the United States. He then served as general counsel for the Cost of Living Council in the Executive Office of the President.

Also of Note
Mullaney, like his mother, Judge Mullaney, received the Durfee Distinguished Alumni Award. His was presented in 1995. They are the only mother-son team so recognized by the school. He is also a member of the Durfee High School Sports Hall of Fame.

He served as a trustee of the Boston Public Library, and was former chair of the Boston Municipal Research Bureau and the New England Legal Foundation. He was a member of the Greater Boston Chamber of Commerce and the World Affairs Council in Boston and the Massachusetts Taxpayers Foundation. Mullaney funded the Judge Beatrice H. Mullaney and Rosemary W. Mullaney Family Services Endowment Fund at the United Way of Greater Fall River, Inc. to benefit residents of Greater Fall River. His family was also recognized for outstanding service by the Massachusetts Society for the Prevention of Cruelty to Children. His generosity benefits the Boston Public Library, as well.

Information gathered from Mr. Mullaney, The Boston Public Library, *Forbes* Magazine and *The Herald News*
—photos courtesy of Mr. Mullaney and the Durfee yearbooks

JAMES F. O'HEARN
Chemical Producer Executive

Profile
James O'Hearn was born in Fall River 1935 and is the third of four children of Eileen and Francis O'Hearn. He grew up in the Maplewood section of the city. He married Sabrina Hu and they have two children and 4fourgrandchildren.

Experience
O'Hearn always wanted to learn multiple languages and eventually serve in the diplomatic corps of the United States. It was teaching that led him to become proficient in more than one language.

He was inspired by his Henry Lord Junior High teachers Bob Nagle and Frank Fanning and he put his skills to work in the Freetown Schools before relocating to Japan as a teacher for the Defense Department. His education in Fall River prepared him to compete internationally.

O'Hearn was inspired to return to Asia after his teaching assignment was complete and he did so while in the employ of Reynolds Metals Co. in 1965 as a regional manager in Hong Kong. By 1972, President Nixon had opened a dialogue with China and trade began with O'Hearn on the ground floor. His ability to speak two Chinese languages fluently gave him an upper hand when he became president of Premier Chemical in 1980. He helped open the door for American business to negotiate contracts with China for textiles and chemicals after the Canton Trade Fair in 1972.

It was not long before Premier Chemical was doing business in the Soviet Union between 1977 and 1980. O'Hearn participated in establishing chemical joint venture factories in Taiwan, Korea, Thailand and China from 1980 to 2003.

Education
Stone School, Henry Lord Junior High School and B.M.C. Durfee High School. He graduated from Providence College, Bridgewater State University and Sofia University in Tokyo.

Skills
Between employment in Japan and China, he worked for Uniroyal in Singapore and later became that firm's European Marketing Director based in Belgium.

Also of Note
He received the Durfee Distinguished Alumni Award in 2003. O'Hearn was elected president of the 1,200 member firms American Chamber of Commerce in Taipei, Taiwan, for a two-year term in the early 1990s. He then served as president of the 1,500-member American Club in China.

Information gathered from Mr. O'Hearn and Durfee Chimes—photo courtesy of Mr. O'Hearn

RICHARD M. ROSENBERG, ESQUIRE
Banking Executive

Profile
Richard Rosenberg was born in Fall River in 1930. He was the only child of Charles and Betty Rosenberg and they lived on New Boston Road in Fall River. He married fellow Durfee graduate, Barbara Cohen, Ph.D. They have been married for fifty-seven years and have two sons and five grandchildren.

Experience
After Rosenberg's father lost his job during the Great Depression and his parents lost their spirit, he wanted to make them proud. A brief experience in the restaurant business as a teen and a desire to become a journalist, editor of the Durfee yearbook, were only part of his life journey. It was West Coast banking where his leadership skills shone. Rosenberg excelled at bank marketing and at Wells Fargo Bank in California; he moved up the ranks to serve as vice chair and director for more than twenty-two years. Following his time at Wells Fargo, Rosenberg moved to Seattle-First National Bank and Seafirst Corporation as president and CEO.

Rosenberg, left, and his wife, Barbara with Jehuda Reinharz who was the President of Brandeis University and Dr. Peter Petri also from Fall River who is head of the International Business School and highlighted herein.

He joined Bank of America, which was headquartered in San Francisco in 1987, and became chair and CEO from 1990 through 1996. During that period, Bank of America acquired Security Pacific Corporation and Continental Bank and achieved record earnings, stock prices and dividend levels.

Education
Highland School, Morton Junior High School and B.M.C. Durfee High School. He graduated from Suffolk and Golden Gate Universities.

Skills
Rosenberg is a retired United States Naval Reserve commander and he served in Vietnam. He is also a member of the California Bar Association.

Also of Note
Rosenberg received the Durfee Distinguished Alumni Award in 1986. He has served on the board of many civic and charitable organizations, including the California Institute of Technology, the San Francisco Symphony and the San Francisco United Way. He has also served on the board of Pacific Life, SBC Communications and Northrop Grumman among others. He and his wife, Barbara, have established The Rosenberg Institute of Global Finance at Brandeis University International Business School. He was recently elected a member of the American Academy of Arts and Science.

Information gathered from Mr. & Mrs. Rosenberg and Brandeis University International Business School
—photos courtesy of Mr. Rosenberg

LIONEL SPIRO
Co-founder Architectural Design Firm

Profile
Lionel Spiro is the son of Caroline and Harry Spiro and grew up with his sister on Lincoln Avenue and Highland Avenue. He is married to Vivian Reubens Kemp Spiro and they have two children. He also has two children from a previous marriage.

Experience
As a youngster, Spiro's first job was in the construction business at his father's lumber yard in Fall River. He knew he wanted to become an architect from the time he was a young man. He excelled in high school in order to move on to college and graduate school to achieve his ambition. Along the way, he and his college classmate's younger brother developed a plan to combine their architectural skills with the needs of the industry and established a large supply house called the Charrette* Company. His business grew and expanded over 33 years with 800 employees at 26 locations.

Charrette did business with manufacturing facilities including Ford, Raytheon, GM and Chrysler along with various design offices within the government. Charrette also manufactured and provided products for structural, mechanical, civil, electrical and electronic engineers as well as designers at advertising agencies, media firms and television shows.

Education
Borden, Westall, Morton Junior High School and B.M.C. Durfee High School (National Honor Society), Harvard and Harvard graduate school.

Skills
Spiro sold the business in 1997 but did not leave the business world. He served on the board of directors of Monro Muffler/Brake, Inc., from 1992 to his retirement in 2010.

Also of Note
* The name of the firm, Charette, is a well known term used in the business. When students and professions in architecture stay up all night to meet a deadline they say they are "charretting." The term came from the leading French school, *Ecole de Beaux Arts*, which would allow students to place their works in a wagon, a charrette, at midnight for teacher consideration.

Spiro was voted most brilliant by his classmates at Durfee in 1956.

Information gathered from Mr. Spiro, *Forbes Magazine* and *The Examiner*—photo courtesy of Mr. Spiro

LEE A. SUNDERLAND
Men's Clothing Manufacturer/Retailer CEO

Profile
Lee Sunderland was born in Fall River in 1940, the second son of Arthur H. and Anne L. Andrew Sunderland. They lived on Bradford Avenue, next to the railroad tracks, near South Park. He married Diane Cote more than fifty years ago and they have three sons and nine grandchildren.

Experience
Sunderland's working career began on the farms of Swansea when he was a teenager. Long days and hard work were ingrained in him at a young age and served him well during his business career. His father and his professor, Dr. William Wilde, were his greatest influences, but listening to adults relate their own stories of success motivated him to work hard and enjoy his own success as a businessperson.

He took a part-time factory stockroom job at one of Fall River's major employers, Anderson-Little, during his college years. Invited to work in the office by the firm's owner, he jumped at the opportunity to learn all aspects of the men's clothing manufacturing business. Sunderland rose through the company ranks, learning all aspects of the business. He traveled all over the world and eventually became president and CEO of Anderson-Little/Richman Bros. He was instrumental in relocating the corporate offices from Ohio to Fall River.

Education
Local Fall River schools, Morton Junior High School and B.M.C. Durfee High School. He graduated from Providence Country Day School and Bradford Durfee College of Technology.

Skills
During his tenure Anderson-Little not only continued to manufacture men's clothes in Fall River and other locations, it became a household retail name with hundreds of retail outlets in malls across the country. Eventually, the firm became a division of Woolworth Company which changed its name to Venator, refocused its business model, and closed the division.

Also of Note
Sunderland served in the U.S. Coast Guard Reserves but spent six months on active duty as well. He felt that basic training in the military was something that all able-bodied citizens should experience to make one a better person.

Actively involved in the community, Sunderland served as general campaign chair and later as chair of the board of the United Way of Greater Fall River, Inc.

Information gathered from Mr. Sunderland—photo courtesy of Mr. Sunderland

CLINTON WOODROW WALKER
International Furniture Manufacturer and Retailer

Profile
Born in 1917, Clinton Walker was the son of Effie Mercer and Harry Walker. He and his brother lived on the family farm in Fall River before moving to Pottersville in Somerset, Massachusetts. Walker married Eleanor Ferguson and they had twp daughters and a son who passed away at a very young age. After Eleanor's death, he married Janet Dustin, a widow herself with two young children. He died in 2006 and is buried in Oak Grove Cemetery in Fall River.

Experience
Walker filled his life with multiple career opportunities. As a teen during the Great Depression—with unemployment in Fall River between 25 and 35 percent and with a need to help support the family— he worked three jobs. He worked as a contractor, soda jerk and night nurse for an elderly man for a total of $61.50 for a 110-hour work week.

While playing football at Durfee, Walker was referred by a classmate to Pacific Oil in Fall River and he landed an office job. He also started a band, Clint Walker's New Englanders, and recruited Eleanor Ferguson as his piano player. He later married Ferguson and they started their family.

At age eighteen, Walker tested for a job at the Naval Torpedo Station in Newport, Rhode Island. He was selected an apprentice machinist trainee. He earned less money per week but followed his mother's advice and it was the training and experience that later paid big dividends.

After the war, it was off to the roofing, siding and insulation business as a door-to-door salesperson on commission only. Then it was time to uproot the family and head to Rutland, Vermont, and the Howe Scale Company where at age twenty-six he was paid $60 per week but refused the position of chief of engineering at $10,000 per year. He continued to work nights at Virginia Pulp and Paper and on weekends he painted houses to earn $100 a week.

Walker's first exposure to the furniture business was at Beecher Falls in Vermont, but after two years he transferred his family to the New York area to get medical treatment for their son while working for T. Baumritter as vice president of manufacturing. The Fall Riverite oversaw two facilities; one in Boonville, NY, and one in Orleans, VT. As the Ethan Allen Gallery idea grew so did Walker's responsibilities at Baumritter. Soon the company's name changed to Ethan Allen with 18 factories and innumerable retail outlets.

He moved the corporate office from New York to Danbury, Connecticut, and was named president after thirty-three years with the furniture manufacture/retailer. As Walker would say, "Not bad for a Fall River lad, a product of the Depression."

Education
Fall River and Somerset elementary schools, B.M.C. Durfee High School, Tufts University, Brown University and an honorary doctorate from Annhurst College in Connecticut.

Skills
"Pappy" Walker joined the military when his bother, Hank, was reported missing in action soon after the bombs fell on Pearl Harbor. After flight training, his mission to bomb Tokyo was canceled when the atom bomb exploded over Hiroshima.

Also of Note
A member of the Greatest Generation, Walker was a member of the Army Air Force as a Bombardier Navigator. He and his wife Jan, established a significant scholarship fund at Durfee High School in Eleanor's name.

Information gathered from *Diary of a Walker* and the Walker family—photo courtesy of the Walker family

1926-Present
Education

Durfee Alma Mater

I

Rise our praises high to Durfee
Alma Mater dear,
Tow'ring high beside the river,
Radiant beacon clear.

II

God preserve for Alma Mater
Standards staunch and true
High aloft we'll lift her banner
Bright with Durfee hue.

Chorus:
Love and praise we render ever,
Voices raised on high.
Loud we sing of Durfee's glory
To the earth and sky.

B.M.C. DURFEE HIGH SCHOOL

SAMUEL T. ARNOLD
First Brown University Provost

Profile
Samuel T. Arnold was born in 1892 in Fall River, the son of Reverend Henry and Annie Tomlinson Arnold. He had a brother and two sisters. He married Vera Stockard in 1920; they had three sons and five grandchildren. He died in 1956.

Experience
Before his long, illustrious career at Brown University in Providence, Rhode Island, Arnold taught evening classes in Central Falls, Rhode Island, as a way to earn extra money.

Arnold was appointed an assistant chemistry professor in 1917 after three years as an instructor. He was promoted to associate and then full professor by 1930. During World War II, Arnold assisted the National Defense Committee to recruit scientists for the Manhattan Project in New Mexico that created the atomic bomb.

Arnold was named Provost in 1949.

Education
Local Fall River schools, B.M.C. Durfee High School, Corinna Union Academy in Maine, Brown University 1913 (Phi Beta Kappa and Sigma Xi, James Manning and Francis Wayland Scholar). Brown also awarded him a masters and doctorate in chemistry in 1916.

Skills
Beside teaching and research, Professor Arnold's service extended to administrative work at the University as Dean. As Dean of the University in 1946, Arnold was responsible for oversight at the Graduate School, Pembroke College and the Veterans College.

Provost Arnold was named the first president of the Naval NROTC Colleges.

Also of Note
Called "Father of Brown", Provost Arnold was recognized with the Arnold Fellowships for graduating seniors and his portrait is located in the Keeney Quad. He served as a member of the Fulbright award selection committee.

To paraphrase Sam Arnold: One must talk with these students, not down to them. One never knows how superior they will be after they leave college.

Information gathered from Bob Deane and Brown University—photo courtesy of Brown University

RICHARD MATTHEW BONALEWICZ, PH.D.
Educator, Coach and Air Force Lt. Colonel

Profile
Richard Matthew Bonalewicz grew up in Fall River, the son of Matthew and Joan Bonalewicz, also Fall River natives. He had two sisters and a brother. Bonalewicz was married to Marcia Will and they had three daughters. Born in 1941, he died in 2011, and is buried in Arlington National Cemetery.

Experience
Bonalewicz is another one of the cream of the crop who might be placed in multiple categories but it was his love of education that warranted this placement.

His first job, however, was sports related: setting duck pins at the Walko Bowling Alley at "Globe Four Corners".

Bonalewicz taught at SUNY Brockport, Rochester Institute of Technology, Gannon University and Mercyhurst College NE.

His career at Gannon University began in 1984 as Director of Pre-Podiatry followed by Department Chair of Sports Science and Human Movement Program. Bonalewicz also served as Director of the General Science Program and Environmental Studies Program. He finished his career as an associate professor of Exercise Physiology from 2002 to retirement.

Bonalewicz's teaching career included classes in biology, earth sciences, exercise science, health and geography.

Education
Greene School and St. Patrick's School, B.M.C. Durfee High School and Colby College. He received his masters at California State University and his doctorate at the University of Oregon, Squadron Officers School, Marine Corps Command and Staff College, Air Command and Staff College.

Skills
Lt. Colonel Bonalewicz was an Air Force navigator in Vietnam and a reserve liaison for the Air Force Academy. He was also a baseball coach for SUNY Brockport, Gannon and RIT. He worked on the field of the 1996 Olympic Games for the United States baseball team, which won the bronze medal.

Also of Note
Lt. Colonel Dr. Bonalewicz is a member of the Durfee High Sports Hall of Fame as a member of the 1957 baseball team and a protegé of Luke Urban in three sports.

He received both the Distinguished Flying Cross and two Air Medals.

Information gathered from the Bonalewicz family and the *Eire Times-News*—photos courtesy of the family

R. JUDSON CARLBERG
President of Gordon College

Profile
Judson Carlberg was the son of Helen Thomas Carlberg and Robert L. Carlberg. He was born in 1940. The family lived on Highland Avenue near Truesdale Hospital while he and his younger two siblings were growing up. He married Janice Dawn Jensen while in graduate school and they have two children and two grandchildren.

Experience
Being a *Herald News* paper carrier and following that up with delivering milk for the H.P. Hood Milk Company was the beginning of delivering a lifetime of service to others for Judson Carlberg.

After teaching stints at Michigan State University and John Wesley College in Michigan, Carlberg returned to Massachusetts as Dean of Faculty at Gordon College in Wenham in 1976. As a senior leader at Gordon over the next thirty-five years, he was able to help shape the institution it is today. His family, his teachers including Miss Mildred Carroll and Faust Fiore, and certainly his strong Christian faith were motivating factors in his success.

Since 1992 when he took over as president of the college, Gordon College has grown from 1,200 to 1,800 students and raised more than $69 million to construct and renovate buildings, advance academic programs and institute studies in foreign countries. He is now President Emeritus.

Education
Highland School and graduated from B.M.C. Durfee High School, Wheaton College in Illinois, Denver Seminary and Michigan State University.

Skills
Carlberg has served on a variety of distinguished boards of higher education. He is an authority in the field of character development and leadership.

Also of Note
Carlberg received the Durfee Distinguished Alumni Award in 2000.

Information gathered from Mr. Carlberg and *The Durfee Chimes*—photo courtesy of Gordon College

FENNER A. CHACE, JR., PH.D.
Carcinologist and Zoologist

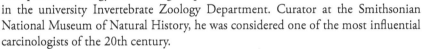

Profile
Born in Fall River in 1908, Fenner A. Chace, Jr., died in 2004. He was married to Janis Dexter Chace and is survived by a grandson and two great-grandchildren. He was the son of Fenner A. Chace, M.D. and Mary Deane Buffinton.

Experience
Chace became curator of Harvard's Museum of Comparative Zoology after serving as a professor in the university Invertebrate Zoology Department. Curator at the Smithsonian National Museum of Natural History, he was considered one of the most influential carcinologists of the 20th century.

Chace retired in 1978 but continued as Zoologist Emeritus.

Education
B.M.C. Durfee High School and Harvard University.

Skills
Chace named more than 200 taxa in the Decapoda and Stomatopoda, most of them shrimp.

Also of Note
Chace served as a first lieutenant then a major in the Army Air Corps before transferring to the Oceanographic Unit of the U.S. Navy Hydrographic Office during WWII. He was part of the Greatest Generation.

PROFESSOR LESTER W. CORY
Electrical Engineer, Educator and Air Force Colonel

Profile
Margaret Grant Cory and Harold R. Cory, Sr. Cory are the parents of three sons. Lester Cory is the youngest. He and his first wife, Judith, had four children and "Buzz" and his second wife, Patricia, have a daughter.

Experience
Lester Cory has always been a busy man. It started when he was a boy. He was a farm boy and there were chores aplenty to do before and after school and animals to care for. Before he learned how to drive the tractor he pulled weeds in the garden and then delivered both editions of the *Fall River Herald News*.

It was engineering that excited Cory. He became a ham radio operator, ran a radio/TV repair business and was an engineer for radio station WALE and television stations in Providence, Rhode Island, and New Bedford, Massachusetts.

Cory was so familiar with electronics that while he attended college as a full-time student, he taught night school classes in ham radio. Soon he was accepted to a teaching position at Bradford Durfee College of Technology.

Cory has been a member of the College of Engineering at UMD since 1963 and retired in 2012 as Chancellor Professor.

Education
Henry Lord Junior High, B.M.C. Durfee High School and graduated from Bradford Durfee College of Technology in 1963. He received his masters from Northeastern University and Bridgewater State University. He also graduated from the U.S. Air Force War College, and was bestowed an honorary doctorate from the University of Rhode Island in 1996.

Skills
Becoming a cross country truck driver was one of Cory's ambitions as a youngster. The closest he came to that was driving an aircraft refueling truck for the U.S. Air Force along with serving as an airborn radio operator aboard an HU-16 Albatross. After receiving his commission he stopped flying and landed a position in ground communication.

Also of Note
Founded in 1981, the Society for Human Advancement through Rehabilitation Engineering (SHARE) Foundation, Inc., is a nonprofit foundation that supports the University of Massachusetts Dartmouth Center for Rehabilitation Engineering and uses rehabilitation engineering to assist clients with physical challenges to communicate.

He spent thirty-six years in the Rhode Island Air National Guard, retiring with the rank of colonel and the recipient of the Rhode Island Star and the U.S. Air Force Legion of Merit.

He is listed in *Who's Who in Science and Engineering, Who's Who in America* and *Who's Who in the World*.

Cory is the 2001 recipient of the Durfee Distinguished Alumni Award. He was also a major force behind the fundraising efforts to relocate the Durfee Bells to a site on the school property.

Information gathered from Professor Cory and UMass Dartmouth—photo courtesy of SHARE

142

THOMAS J. CURRY, PH.D.
Professor of Electrical and Computer Engineering

Profile
Thomas J. Curry is the son of Raymond F. and Olympia M. Curry. He was born in Fall River in 1942. He had one brother, Ray. He married Carolyn E. Sullivan and they are the parents of three daughters and grandparents to eight grandchildren.

Experience
Curry's career began with the government at the Naval Underwater Systems Center from 1966 to 1981. He was selected as the first Naval Science Advisor to the Commander, Submarine Force Pacific Fleet in Pearl Harbor. He was the link between the admiral of the submarine fleet and the nation's research and development labs.

In 1981, Curry worked for Gould Ocean Systems Division as Director of Research and Engineering until founding his own firm, Technology Applications, Inc., in 1983. He joined the faculty at University of Massachusetts Dartmouth the same year in the College of Engineering with his colleague, Lester Cory (also included herein).

Curry served as department chair, dean, provost and Vice Chancellor for Academic Affairs and director of the Advanced Technology and Manufacturing Center now located in Fall River on the site of the former Kerr Mill on the South Watuppa Pond.

In 1988, Curry conceived and established the Center for Marine Science and Technology at the University and became its founding director. In 2003, he took the position of director at the Advanced Technology and Manufacturing Center. In 2006 Curry retired but returned as a special assistant to the chancellor.

Education
Davis School, B.M.C. Durfee High School, Bradford Durfee College of Technology (BS), Worcester Polytechnic Institute (MS), University of Rhode Island (Ph.D.) and Harvard Graduate School of Business.

Skills
Project Engineering, Marine Science and Technology, Strategies for College Selection at University of Massachusetts Dartmouth.

Also of Note
Curry is the 2009 recipient of the Durfee Distinguished Alumni Award. He is listed in *Who's Who in Technology* and *Who's Who in America*.

Information gathered from Dr. Curry and *The Durfee Chimes*—photo courtesy of Dr. Curry

ROBERTA KEVELSON, PH.D.
Professor of Semiotics

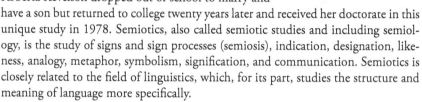

Profile
Born in Fall River in 1931, Roberta Kevelson died in 1998. She is the daughter of Helen and Barney Kahan. She had a younger sister. She married Seymour Kevelson at age seventeen and they had a son.

Experience
Roberta Kevelson dropped out of school to marry and have a son but returned to college twenty years later and received her doctorate in this unique study in 1978. Semiotics, also called semiotic studies and including semiology, is the study of signs and sign processes (semiosis), indication, designation, likeness, analogy, metaphor, symbolism, signification, and communication. Semiotics is closely related to the field of linguistics, which, for its part, studies the structure and meaning of language more specifically.

Education
Morton Junior High and B.M.C. Durfee High School. She attended Bryant and Goddard Colleges and received her doctorate from Brown University.

Skills
Kevelson introduced the idea of legal semiotics and subsequently established an international cross disciplinary center for its study in 1984.

Also of Note
Kevelson was a founding member of the Semiotic Society of America. She also spent time working at the Women's Center at Bristol Community College in Fall River.

Information gathered from *Wikipedia* and her son—photo courtesy of her son

MALCOM G. KISPERT
Aeronautical Engineer

Profile
Born in Fall River in 1923, Malcom G. Kispert was the son of Edward and Margaret Kispert and lived on Warren Street. He married his wife, Janice, and had two sons and two daughters. He died at fifty-two in 1975 and is buried in Dover, Massachusetts.

Experience
After receiving his degrees from Massachusetts Institute of Technology in 1944 and 1946 and serving his country, Kispert returned to the Institute and was named assistant to the president. In 1952, he became Executive Assistant to the President and then Assistant Chancellor in 1956. In 1961 he was named Vice President, and ten years later Kispert was named Secretary and Vice President until his untimely passing four years later.

Education
Local Fall River schools, B.M.C. Durfee High School and S.B. in Engineering from M.I.T. in 1944.

Skills
Kispert was a member of the Greatest Generation and served in the Navy in the Pacific Theater as an aeronautical engineer during World War II.

Also of Note
Kispert received the William Barton Rogers Award at M.I.T. and he is remembered today with the presentation of the Malcom G. Kispert Award to the male and female scholar-athletes of the year.

Information gathered from M.I.T. and Boston *Herald American*—photo courtesy of M.I.T.

JOHN C. MANNING, PH.D.
International Reading Expert
Marine Corps Colonel

Profile
John C. Manning was born in 1930, raised in Fall River and died in Minnesota in 2010. He was the son of John W. and Ida Chorlton Manning. He had three children by his first wife, Gloria Audet of Fall River, and was also married to Marie Manning in California. He is survived by his companion, Verla, his three children and three grandchildren, a brother and three sisters.

Experience
Manning began his teaching career at Slade School and Morton Junior High in Fall River. He became an international authority on beginning reading instruction. Manning was a professor at University of Minnesota. He also was a visiting professor and lecturer at more than 300 colleges and universities throughout the country.

Manning was an author and educational consultant and served as a president of the International Reading Association. He was named Professor Emeritus at the University of Minnesota in 2006.

Education
St. Mary's School, Monsignor Coyle High, Providence College and advanced degrees from Bridgewater State College and Boston University.

Skills
Manning was a Marine Corps veteran of the Korean Conflict and as colonel he commanded the Newport, Rhode Island, Marine Corps Detachment.

Also of Note
He received a lifetime achievement award from the International Reading Association in 2010 and is recognized yearly with a Public School Service Award presented in his name.

Information gathered from the University of Minnesota—photo courtesy of the University of Minnesota

JEROME NAMIAS, PH.D.
Meteorologist

Profile
Born in Bridgeport, Connecticut, in 1910, Jerome Namias was raised in Fall River with his brother. He was the son of optometrist Joseph and Sadie Jacobs Namias. He married Edith Piapert in 1938 and they had a daughter. He died of pneumonia in 1997.

Experience
Namias began his career in meteorology in the 1930s by studying the phenomena of the Dust Bowl. For 30 years beginning in 1941 he was Chief of the Extended Forecast Division of the United States Weather Bureau. In 1940, he developed the five-day forecast and by the 1960s he had developed monthly and seasonal forecasts. Namias was involved in the research of the El Niño phenomenon in the Pacific Ocean and its effect on world climate.

After joining the Scripps Institution in 1971, Namias established the first Experimental Climate Research Center, which greatly assisted a domestic policy response during the 1973 Arab Oil Embargo.

Education
Local Fall River schools, B.M.C. Durfee High School, University of Michigan, M.I.T. and a Ph.D. from the American Institute of Aerodynamics and Astronautics as well as honorary doctorates from Clark University and University of Rhode Island.

Skills
Namias was responsible for forecasting weather for the Allies during WWII in North Africa. He also developed the system of passenger flight weather forecasting and researched the interaction between oceans and atmosphere.

Also of Note
Namias is the 1968 recipient of the Durfee Distinguished Alumni Award. He was elected as a fellow into both the National Academy of Sciences and the American Academy of Arts and Sciences. Awarded the Gold Medal of the U.S. Department of Commerce for distinguished achievement, he published more than 200 papers and continued to work in meteorology until 1989.

"Predicting human behavior was the most complex problem."

DR. JEROME NAMAIS

Information gathered from *Wikipedia* and The National Academies Press—photo courtesy of *Wikipedia*

PETER A. PETRI, PH.D.
Professor of International Finance

Profile
Peter A. Petri is the son of George and Margaret Petri, Hungarian immigrants who migrated to Fall River. George was a machine engineer for Ashworth Brothers off Bay Street and Margaret worked at FR Knitting. Petri lived on High Street and enrolled in junior high school in Fall River. He married Jean Lawrence and they have two sons.

Experience
Petri started his career at Brandeis University in 1974 and served as the founding dean of the Brandeis International Business School from 1994 to 2006. He is the Carl J. Shapiro Professor of International Finance and a senior fellow of the East-West Center.

Education
Morton Junior High, B.M.C. Durfee High School and Harvard for undergraduate and doctorates.

Skills
Petri has written or co-authored more than 25 articles and books on Asian economic development.

Also of Note
Petri is the former chair of the U.S. APEC Study Center Consortium.

Information gathered from Brandeis University and Fall River City Directory—photo courtesy of Dr. Petri

MICHELE KAUFMAN RALLIS, PH.D.
Ph.D. Professor of Physics and Astronomy

Profile

Michele Kaufman Rallis is the daughter of Rose Lepes and David Kaufman. She grew up in Tiverton, Rhode Island, with her younger sister Linda, who does research in scientific computing. She was married to Steve Rallis, an internationally recognized mathematician.

Experience

Michelle and her husband, Steve, in his office at Ohio State University.

Kaufman's first real job was as a professor of physics at Brown University after her first workplace experience at the ticket booth at the Ponta Drive-in Theater in her hometown of Tiverton. She was drawn to her career path at a young age by Durfee teachers like Mr. McIlwaine, her chemistry teacher and Mr. Whitman, her Latin teacher. However, as is true in so many of these success stories, her mother, a playwright, was her greatest motivator. At eight years old, a visit to the Hayden Planetarium in New York City moved the young Kaufman girl towards astronomy—not to star gaze but to understand the physics of stars and galaxies.

After her tenure at Brown, she moved on to the University of Notre Dame and Swarthmore College, and eventually to Ohio State University, where she taught and conducted research from 1977 to 2012. In 1999, she and her colleagues wrote about their Hubble space telescope observations. The image from this article appeared on the front page of the *New York Times, CNN* and *Life* Magazine. The articles refer to two galaxies brushing against each other more than 100 million light years away and the moment was captured in a striking photo maintained by the Space Telescope Science Institute.

Education

Kaufman Rallis graduated from B.M.C. Durfee High School after attending Tiverton, Rhode Island, elementary schools. She went on to Harvard for both her undergraduate, graduate and doctorates from 1958 to 1968.

Skills

Kaufman Rallis also played violin in school and with both the Fall River Symphony and the Rhode Island Youth Orchestra. She has written more than 60 astronomy research articles, most of which have appeared in professional journals.

Also of Note

She is the 1996 recipient of the Durfee High School Distinguished Alumni Award.

Information gathered from Michele Kaufman Rallis and Ohio State University—photo courtesy of Mrs. Rallis

IRA SHARKANSKY, PH.D.
Professor of Political Science

Profile
Ira Sharkansky was born in Fall River in 1938, the only child to Beatrice Mines and Eugene Sharkansky. They lived on Montgomery Street. He was married twice—once during graduate school where he started his first family and later in Israel where he started a second family with Varda and their four children.

Experience
Sharkansky wrote his thesis from Wesleyan University on *The Portuguese of Fall River: A Study of Ethnic Acculturation*. It was the education provided by Mr. McIlwaine, his chemistry teacher, and Mr. Sperduti, his Spanish teacher, that helped point him toward a career in social sciences as well as international travel and living.

Sharkansky was named an assistant professor at Ball State University in 1964, the same year he earned his doctorate. He moved on after a year to Florida State University and then to the University of Georgia. From 1968 to 1971 he returned to University of Wisconsin and was named a full professor from 1971 to 1975.

In 1975, he became a professor of political science and public administration at the Hebrew University of Jerusalem, where he still holds the title of Professor Emeritus.

Education
Highland School and B.M.C. Durfee High School, Wesleyan University and a doctorate at the University of Wisconsin.

Skills
Sharkansky is a prolific author on policy and politics in Israel and the United States. A prominent political theorist, he looks at how religion and politics intersect, using Israel as the example.

Also of Note
In 1979, he became a fellow of the National Academy of Public Administration.

Information gathered from Dr. Sharkansky and *Wikipedia*—photos courtesy of Dr. Sharkansky

JOHN G. SHERMAN, PH.D.
Behavioral Psychologist

Profile
Jack G. Sherman was born in 1931 and raised in Fall River. He was the only child of Margaret Stockman Sherman. He was a summer resident of Westport while he lived in Washington, D.C., and Key West, Florida. He died of cancer in Fall River in 2006 at age seventy-five with no immediate survivors.

Experience
Sherman's first teaching assignment was at the University of Brasilia in Sao Paulo, Brazil. He followed that by joining the faculty at Barnard College and Arizona State University before going to Georgetown University in 1969.

Sherman, also known as Gil, was a behavioral psychologist and former chair of the Psychology Department at Georgetown University. He studied with B. F. Skinner and became one of the creators of the Personalized System of Instruction (PSI). In 1981, Sherman served on a panel of advisors for the D.C. school system as it developed a new curriculum. He was a visiting professor at M.I.T., Harvard and the University of Brasilia.

Education
He attended the Highland School in Fall River and then moved to Rhode Island for high school. Sherman graduated from Bowdoin College and did graduate study at University of Edinburgh before earning a masters and doctorate at Columbia.

Skills
Sherman wrote seven books and dozens of professional articles. He served as the director of the Center for Personalized Instruction, taught himself sign language and was a part-time faculty member at Gallaudet University. He taught signing at Georgetown as well.

Also of Note
Sherman was a fellow of the American Psychological Association and the American Association for the Advancement of Science, a member of the National Humanities Faculty and the Registry of the Interpreters for the Deaf.

Information gathered from the *Washington Post*—photo courtesy of his friends

PHILIP T. SILVIA, JR., PH.D.
History Professor and Fall River Historian

Profile
Philip T. Silvia, Jr. was born in Fall River, the oldest of six children of Rita Burke Silvia and Philip T. Silvia, Sr. He is the grandson of the first Portuguese judge, Frank M. Silvia, who is also highlighted in this book. He is married to Geraldine Holleran, also from Fall River. They are the parents of three children.

Experience
Silvia bussed tables for the Ney family at Stone Bridge Inn in Tiverton, Rhode Island, but it was his family that inspired hard work and a formal education. Silvia decided in college that history and the history of Fall River, specifically, would be his focus. His doctoral dissertation entitled: "The Spindle City: Labor, Politics, and Religion in Fall River" set him on his course and he hasn't looked back.

Silvia joined the faculty in the Bridgewater State University History Department in 1968. He taught young people history, particularly of this area and specifically Fall River.

Education
He attended Highland School, Morton Junior High, DeLaSalle Academy and graduated from Providence College with advanced degrees from Fordham University.

Skills
He is the editor of three volumes of Fall River history: *Victorian Vistas* (often referenced in this publication) as well as his fascinating booklet, *Greater Fall River Baseball* (also often referenced herein.)

His research and professional journal writings have focused on immigration and labor topics.

Also of Note
In 2008, Bridgewater State University awarded Silvia a Lifetime Faculty Research Award, forty years after beginning his career at the University.

Information gathered from Dr. Silvia and *Fall River Spirit*—photo courtesy of Dr. Silvia

ARTHUR ALVES TEIXEIRA, PH.D.
*Agricultural and Biological Engineer
and Educator*

Profile
Arthur Alves Teixeira was born in Fall River to Emilia
Alves Teixeira and Arthur Araoujo Teixeira. He is the
oldest of three siblings. They grew up on Plain Street
near Ruggles and Columbus Parks. His first wife
passed on at age thirty-seven and he was left with two
teenage sons to raise. He remarried twenty-six years
ago and lives in Florida.

Experience
Teixeira is fluent in Portuguese, which made him a valuable member of the stock
room staff at Bedford Street Hardware when he was fifteen. Those leadership talents
at the hardware store translated into student governance as class vice president at
Durfee. He passed up job offers at Firestone and Kodak to go on to graduate school
and earned international recognition as an expert in food and agricultural engineering.

Teixeira earned degrees in Mechanical and Aerospace Engineering as well as Food
and Agricultural Engineering. He is a Registered Professional Engineer in both Massachusetts and Florida.

Teixeira's first research position was with Ross Laboratories, the maker of Similac
infant formula. He also worked for a time with Arthur D. Little before he went off
to teach and research food to help provide safety and quality assurance all over the
world.

Education
Brown, Lincoln, and Davis schools, B.M.C. Durfee High School 1962 and University of Massachusetts, Amherst, for all engineering degrees.

Skills
He has published two books and more than 90 journal articles. He has taught and
conducted research in twenty countries and five continents.

Also of Note
Dr. Teixeira is the 2007 recipient of the Durfee Distinguished Alumni Award. Twice
selected as a Fulbright Scholar and a NATO Guest Fellow, he has received the Distinguished Food Engineer Award and multiple teaching awards.

Information gathered from Dr. Teixeira and *The Durfee Chimes*—photo courtesy of *The Durfee Chimes*

MEL B. YOKEN, PH.D.
French Linguist

Profile
Mel B. Yoken was born in 1938 and has a younger brother, Stephen. They are the sons of Sylvia S. Yoken and Albert B. Yoken and lived on Archer Street in the Highland section of Fall River. He is married to Cynthia Stein and they have three sons and two grandsons.

Experience
Yoken seems to have been strongly influenced primarily by his parents but also by four well-known Fall River teachers: Jean Judge, Margaret Dailey, Mildred Carroll and Anna McCarthy.

He spent more than forty0five years teaching French. His first three years were at the high school level and for the next forty-three at the university level at University of Massachusetts, Dartmouth.

For the past twenty-five years, Yoken has headed the Boivin Center for French Language and Culture at UMD. Not only has he taught French, but he has shared his love of the language and culture with students and the general public. He has lectured nationally and internationally on some of his specialties: contemporary French and Quebec poetry, twentieth century French, and Quebec Novello Theatre and nineteenth century French poetry.

Education
Highland School and Morton Junior High School, B.M.C. Durfee High School, University of Massachusetts Amherst and Brown University for a masters degree followed by a doctorate from University of Massachusetts Amherst. Yoken did advance study at Mt. Holyoke, Hampshire, Smith and Middlebury Colleges.

Skills
Yoken has also hosted radio programs over the years and published seven books. He served as President of the University Library Associates at UMass Dartmouth.

Also of Note
Yoken is the 1998 recipient of the Durfee Distinguished Alumni Award. He also received the 2013 Distinguished Alumnus Award from University of Massachusetts Amherst. He received recognition from the French Academy and the French government among other awards.

Information gathered from Dr. Yoken and the Boivin Center—photo courtesy of Dr. Yoken

AREA SCHOOL SUPERINTENDENTS WHO RECEIVED SOME EDUCATION IN FALL RIVER

Fall River School Department

William S. Lynch	1945-1963
Robert J. Nagle *	1963-1980-Durfee Distinguished Alumni Award recipient in 1979
John R. Carreiro	1980-1993
James M. Gibney	1993-2000-An Olympic Torch bearer for the 1996 Summer Games
Richard D. Pavao	2002-2005

Diman Regional Vocational School

John P. Harrington	1956-1979
John G. Connell**	1989-1992
Joseph Martins	1992-2001
Roger Ramos	2001-2009

Tiverton Schools

Stan Sincoski	1971-1988

Westport Community Schools

Margot J. desJardins	1990-2001

Fall River Diocese

Monsignor Patrick J. O'Neil, D.Ed.	1960-1976

*There is a scholarship in his memory at Durfee High School that benefit graduates.
**Member of the Durfee High School Sports Hall of Fame.

1926-Present

Government

———◆———

"If one advances confidently in the direction of his dreams,

and endeavors to live life which he had imagined,

he will meet with success unexpected in common hours."

———◆———

HENRY DAVID THOREAU

SHAY D. ASSAD
Defense Department Procurement Officer

Profile
Shay D. Assad was born in Fall River, the son of Shady and Olim-
pia R. Macedo Assad. He is the oldest of four children. Now married to Christine Kelleher of New Bedford, he has three daughters
from his first marriage.

Experience
If you talk with Assad, he is just a kid from the Flint who has never forgotten his roots. The
Flint was where everyone knew everyone and in a town where hard work, family and commitment were vital. What distinguished him from others in his era is leadership. From football
captain and class president at Bishop Stang High School to Outstanding Junior Officer in the
Fifth Naval District, executive vice president and CEO at Raytheon and Department of Defense Director of Procurement, Assad has demonstrated his leadership ability throughout his
career. He, like many others in this book, could appear in more than one category.

He was influenced by his parents who encouraged and supported along with teachers includ-
ing Miss Logan, Baron Baroody and Miss O'Neil. He idolized naval captain and cousin Martin
Zenni, who served in Fall River city government during the Carlton Viveiros administrations.
Like many others in this book his first job was as a paper carrier for the *Fall River Herald News*.

Education
Aldrich and Davis Schools, Bishop Stang High School and the U.S. Naval Academy.

Skills
As a Naval Academy midshipman, Assad served as a deck officer during Typhoon Rose in
1971. He served two tours of duty as an ensign on naval destroyers after graduating with distinction from the Academy in 1972. His first tour as a commissioned officer included saving
shipmates from a fire on board ship. Following his sea tours, he served as a Naval Procurement
Officer at Naval Sea Systems Command.

Following those tours, in 1978, Assad joined Raytheon and gained experience in defense, commercial and international contracting. He became intimately involved with the Patriot, Hawk
and other ballistic missile defenses. His leadership skills were again recognized in 1997 when as
senior vice president, he was responsible for the contracting of 20 billion dollars of Raytheon
business. He eventually was promoted to Raytheon Executive Vice president, serving as chair
and CEO of Raytheon's Engineering and Construction business.

Also of Note
After retiring from Raytheon in 2001, Assad established a small company providing consulting
and retail services. In 2004, he held the position of the Marine Corps' senior civilian contrac-
tion official. Today, Assad is responsible for overseeing all contract pricing activities within the
Department of Defense.

He is especially proud to have been recognized a number of times within the federal government for his leadership and advocacy for the employment of the blind and severely disabled.

Information gathered from Mr. Assad and the Department of Defense—photo courtesy of Mr. Assad

MARY LEITE FONSECA
Massachusetts State Senator

Profile
Mary Leite Fonseca was born in Fall River in 1915, the daughter of Portuguese immigrants Jose and Mary Botelho Leite. The oldest girl of twelve children, she died in Swansea at age ninety and is buried in St. Patrick's Cemetery. Fonseca married John C. Fonseca, Jr., and had a son and a daughter and two grandchildren.

Experience
Senator Fonseca was unable to attend college because as the oldest daughter in her family of twleve, she was forced to go to work and help support her siblings. She worked at the Fall River Public Library. She also worked as a legal secretary for the United States Census Bureau and the Civil Defense. She was elected as a school committeeperson, an unpaid position at the time, and followed that elected position with state senator in 1952 and served until 1984. She was the first woman of Portuguese-American descent elected to the Massachusetts State Senate and the first woman to hold a senate leadership position. From 1973 to 1984 she was the Assistant Majority Leader. She was a model for female elected officials from her district who followed her.

Fonseca would often lecture her fellow legislators about the importance of supporting women's causes—working mothers, in particular.

Education
Watson School and B.M.C. Durfee High School.

Skills
Fonseca was not only known for her commitment to education in the Southcoast area through years of support for UMass Dartmouth and Bristol Community College but for her penchant for big hairdos and flashy hats. She was also known as the "Queen of Installations" as she conducted hundreds for local clubs and organizations. Fonseca was an old-fashioned politician who shook thousands of hands and attended hundreds of wakes and funerals.

Also of Note
The University of Massachusetts Dartmouth created a scholarship in Fonseca's name and her personal papers are archived at the University library. The purpose of the scholarship is to support incoming freshmen from Fall River, especially female students with high academic achievement who plan to major in political science.

Senator Fonseca was recognized as a Distinguished Alumni Recipient at Durfee High School in 1980.

Information gathered from UMass Dartmouth and the *Fall River Herald News*—photo courtesy of UMass Dartmouth

ROBERT HARGRAVES
Supervisory Special Agent F.B.I.

Profile
Robert Hargraves was an only child, son of Charles and Marion McDonald Hargraves. He married Mary Elizabeth McDonald and they have four children and six grandchildren.

Experience
Most of his Federal Bureau of Investigation career was spent in the Organized Crime and Drugs division. He spent fourteen years in the Midwest and returned to the New England area in 1978. He was a Supervisory Special Agent and was involved in the arrest and successful prosecution of Raymond L.S. Patriarca, head of the New England La Cosa Nostra.

Education
Greene School, Henry Lord Junior High School and B.M.C. Durfee High School. He graduated from College of the Holy Cross and did graduate study at Brown University.

Skills
Hargraves was employed at the Berkshire-Hathaway Mills and like so many others was a *Fall River Herald News* paper carrier as a youngster. An outstanding high school athlete, Hargraves's first "real" job was football. He was influenced by his parents and teachers like Bob Murray, Luke Urban, Nick Olivier, Joe D'Adamo and Millie Carroll. The key to his positive Fall River upbringing was how he learned to get along with people from all classes of society.

Also of Note
Hargraves, like many others in this book, gives special praise to his wife, Mary Lib. With four children and like many women at the time, Mary Lib was a stay-at-home mom. When their children grew up, she returned to work, supplementing the family income. She and other spouses in this book raised the children and were very supportive of their spouse's careers.

When his career with the F.B.I. ended, he took a position as Director of Investigations at Foxwoods Resort Casino in Connecticut. He is an elected a member of the Durfee High School Sports Hall of Fame.

Information gathered from Mr. Hargraves—photo courtesy of Mr. Hargraves

GRACE HARTLEY HOWE
Postmaster

Profile
Born in Fall River in 1874, Grace Hartley Howe was the daughter of Dr. James W. and Mary Borden Hartley. She married Louis McHenry Howe. They had a son, a daughter and five grandchildren. She died of a cerebral hemorrhage at Union Hospital at the age eighty in 1954.

Experience
Grace Hartley met Louis McHenry Howe when she was in her second year of college and he was a political reporter for the *New York Herald*. In 1913, when Franklin D. Roosevelt joined the Wilson administration, her husband became his assistant. After eight years they planned to return to private life but, out of loyalty to FDR who had just contracted paralysis, they stayed on. When FDR was elected President, the Howes were thrust back into the limelight as he became the president's Secretary (now known as the Chief of Staff) and often referred to as "the man behind Roosevelt."

Howe did return to Fall River while Louis continued his busy schedule with the President. He spent more time in Washington than in his home in Fall River. Mrs. Howe continued her busy schedule in Fall River after the death of her husband during FDR's first term.

Howe was named Fall River Postmaster by President Roosevelt after her husband's death. She served from 1936 until 1951 and was compensated at $4,000 per year. She had been the regional leader of the Franklin Delano Roosevelt Infantile Paralysis Commission which helped care for stricken children. The March of Dimes was an outgrowth of this commission. Unfortunately, Howe passed on before the announcement of the Salk vaccine and the eventual cure of the disease she had fought so long for.

Education
Local Fall River schools, B.M.C. Durfee High School and Vassar College.

Skills
Howe served on a plethora of charity boards and organizations in Fall River, including but not limited to the Family Welfare Association, Historical Society, Ninth Street Day Nursery and the League of Nations Association. None of these charitable undertakings provided her with any money to live and her husband had left her less than $20,000.

Also of Note
Howe served as a delegate to the National Democratic Convention in 1936. She served as secretary of the Massachusetts State Democratic Committee for years. While in Fall River, she also served as vice chairman of the City Democratic Committee, the Fall River Public Library and Bristol County Agricultural School.

Information gathered from Fall River Historical Society and the *Providence Journal*
—photo courtesy of the Fall River Historical Society collection

ERNEST MONIZ, PH.D.
Department of Energy Secretary
World Renowned Physicist

Profile
Ernest Moniz is the only child of the former Georgina Pavao and Ernest P. Moniz. They lived on Diman Street near Kennedy Park. He married Naomi Hoki in Paris.

Experience
During the writing of this book Moniz was appointed by President Obama to the cabinet position of Energy Secretary. During President Obama's State of the Union message on January 28th, 2014, Moniz was the "designated successor." That is the member of the cabinet who was not in attendance in the House chamber in case of an attack. He was placed in an undisclosed location in case there was a catastrophe and all other top officials died. Before that appointment, he held the position of physicist at Massachusetts Institute of Technology. Does he belong in the education section or the government section? Since he had previously served as Under Secretary of the Energy Department during the final four years of the Clinton administration, he was assigned here. Earlier, he was Associate Director for Science and Technology Policy, Executive Office of the President. Moniz had served on the M.I.T. faculty since 1973 and was the director of the Bates Linear Accelerator Institute.

Moniz with President Obama and other appointees at the announcement ceremony.

He developed the nuclear framework for understanding meson-nucleus interactions, guided the experimental nuclear physics research program at Bates lab, put U.S.-Russian nuclear nonproliferation programs back on track and founded the M.I.T. Energy Initiative.

Education
Local Fall River schools, B.M.C. Durfee High School, Boston College and a doctorate from Stanford University. He was awarded honorary degrees from the University of Athens, University Eriangen-Nurenburg and Michigan State University.

Skills
Moniz wanted to be a scientist or engineer when growing up. His parents stressed education and both Mr. Dallier and Mr. Carey at Durfee High School were motivators in his life. When it was time to go away to college, Moniz gave up tennis and baseball in the Fall River parks and was challenged instead by Professor Chen at Boston College and Professor Walecka at Stanford—far from Kennedy Park.

Also of Note
Moniz was formerly on the advisory council of King Abdullah Petroleum Studies and Research Center in Saudi Arabia, a former consultant for British Petroleum and a former board member of NGP Energy Technology. He was a former advisor to General Electric Ecomagination Advisory Board, among other international firms where he served as either a past consultant or as a past advisor.

He was also a former senior associate at the Washington Advisory Group, the Gas Technology Institute and a past advisor at Riverstone Equity Holdings LP.

Moniz is another recipient of the Distinguished Alumni Award from Durfee High School awarded in 2004.

Information gathered from *The Durfee Chimes*, M.I.T., the *Boston Globe* and Dr. Moniz
—photos courtesy of Dr. Moniz and The White House

WILLIAM J. PORTER
Ambassador

Profile
William J. Porter was born in 1914 in England and died in 1988 at the Rose Hawthorne Lathrop Cancer Home in Fall River. He was the son of Sarah Day Porter and William Porter. He met his wife, Eleanore Henry, an Army nurse, while they both served in Syria. He and Eleanore had a son and daughter and six grandchildren. Ambassador Porter lived in Westport from 1977 to his death in 1988. He became a naturalized citizen in 1936.

Experience
Porter became famous when President Richard M. Nixon appointed him to head the Paris Peace Talks to end the Vietnam War and later as Under Secretary of State for Political Affairs after the talks ended.

Before serving in that very visible diplomatic post, Porter began his career as a secretary to the United States Ambassador to Hungary. Subsequent to spending one year in that position, he joined the United States Foreign Service. He then spent time in Iraq, Lebanon, Syria, Cyprus and in Washington at the State Department at both the Palestine and Greek desks. Next came assignments in Morocco, North Africa and then on to Algeria as the first U.S. Ambassador to that newly independent country. He became deputy ambassador to South Vietnam until President Lyndon B. Johnson named him as Ambassador to South Korea.

Education
Local Fall River schools, B.M.C. Durfee High School, Thibodeau College of Business and Boston College.

Skills
Porter received diplomatic appointments from Presidents Kennedy, Johnson, Nixon and Ford until his retirement in 1977.

Also of Note
President Richard M. Nixon appointed Porter as Ambassador to Canada in 1974 and 1975.

President Gerald R. Ford selected Porter as the United States Ambassador to Saudi Arabia, where he presented his credentials in 1976 until May 1977.

Porter was a recipient of the Durfee Distinguished Alumni Award in 1973.

Information gathered from *Wikipedia* and the *Fall River Herald News*—photo courtesy of *Wikipedia*

WILLIAM F. "ACE" POWERS
Public Safety Commissioner and Author

Profile
William F. Powers was born in Fall River in 1928, son of Francis M. "Dick" and Ann Dickinson Powers. He was the oldest of three children. He married Lois V. Grover in 1954. They had five children and were married more than fifty years. He died in 2009 and is buried in St. Patrick's Cemetery.

Experience
Powers left school at age sixteen to work in a nearby mill, then as an H.P. Hood milk delivery person and gas station attendant with his dad on Durfee Street. He lived in a three-family home on 18th Street like many in this book and his asphalt driveway was his park for sports. Shortly after dropping out of school, Powers joined the Coast Guard and was a veteran at age seventeen. He was at Pearl Harbor ready to deploy for Japan when President Truman dropped the A-bomb. Powers graduated from the Massachusetts State Police Academy in 1949. Not only was he a well-respected law enforcement official, he was also State Police historian and author. In 1957, Powers graduated from Northwestern University's famed Traffic Institute. His many assignments included providing the motorcycle escort for Mrs. Eleanor Roosevelt during her attendance at Mrs. Louis McHenry Howe's funeral in Fall River and for President Harry S. Truman. He was then assigned to General Headquarters in Boston and served in the Traffic Bureau, directed statewide public affairs and was an instructor at the Academy. Governor Francis W. Sargent named Captain Powers the head of the Massachusetts State Police and Commissioner of Public Safety in 1969. He was the first uniform officer to be named top cop in Massachusetts. Powers continued in law enforcement over the next two decades.

Education
Sacred Heart School, Morton Junior High and B.M.C. Durfee High School, Thibodeau Business School and Boston University. He received degrees from John Jay College and Nova Southeastern University.

Skills
Appointed the Justice Department's Regional Administrator for the Law Assistance Administration, Powers also became founding director of the federal National Public Safety Officers' Safety Program, serving until his 1994 retirement.

Powers wrote three volumes on the history of the Massachusetts State Police. In 1998, he wrote the final part of the trilogy, *Enforcement Odyssey*. He was posthumously named Historian Emeritus by the State Police. While on loan to the Rhode Island State Police, he wrote that organization's history.

Also of Note
Reminiscing about his Fall River days was one of Powers's favorite things to do. He loved to tell stories of delivering milk in five-gallon cans to local hospitals, mill fires, the Old Fall River Line and playing ball at Ruggles Park. He so loved his home town that he would wear a Corky Row hat and he departed this world with a Durfee tie around his neck. Powers was a recipient of the Durfee High Distinguished Alumni Award in 1994.

> "When Time who steals your years away
> Shall steal your pleasures too
> Then memories of the past will stay
> And half your joys renew."
> THOMAS MOORE

Powers' favorite poem.

Information gathered from Mrs. Powers and the *Fall River Herald News*—photo courtesy of Mrs. Powers

HONORABLE WILLIAM K. REILLY
Environmental Protection Agency Administrator

Profile
William K. Reilly was born in 1940 to Margaret M. Kane and George P. Reilly. He was grew up on Walnut Street near Ruggles Park. He married Elizabeth Buxton and they have two daughters and three grandchildren.

Reilly with President
Bush 41

Experience
After law school, Reilly entered the Army and served as a captain from 1966 to 1967 in Europe with intelligence planning. He subsequently returned to Columbia and received a degree in urban planning, which he put to work for Urban America, Inc.

Reilly became a senior staff member in the Nixon Administration on the President's Council on Environmental Quality. Back in the private sector for a number of years, Reilly was president of the Conservation Foundation, which merged with the World Wildlife Fund. He served as president of that successor organization before joining the George H.W. Bush administration as administrator of the Environmental Protection Agency from 1989 through 1992.

Education
Sacred Heart School, B.M.C. Durfee High School, Yale and Harvard Law School and Columbia University School of Urban Planning. He is one of the first recipients of a Citizens Scholarship in Fall River, the organization created by Irving Fradkin (who is also referenced in this book).

Skills
Reilly was asked by President Obama to serve as co-chair with Senator Bob Graham (D., FL) of the National Commission on the BP Deepwater Horizon Oil Spill in 2010 and 2011 to study the spill and related issues of offshore drilling.

Also of Note
Reilly is a founding partner of Aqua International Partners, L.P., a private equity firm dedicated to investing in firms engaged in water and renewable energy. He is a director of DuPont, Conoco Philips, Royal Caribbean International, the National Geographic Society and the Packard Foundation. He was chair of the World Wildlife Fund. Reilly has also been a visiting professor of International Studies at Stanford University.

Reilly was the recipient of the Vincent Scully Prize at the National Building Museum for his commitment to smart environmental planning, comprehensive land use and preservation of open space.

Reilly was also a 1992 recipient of the Durfee High School Distinguished Alumni Award.

Information gathered from Secretary Reilly, *Wikipedia* and Aqua International Partners—photos courtesy of Mr. Reilly

RICHARD P. RILEY
Secret Service
Director of White House Military Office

Profile
Richard P. Riley was born in 1940 in Fall River and died in Washington, D.C. in 2010 at age seventy. He was the youngest of three children of Irene Castonguay Riley and Francis J. Riley, II. He married Fall Riverite Frances White; they were married for forty-three years and had three daughters and four grandchildren.

Experience
Law enforcement was Riley's lifelong interest. After graduating from Monsignor Coyle High, where many others in this book attended school, Riley joined the military. As an Air Force military police officer, he was honorably discharged after four years. Riley worked for the Central Intelligence Agency before attending college. During his college years, he signed on to the Hyannis police force where he had the opportunity to work with the U.S. Secret Service as they protected President John F. Kennedy at the compound in the early 1960s.

In 1969, Riley joined the Secret Service and began his career as a Special Agent in Boston. He spent twenty-two years with the Service from 1969 until retirement in 1990. During his career, he was appointed Special Assistant to the White House Chief of Staff Donald T. Regan and then became Deputy Assistant to President Ronald W. Reagan and Director of the White House Military Office. In 1985, Riley was named director of the White House Military Office and was a deputy assistant to President Ronald W. Reagan.

Education
Sacred Heart School, Monsignor Coyle High School and California State University.

Skills
He began his career in Boston and Providence investigating counterfeiting and forgery. He was part of the protection team for many high level dignitaries including Pope John Paul II, Queen Elizabeth II and Fidel Castro.

After leaving the White House, Riley served as Director of Security of the United States Department of the Treasury.

Also of Note
Riley served under four Presidents—Nixon, Ford, Carter and Reagan. He earned the Department of Defense Distinguished Civilian Award in 1987 for his exceptional contributions as Director of the White House Military Office.

Information gathered from Mrs. Riley and Waring-Sullivan Home of Memorial Tribute—photo courtesy of Mrs. Riley

MAYORS WHO WERE EDUCATED IN FALL RIVER

W. Harry Monks	1927-1928	Law Enforcement
Edmond P. Talbot	1929-1930	Druggist
Daniel F. Sullivan	1931-1932	Retired
Joseph L. Hurley, Esq.	1933-1934	Law
Alexander C. Murray	1935-1945	Engineer
William P. Grant, Esq.	1946-1951	Law
John F. Kane	1952-1957	Bus Driver
John M. Arruda	1958-1963	State Tax Examiner
Roland G. Desmarais, Esq.	1964-1967	Law
Nicholas W. Mitchell	1968-1971	Druggist
Wilfred C. Driscoll	1972-1978	Funeral Director
Carlton M. Vivieros	1979-1990	State Relocation Expert
Daniel E. Bogan* **	1990-1991	Industrialist
John R. Mitchell, Esq.	1991-1996	Law
Edward M. Lambert	1996-2007	Educator
William F. Whitty	2007-2008	Engineer
Robert Correia	2008-2010	Educator
William A. Flanagan, Esq.	2010-	Law Member Diman Vocational Technical High School Hall Of Fame

* Received the Durfee Distinguished Alumni Award in 2005
* **There is a scholarship in his honor at Durfee High School to benefit graduates.

FIRE AND POLICE CHIEFS EDUCATED IN FALL RIVER

FIRE CHIEFS

Jeremiah F. Sullivan	1922-1937
Dennis D. Holmes	1937-1940
George E. McGaw	1941-1955
Francis J. McDonald	1956-1969
Thomas J. Moore	1970-1975
Antone R. Medeiros	1976-1977
Louis A. Shea	1978-1990
Edward J. Dawson	1990-2005
David L. Thiboutot	2005-2008
Paul D. Ford	2008-2011 Member Diman Vocational Technical High School Hall Of Fame
William A. Silvia	2011-2013
Robert Viveiros	2014-present

POLICE CHIEFS

Abel J. Violette	1931-1946
Edward McMahon	1946-1952
Charles A. McDonald	1952-1956
Norman Bowers	1957-1969
James E. Powers	1969-1974
Henry Ramos	1974-1980
Raymond E. Conroy	1981-1985
Ronald J. Andrade	1985-1989
Francis J. McDonald	1989-2001
John M. Souza	2001-2010
Daniel S. Racine	2010-present

1926-Present
Local

———◆———

The secret in business is to know something

that nobody else knows.

———◆———

ARISTOTLE ONASSIS

MARIANO S. (BISPO) BISHOP
Union Leader

Profile
Mariano S. Bishop was born on Sao Miguel, Azores, in 1906 to Joao and Emilia Medeiros Bispo. He died suddenly in 1953 of a heart attack at the age of forty-six while driving his car in New Jersey on the way to a union meeting. Bishop was married to Mary Souza; they had three daughters and lived on Tower Street in Fall River.

Experience
As the industrial New England labor movement formed in the early 1930s, Bishop was caught up and rose in the local leadership ranks. He led the massive 1934 textile strike in Fall River, which was still one of the largest producers of cotton goods in the world. It became the largest strike in American history as more than 400,000 textile workers across the nation walked out. The strike ended unsuccessfully and destroyed the United Textile Workers Union in the process.

The Textile Workers Union of America was created in 1939 and Bishop was its principal organizer. Although he did not hold an official position until 1943, he was a key figure in unionizing most New England textile workers and more than 70,000 Southern workers as well.

In 1952, Bishop became the international executive vice president of the Textile Workers of America (TWUA).

Education
Local Fall River schools.

Skills
As a young man, Bishop was a star of the famous Ponta Delgada Football Club and played with many of the greats who are included in the soccer sections of this book.

Also of Note
One of Fall River's busiest thoroughfares, Mariano Bishop Boulevard is named in his honor. Bishop was also known as one of "The Most Important Americans of Portuguese Descent".

FLORENCE C. BRIGHAM
Historian

Profile
Florence Cook Brigham was the daughter of Judge Benjamin and Hattie-May Clark Cook, and had two sisters. She married Richard C. Brigham and they had a son and two daughters. She was born in 1899 and died at age 100.

Experience
Brigham began her career as a payroll clerk in the Luther Mill during WWII. She then worked for the Fall River Tuberculosis Association for twenty-five years until retiring from that group in 1967 to pursue her historical interest in the city as assistant curator of the Fall River Historical Society. Brigham was appointed curator in 1976 and educated scholars and curious visitors alike on the people, places and events that have made Fall River famous.

Education
Local Fall River schools, B.M.C. Durfee High School and Mount Holyoke College in 1921.

Skills
Brigham and her husband, Richard, were avid meteorologists and both served for years as the Fall River weather observers, recording information for daily newspaper publications.

Also of Note
Brigham received the Durfee Distinguished Alumni Award in 1982. In 1990, the Fall River Historical Society named an annex of the building in her honor.

Florence Cook Brigham often remarked: "There is much more to the history of Fall River than Lizzie Borden." *Mrs. Brigham, this author totally agrees and that is one reason for this book and the absence of a Miss Borden profile.*

Information gathered from the Fall River Historical Society, the *Fall River Herald News* and *Parallel Lives*—photos courtesy of the Fall River Historical Society Collection and Waring Portrait Art Photography

BETTY WONG CHANG
Restaurateur

Betty far left and her parents far right

Profile
Betty Wong Chang is the daughter of Chung Gong Wong and Mrs. Wong. She was born in Hong Kong in 1943 and migrated here when she was five years old. She married Walter Chang and they have two daughters and four grandchildren.

Experience
Chang's father migrated from China in 1932 and headed to the Golden Mountain, as America was called then. He was forced to leave his wife and baby daughter in China for many years due to American law. Traveling from China, Mr. Wong came across a restaurant set in ancient artistic Chinese decor. That memory remained with the Wong family as they opened and ran the China Royal in 1949 for twenty-five years on Main Street in downtown Fall River until the property was bought and a high-rise bank took its place.

Mr. Wong's "Dream" opened in 1974 on Pleasant Street with Betty Wong Chang taking it to the next level.

During that time, their only child, Betty, worked in the restaurant while attending to her education. Her father was convinced that the opportunity presented itself in the early 1970s to make the family dream a reality by recreating the restaurant on Pleasant Street and Plymouth Avenue. At the time she was working full-time as a registered physical therapist but returned to her home town to manage the new grand facility. It remained open under Betty's direction for more than thirty years. The restaurant with banquet facilities and fine Chinese dining and take out made Wong's dream a successful reality. It was complete with a smiling Buddha in the lobby to welcome hungry guests while stone lions guarded the front door from unwanted visitors.

Like other traditional local banquet halls of American cuisine, the China Royal offered facilities for weddings and other large gatherings. For a time the facility presented entertainment from the Pacific Islands.

When her husband, Walter, was not traveling to China on business (he was Vice President of Marketing for General Electric), he would assist his wife with the financial end of the business. Betty had no brothers or sisters to share the work load of running a major business with more than 100 on staff and hours of operation from 11 a.m. to 2 a.m. 365 days a year.

Education
Local Fall River schools and Sacred Hearts Academy, Tufts and Boston College.

Also of Note
Chang found time to serve her community as well. She was a member of the Board of Directors of the United Way of Greater Fall River and the University of Massachusetts Dartmouth Foundation Board.

She and her husband, Walter, also established a scholarship at the University to benefit local needy students.

Information gather from Mrs. Chang and the *Fall River Herald News*—photos courtesy of the *Fall River Herald News*

JOHN F. DATOR
Realtor and Insurance Executive
Somerset Selectman

Profile
John F. Dator, born in 1930, was raised in Fall River and lived on Adams Street. He was the only child of Laura Beckett Dator. He was previously married to Norma Dator and they had three children.

Experience
Dator's first job, like many others listed here, was in a market—the Highland Market. That experience did not seemingly have any influence in either direction on his eventual life's work, which was insurance and real estate. Dator began his work in insurance as a Berkshire Life representative in 1957 and qualified for multiple sales awards over the years.

He enjoyed his teachers and was influenced by family friend Austin McCauliff when growing up.

He retired from the insurance business within the past decade but still sells commercial real estate in the Greater Fall River community.

Education
Dator went to the Highland School, B.M.C. Durfee High School and graduated from Brown University.

Skills
Dator served in the U.S. Navy on Guam. Later in life he served on the Somerset, Massachusetts, Board of Selectmen, including time as chair.

Leadership is Dator's greatest asset. He has led a variety of civic and charitable organizations from a very young age, including the United Way and The Boys and Girls Club. He also served as chair of the board of directors of the Fall River Five Cent Savings Bank (Bank 5) for many years.

Also of Note
Dator has received multiple awards for his volunteer leadership in multiple Fall River organizations, including the first Chamber of Commerce Outstanding Citizen award in 1967. He was appointed a member of the Massachusetts Bay Transit Authority by former Governor Edward J. King in the late 1970s.

Dator was president of the Massachusetts Association of Realtors in 1977, only the second realtor from Fall River to be so designated. He was also the 1988 recipient of the Milton Shaw Distinguished Service Award from the state association.

He served as general campaign chair and board chair of the United Way of Greater Fall River. He was also a director at Truesdale and Charlton Memorial Hospitals as well as many other civic and charitable organizations.

Information provided by Mr. Dator and the Fall River Association of Realtors—photo courtesy of Mr. Dator

GEORGE R. DUCLOS
Commercial Ship Builder

Profile
George R. Duclos was born in 1933 and raised in Fall River. He and his step brother were raised in the Maplewood section of the city by their parents Raymond and Bertha Chenard Duclos. He is married to Pauline Duperre and they have four children (three of whom are in the family business today) and eight grandchildren.

Experience
Building boats was always in Duclos's blood. At age 13, he was building and repairing boats on Wattuppa Pond in Fall River. After working on design for various local ship builders, Duclos joined his mentors, Preston Gladding and Richard Hearn, in their boat building firm in Somerset on the banks of the Taunton River. Since 1955, he has constructed more than 400 vessels.

The team had constructed more than 250 vessels by 1982 when Gladding and Hearn decided to retire and sell the business to Duclos. It was then that Duclos acquired the license to build the world's leading catamaran fast ferries. More than 100 skilled craftspeople now work at the Somerset shipyard, designing and building ferries for worldwide consumption. The firm is also recognized as one of America's premier builders of small, custom steel boats. Today, passengers take Duclos's ferries daily in and out of New York City at speeds of up to 45 m.p.h.

Education
Saint Jean the Baptiste School and B.M.C. Durfee High School. Duclos received an honorary doctorate from Massachusetts Maritime Academy.

Skills
It was his uncles Edgar, Albert and Arthur Chenard who greatly influenced the ship-builder. It was also Durfee High teachers Fred Gotwald and George Mitchie who helped make dreams reality for this young entrepreneur whose first designs were fishing craft followed by tug boats and pilot boats.

Also of Note
Duclos received the Durfee High Distinguished Alumni Award in 2007 and the Small Business Person of the Year in the same year. Duclos was a founding member of the Marine Museum at Fall River and was a volunteer at the 1980 Olympic sailing trials in Newport, Rhode Island.

Information gathered from George Duclos and MarineLink—photo courtesy of Mr. Duclos

JOSEPH H. (JOE) FEITELBERG
Insurance Executive

Profile
Joseph Feitelberg is the oldest of Henry J. Feitelberg's five children. His mother, Mary V. Kepple, passed away at a young age. His father later married Ann B. Kuss. Feitelberg is married to Sheila D. Feitelberg and they are the parents of six children and grandparents of ten.

Experience
After working as a teen in construction and warehouses, Feitelberg followed college with Navy Destroyer service. He then enjoyed a stellar local and national career in the insurance industry. It began when he returned to his home town in 1959 and joined his father in an agency and brokerage business that his grandfather founded in 1916. The firm, then on North Main Street, had seven employees. When he, Tony Abraham and seven other stockholders sold the business to Citizens Bank in 2003, the staff was 50 with multiple locations. The Feitelberg Company's contemporary headquarters was on Milliken Blvd., where they represented a broad number of insurers and bonding companies.

Beginning in 1990, Feitelberg Company made a commitment to the emerging culture of "Continuous Improvement" and the ISO standards it exemplified. The critical success factor was to exceed customer expectations by reducing the human factors of rework. The insurance world took notice and provided national and state recognition. In 2006, the business became part of HUB International New England, LLC .

Education
Highland School, St. Joseph's Academy in Wellesley, Tabor, Monsignor Coyle and then three years at Cranwell Prep in Lenox preceded his graduation from the College of the Holy Cross in 1956. Feitelberg also completed the Advanced Management Program at the Harvard Business School.

Skills
Serving as President of the USS *Massachusetts* Memorial Committee, Feitelberg had the privilege in 1965 to sign for and accept custody of the Battleship. With a small group of talented volunteers, Battleship Cove was then developed. His experience in Holy Cross's NROTC program and three years of active duty in the U.S. Navy aided him greatly.

He was also president of the Fall River Regional Task Force. This group of public and private individuals during the '70s and '80s helped elected officials to reorganize Fall River's city government. The group also initiated a program presently still in place to modernize the city's public schools. Healthcare, banking and the Catholic Church also held his focus and interest.

Also of Note
In 2003, UMass Dartmouth presented him with an honorary business degree. In 1997, the Independent Insurance Agents of America presented him its highest award, the Woodworth Memorial. He also received recognition from the Fall River Chamber of Commerce and Bristol Community College. The Catholic lay religious Order of Malta has also recognized his work.

Information gathered from Mr. Feitelberg—photo courtesy of Mr. Feitelberg

MONSOUR, RONALD & MONTE FERRIS
Restaurateurs

Monsour, seated with his sons—
Ron, also seated, and Monte
standing in the lobby of The Venus
de Milo.

Profile
Monsour Ferris was born in Providence, Rhode Island, and was the second oldest of seven children of John and Rose Ferris. He married Somaya Sarkees and they had a daughter as well as two sons. They lived in the Flint section and had seven grandchildren. Monsour is buried in Notre Dame Cemetery.

Ronald J. Ferris was the oldest child and was born in Fall River in 1942, as were his brother and sister. He married Dale Parker and they had two children. He died of cancer in 2009 and is buried in St. Patrick's Cemetery.

Monte Ferris, who was married and has two sons and a daughter, is now the sole owner of the Venus de Milo restaurant. He also owns the Quality Inn and Jillian's Sports Pub in Somerset, Massachusetts, as well as commercial real estate in downtown Fall River.

Experience
Monsour worked at and then owned and operated the former Empire Bowling alley on the second floor of a Pleasant Street building in downtown Fall River and the Somerset Bowing Alley. Since there was no room for growth or expansion possibilities, he bought land in Swansea, Massachusetts and built a modern 20-lane duck pin facility with automatic pin setters (no more kids on the lanes) and added a snack bar in 1960.

Ferris, Sr., opened the Venus de Milo Restaurant alongside the alleys but it was the vegetable minestrone soup (Venus Soup as most called it, despite the fact it and the chef came from the Hotel Mellen in Fall River), that launched the banquet business. From that initiative came a deal with a Fall River fish market, 600 quality scaleless schrod in exchange for hiring Portuguese employees at the facility. As his sons finished their educations they entered the family business, which then was thriving and needed more management help. By 1987, Dun and Bradstreet rated the Venus among the top 10 restaurants in sales in New England. Not only was the Venus a popular family eating establishment, it was one of the largest and most respected banquet halls in New England. Special events, weddings and gatherings from 200 to 2000 were held in the main dining room and hot meals such as baked stuffed lobsters and prime rib, served as you like it, were presented by the waitstaff.

Education
Local Fall River schools; Monsour graduated from B.M.C. Durfee High School, Ron graduated from Assumption Prep and Merrimack College, he also attended UCLA and Boston University. Monte graduated from Suffolk University and Cornell University Restaurant and Hotel School after graduating from Durfee High School.

Skills
While Monsour concentrated his efforts on the hospitality business, both his sons ventured into real estate development and other forms of hospitality.

Also of Note
Monsour (1979) and Monte (1997) were both named Fall River's Outstanding Citizens by the Chamber of Commerce where Monte also served as board chair. Ron served on the board of directors of the Durfee Attleboro Bank as well as other organizations and was first president of Greater Fall River ReCreation, Inc.

Information gathered from the Ferris Family and the *Fall River Herald News*—photo courtesy of Dale Ferris

PAUL A. GIROUX
General Certified Appraiser

Profile
Born in 1923 to Aime and Cora Lariviere Giroux, Paul A. Giroux is one of three children who grew up in the area of South Park. He married the late Jeannine Ledoux and they had two sons, seven grandchildren and five great-grandchildren. He is presently married to Margarete Feil.

Experience
Giroux began in the real estate business in 1947 when he joined the firm, Giroux and Company, which was founded by his father two years earlier. He has been an active appraiser since 1954. He was influenced most by his long-time friend, Bob Fisette, and the brothers at Prevost who taught him, among other things, public speaking, which has served him well in his occupation.

Giroux's father had him collecting rents at a young age and he had designs on becoming a chemist, but it was his close contacts with local attorneys that led him toward forensic appraisal work.

Giroux is a professionally designated appraiser and consultant specializing in forensic appraising and providing litigation support on real estate matters. Specializing in eminent domain land takings, land, improved property, water rights, land fills, he is qualified as expert in real estate by the Federal District Court, Massachusetts Superior Courts; Superior Courts in Rhode Island and New Hampshire.

Education
Giroux attended the Dominican Academy and St. Anne's Elementary School followed by Monsignor Prevost High School, Northeastern University, Ohio State University, and University of Grenoble, France. He studied Urban Land Economics and Real Estate Appraisal, University of Rhode Island, completed American Institute of Real Estate Appraisers courses at Harvard Business School, and courses II and IV (eminent domain), University of Connecticut.

Skills
Giroux is a Member of the Greatest Generation. He landed on the beach in Normandy, France on D-Day+10, where he served as a French interprepter with the combat units in the 1st and 3rd Army. He also participated in the Battle of the Bulge. Recalled to active duty during the Korean Conflict in 1951, Giroux was assigned as a special agent in counter intelligence in Frankfurt, Germany, and retired from the service in 1952 as an Army Captain in Military Intelligence.

Also of Note
Giroux served as both a French and German interpreter during WWII and remains fluent in both.

Information gathered from and photo courtesy of Mr. Giroux

EDWIN A. JAFFE
Manufacturer

Profile
Ed Jaffe moved to Fall River at age ten in 1932 when his father started what turned into a family business. He was born in 1922 to Etta Sundel and Meyer Jaffe and was the middle child. They lived on Highland Avenue. He married Lola Schweitzer and they had three sons and a daughter and six grandchildren. Jaffe died in Stockbridge, Massachusetts, at age eighty-four in 2007.

Experience
From the time of his father's death in 1964, Jaffe built J&J Corrugated Box Corporation into the largest privately-owned converter of corrugated containers in the nation. Jaffe had factories not only in Fall River where the corporate office was based but in Virginia, Georgia and Alabama as well. Known for re-investing in modern equipment, Jaffe's corporate culture was one that valued long-term employment of staff until the sale of the company in 1986.

Education
Local Fall River schools, B.M.C. Durfee High School and Yale University.

Skills
A member of the Greatest Generation, Jaffe served in the Army Air Corps. His passions were helping others through his generosity, particularly in the arts where he was a long-time patron, and his near life-long hobby of photography.

Also of Note
Jaffe was active in whatever community in which he lived including Fall River, Providence, Rhode Island, and Stockbridge, Massachusetts. He was a campaign chairman for the United Jewish Appeal in Fall River and an early major supporter and president of the Stanley Street Treatment and Rehabilitation Center (SSTAR). He served as chairman of the board of Miriam Hospital in Providence and was founding chairman of Berkshire South Regional Community Center in Great Barrington, Massachusetts.

Information gathered from the Jaffe family and *The Berkshire Eagle*

JAMES J. KARAM
*Businessperson, Educator
and Media Owner*

Profile
James J. Karam is the youngest child of
Thomas and Barbara Karam. He and his
two brothers lived in the Flint section of Fall
River. He married Janis Bisko, also from Fall River, and they have four children.

Experience
Karam began his career with the former Industrial National Bank in Rhode Island, as
part of a team that marketed a new idea, credit cards, and oversaw the expansion of
INCard (which eventually became MasterCard).

Karam is a developer in the southern New England area. He is the owner of First Bristol Corporation, which holds more than 4 million square feet of shopping centers,
hotels and office buildings throughout New England.

Education
Local Fall River schools, B.M.C. Durfee High School and University of Massachusetts Dartmouth. He is the recipient of two honorary doctorate awards from both the
University of Massachusetts Dartmouth and Southern New England School of Law.

Skills
Karam served for ten years and most recently as chair of the University of Massachusetts System Board of Trustees and was recently appointed to the Board of Directors
of Edward M. Kennedy U.S. Senate Library within the John F. Kennedy Presidential
Library.

He is co-owner of local radio stations WSAR and WHTB with his brother, Bob
Karam.

Also of Note
Karam received the Durfee Distinguished Alumni Award in 2011, was named Fall
River's Outstanding Citizen in 2002 by the Fall River Area Chamber of Commerce
and the Entrepreneur of the Year by University of Massachusetts Dartmouth. He
serves on the Board of Trustees of Stewart Health Care Systems and is past chair of
the University of Massachusetts Dartmouth Foundation and the Southcoast CEO
group.

Information gathered from Karam and the *Durfee Chimes*—photo courtesy of Mr. Karam and UMass Dartmouth

ROBERT S. KARAM
Businessperson, Educator
and Media Owner

Profile
Robert S. Karam is the middle child of Thomas and Barbara Assad Karam. Both his brothers are also included in this book. They grew up in the Flint section of Fall River in the heavily ethnic, Lebanese neighborhood of the community. He married another Fall Riverite, the late Sue Hutchinson, and they had two children and five grandchildren.

Experience
After working as a counter boy at the Kerr Mill and then as a bank teller, Karam's dream of becoming an engineer faded when he realized he was a good salesperson—especially of financial products and services.

Karam is the principal of Karam Financial Group, concentrating on design, funding and administration of executive benefit programs and other qualified plans. He has been a life insurance agent and broker since 1969.

He is currently a director of Savings Bank Life Insurance of Massachusetts and with his son is a founder of Karam Financial Group located in Fall River, Boston and Providence, Rhode Island.

Education
Local Fall River schools, B.M.C. Durfee High School and University of Massachusetts Dartmouth. He received an honorary doctorate from University of Massachusetts Dartmouth and Southern New England School of Law. He is a Chartered Life Underwriter (CLU), a Chartered Financial Consultant (ChFC) and a Registered Employee Benefit Consultant (REBC).

Skills
Karam and his brother, Jim, own the local radio stations, WSAR and WHTB. He also develops industrial and residential real estate in the Southcoast area. He and his partners operate multiple properties of approximately 100,000 square feet in the Fall River Industrial Park.

Also of Note
Karam was named Fall River's Outstanding Citizen in 1987 by the Fall River Area Chamber of Commerce. He is a past chair of the Board of Trustees of Southeastern Massachusetts University (UMass Dartmouth). He has established the Robert S. Karam Scholarships available to students attending any of the UMass campuses.

Information gathered from Mr. Karam, American Lebanese Foundation and UMass Dartmouth
—photo courtesy of Mr. Karam

STANLEY A. KOPPELMAN
Law Professor and Businessperson
U.S. Treasury Deputy Tax Legislative Counsel

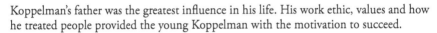

Profile
Stanley Koppelman was born in 1946 and raised in Fall River. He is the only child of Jeanette and Joseph Koppelman. Formerly married to Michele Koppelman, M.D., they have three adult daughters.

Experience
Started by his family in 1947, Fall River Florist Supply Company has grown and expanded under Koppelman's direction. The business employs more than 150 people in Fall River at a facility encompassing over 130,000 square feet.

Koppelman's father was the greatest influence in his life. His work ethic, values and how he treated people provided the young Koppelman with the motivation to succeed.

After Koppelman worked as a tax lawyer in a large Philadelphia law firm where he became a partner, he then worked for the U.S. Treasury Department before becoming a tenured Professor of Law at Boston University. Koppelman then took the family business to a new level based on developing an acquisition and distribution system designed to provide customers with the freshest top quality cut flowers. The firm also imports an extensive line of floral supplies and maintains a fully stocked greenhouse with a wide selection of quality, popular plants.

Education
Local Fall River schools, Morton Junior High and B.M.C. Durfee High School. He graduated from both the University of Pennsylvania and the University of Pennsylvania Law School.

Skills
As a law professor, Koppelman wrote and taught law at Boston University and worked with Congress on tax issues through two administrations. At the Treasury Department he worked on guidelines to broaden the tax base and reduce tax rates. This approach was used in 1986 Tax Reform Legislation and has more recently been proposed in the Bowles-Simpson tax package. He also worked on legislation that substantially limited tax shelters.

Also of Note
Committed to improving the quality of life for area residents, Koppelman has served as campaign chair of the United Way of Greater Fall River's annual appeal and as a long-term member of its board of directors. He is a director of the Koppelman Family Foundation with his mother.

Information gathered from Mr. Koppelman and Fall River Florist Supply—photo courtesy of Mr. Koppelman

RICHARD L. LAFRANCE
Hospitality Entrepreneur

Profile
Richard L. Lafrance is the only child of Roland Aime and Rita Fallon Lafrance. He was born in Fall River in 1947. He married Fall Riverite from the Flint, Muriel Baraby. They are the parents of four children and ten grandchildren.

Experience
It was 1955 when Aime and Rita took a massive leap forward by opening White's of Westport at the Narrows. Their young son worked as a bus person but never gave much thought to joining the family business until he spent some time working on Wall Street as a computer analyst after college and the service.

After years away from home and with four children, the young Lafrance family returned to the family business. Lafrance has not only run the banquet and restaurant business, but expanded it into a full-fledged hospitality business with hotels, banquet halls, catering and multiple restaurant locations.

Lafrance opened the Hampton Inn next door to White's in 1989, followed closely by two more hotels in the 1990s.

He then bought and updated Bittersweet Farm Restaurant in 1998 and Rachel's Lakesider, formerly Stevenson's, near the now closed Lincoln Park in North Westport on the Dartmouth town line.

Multiple hotels and restaurants have been part of the Lafrance stable over the last decade in various states; most recently opening, Ten Cousins Brick Oven, a family dining restaurant located in the Central Village section of Westport. His team now includes his three sons and son-in-law as well as his wife and oldest child, Rachel, and his grandchildren.

Education
St. Joseph's School, Monsignor Prevost High School, Notre Dame University and graduate classes at the University of Rhode Island.

Skills
Lafrance served in the Army for three years after he was drafted and attended Officers Candidate School.

Also of Note
He was named Fall River's Outstanding Citizen in 2007 by the Chamber of Commerce. He was also an official Olympic Torch bearer for the 1996 Summer Games in Atlanta.

Information gathered from Richard Lafrance—photo courtesy of Mr. Lafrance

THOMAS A. RODGERS, JR.
Manufacturer, Entrepreneur
and Philanthropist

Profile
Tom Rodgers was the oldest of three sons of Ella Walsh and
Thomas A. Rodgers, Sr. (His brother, Ted, is also highlighted
in this book.) Born in Fall River, he grew up in the Maplewood
section of the city. Rodgers and his first wife, Rita, had four
children, seven grandchildren and two great-grandchildren. He
remarried Phyllis Kitowski and had three stepchildren and two step-grandchildren. He
died at age ninety-two in 2006.

Experience
Rodgers was the founder, president and CEO of Globe Manufacturing Company, which
was headquartered in Fall River beginning in 1947 with additional manufacturing facilities in the United Kingdom and Alabama. Globe was the world's largest producer of
natural latex thread with manufacturing facilities in Fall River and Tiverton, England.
The company developed the revolutionary product known as Spandex with production
facilities in Fall River, North Carolina and Alabama. Globe, under Rodgers's direction,
produced rubber that was used by makers of undergarments for men and women.

Globe Manufacturing Company was an ISO-9001 registered industry leader in
elastication and had a fiber weight, power match and delivery system for any existing or
imagined construction application.

Education
Saints Peter and Paul's School and B.M.C. Durfee High School. He attended the
University of Rhode Island, Providence College and received honorary degrees from
University of Massachusetts Dartmouth, Bristol Community College, Salve Regina
University and St. Anselm's College in New Hampshire.

Skills
Rodgers was the original founder of Goat Island in Newport, Rhode Island, and served
on the board of directors of Salve Regina University, First Federal Savings Bank and St.
Anne's Hospital in Fall River. For a time, Rodgers also owned the former R.E. Smith
Printing Company also located in Fall River.

Also of Note
Rodgers received the Durfee Distinguished Alumni Award in 1970. The Rodgers Rec-
reation Center at Salve Regina University is named in his honor. He also received the
Benefactor award of the National Council of Resources Development while he served
as a member of the Bristol Community College Foundation. He founded the Rodgers
Family Foundation.

Information gathered from his family and the *Fall River Herald News*—photo courtesy of the Rodgers family

SUMNER JAMES WARING, JR.
Funeral Service Professional

Profile
Jim Waring was born in Fall River in 1936, died in Fall River at age sevemty-four in 2010 and is buried in Beech Grove Cemetery in Westport. He was the son of Louise S. Borden and Sumner J. Waring, Sr. Waring was the youngest child with two older sisters and grew up in the Highlands. He was married to Elizabeth Westgate for forty-five years and they had a son, who is also highlighted herein, and a daughter Christine. They have three granddaughters.

Experience
Waring was a fourth generation funeral professional for more than fifty years. First Congregational Church Minister Lex King Souter inspired Waring, saying, "God only gives what one can handle." It was Waring's inspiration.

Waring joined his father, Sumner, in the funeral profession in 1958. He not only served community families with dignity and dedication but also began a process of uniting funeral services within the city. He united several funeral services in the Southcoast into one and expanded into Boston with a total of 17 locations.

In 1996, Waring Sullivan Homes of Memorial Tribute became affiliated with Service Corporation International, the largest publicly owned funeral and cemetery provider. The regional headquarters remained in Fall River due to Waring's influence and the quality of local employees.

Education
Highland School, Morton Junior High, Choate Prep School, Babson College and Mt. Ida College. He received an honorary doctorate of law from Mt. Ida.

Skills
Waring was an avid reader of newspapers. He read seven papers daily and aspired to own a newspaper in his later years. He collected books on politics, history and sports.

Also of Note
He was not only appointed as a UMass Dartmouth trustee, he also served as a Massachusetts Judicial Nominating Committee member. Waring was named Fall River's Outstanding Citizen in 1986 by the Fall River Area Chamber of Commerce. He was president of the National Funeral Directors of America in 1979-1980 and served as the youngest president of the Fall River Chamber of Commerce at age twenty-nine and chair of the board of Adams House for twenty-five years. Waring was also a director at Truesdale and Charlton Memorial Hospitals and the former Fall River National Bank and Lafayette Cooperative Bank. He was honored by the Moby Dick Council of the Boy Scouts of America with their Good Scout Award in 1996 and as a Rotarian he was named a Paul Harris Fellow. There is a scholarship in his memory at Durfee High School to benefit graduates.

Information gathered from Mrs. Waring, the *Boston Globe* and the *Fall River Herald News*
—photo courtesy of Waring Portrait Art Photography

WONG BROTHERS-ALBERT AND ALFRED
Food Distributors

Albert, left, with Alfred, right, and four of their five sisters in 1990.

Profile
Both Albert T. Wong, 1926, and Alfred G. Wong, 1932, were born in Fall River. They were the sons of Frederick and Lena Wong, who were both born in China. They grew up in Fall River with their five sisters. Albert married Canton-born Barbara and they had six children. He died in 1995.

Experience
The Wong family founded the Oriental Chow Mein Company in Fall River in 1926, as a side business to Frederick Wong's Hong Kong Restaurant on South Main Street. Soon his two sons joined the business to make it a Fall River institution. The sons were motivated by their father to excel, be strong family oriented men and work hard in the business to build the business to what it is today.

Alfred, who is still working in the family business, joined their father after high school graduation.

The Wong family has been producing the "Hoo Mee" brand fried chow mein noodles in the yellow box for restaurants, schools, hospitals and supermarkets for more than seventy-five years. In the mid-1970s, Fall River had the largest per capita consumption of chow mein noodles in the country and had more Chinese restaurants per capita than Boston.

Education
Local Fall River schools and B.M.C. Durfee High School. Both graduated in the top ten of their classes in 1944 and 1950, respectively. Albert attended M.I.T. and Alfred graduated from Boston University.

Skills
Three of Barbara and Albert Wong's six children and twelve other employees still work for the family-run and owned company along with Alfred.

Also of Note
In 2009, a fire broke out while noodles were being fried at the Eighth Street facility, causing slight damage but enough to prevent the day's deliveries. It might have proven an opportunity for the octogenarians to retire, but retirement is clearly not in their blood.

Information and photo gathered from the Wong family—photo courtesy of the Wong family

BANK PRESIDENTS EDUCATED IN FALL RIVER 1926-PRESENT

William R. Eccles, Jr.	Bank Five
John S. Brayton III	B.M.C. Durfee Trust Company
John S. Brayton IV	B.M.C. Durfee Trust Company
Leeds Burchard	Citizens Savings Bank
Joseph D. Milne	Citizens Savings Bank
James E. Osborn	Citizens Savings Bank
John T. Swift	Citizens Savings Bank
Donald A. Bogle	Fall River Five Cent Savings Bank
Nathan Durfee	Fall River Five Cent Savings Bank
Charles L. Holmes	Fall River Five Cent Savings Bank
Douglas J. Richardson	Fall River Five Cent Savings Bank
William F. Staples	Fall River Five Cent Savings Bank
Frederick W. Watts	Fall River Five Cent Savings Bank
John C. Batchelder**	Fall River National Bank
Louis F. Fayan	Fall River National Bank
Frank P. Coolidge	Fall River Peoples Co-Operative Bank
William D. Palmer	Fall River Peoples Co-Operative Bank
Milton Reed	Fall River Peoples Co-Operative Bank
Thomas Bassett	Fall River Savings Bank
Charles R. Murray	Fall River Savings Bank
Alston Rigby	Fall River Savings Bank
Robert F. Sykes	Fall River Savings Bank
James A. Buffington	Fall River Trust Company
Joseph A. Faira	Fall River Trust Company
George W. Graham	Fall River Trust Company
Thomas H. Nabb	Fall River Trust Company
Anthony Perry	Fall River Trust Company

BANK PRESIDENTS EDUCATED IN FALL RIVER 1926-PRESENT

Robert A. Clark *	First Federal Savings and Loan
Paul McDonough	First Federal Savings and Loan
Edmond Cote	Lafayette Co-Operative Bank
Pierre F. Peloquin	Lafayette Co-Operative Bank
Donald T. Corrigan	Slades Ferry Trust Bank
Edward S. Machado	Slades Ferry Trust Bank
Harold Regan	Slades Ferry Trust Bank
Donald Ashton	Union Savings Bank
Cyrus Roundsville	Union Savings Bank

* There is a scholarship in his memory at Durfee High School that benefits graduates.

** Batchelder served as president of more than one bank over the years.

1926-Present
Media

Road to Success

Throw away all ambition beyond

that of doing the day's work well

The travellers on the road to success live in the present,

heedless of taking thought for the morrow.

Live neither in the past nor in the future,

but let each day's work absorb

your entire energies, and satisfy your wildest ambition.

WILLIAM OSLE

MORTON DUBITSKY DEAN
News Correspondent and Television Anchor

Profile
Born in Fall River in 1935, Morton Dubitsky Dean lived on New Boston Road, Farnham and Ray Streets when growing up. He was the second son of Joe and Celia (Tillie) Schwartz Dubitsky. He is married and has three grown children and three grandchildren.

Experience
When Dean was at Durfee High School and Emerson College he was fortunate enough to have summer jobs at local media outlets such as radio station WALE (owned by George Sisson, also cited herein), WHIM and WJAR in Providence and WNBC in West Hartford, Connecticut. After college, Dean landed positions with WVIP in Mt. Kisco, New York, and WBZ Radio in Boston. Dean not only had a voice for radio, he had

Dean, right, with the author at ABC News.

the looks for television and he went to work in Manhattan for WCBS-TV, then CBS, and retired from ABC News, all in New York.

Dean's childhood dream was to become a news reporter and travel the world and he succeeded many times over. He became a news correspondent, reporting particularly on space travel and the war in Vietnam, to where he has occasionally returned. A gifted writer and storyteller, he was one of this nation's most trusted and respected news correspondents and a top notch news anchor.

Education
Spencer Borden and Highland Schools, B.M.C. Durfee High School and Emerson College. He also has a number of honorary degrees including one from UMass Dartmouth.

Skills
Dean was the captain of the Emerson College basketball team after gaining experience with coach Luke Urban at Durfee. More recently, Dean has done voiceovers for documentaries on A&E and the History Channel. He also narrated a slide show to help promote the United Way of Greater Fall River in the mid-1980s.

Also of Note
Dean was a recipient of the Durfee Distinguished Alumni Award in 2003. The media center at Durfee High School is named in his honor. He was also the first recipient of an honorary degree from Ringling Brothers, Barnum and Bailey Clown College. Most significantly, Dean has been the recipient of Emmy Awards and awards from United Press International.

Information gathered from Mr. Dean, *Durfee Chimes* and *Wikipedia*—photos courtesy of Mr. Dean

E.J. DIONNE, JR.
Syndicated Columnist, Author and Journalist

Profile
E.J. Dionne, Jr., was born in Boston in 1952 to Dr. Eugene Dionne, a dentist, and Lucienne Dionne, a school teacher. He grew up in Fall River with his sister. He is married to Mary Boyle and they have three children.

Experience
Brought up in a Catholic environment, Fall River was always a hot bed of politics, the Red Sox, and faith. Despite living in the wealthy Highland section of the city, Dionne's exposure to underclass families seemed to influence his desire to expose and correct injustice.

A nationally syndicated journalist and political commentator, Dionne is also a senior fellow at the Brookings Institute, a professor at Georgetown University, a research fellow at Saint Anselm College and a National Public Radio commentator.

His columns appear in *The Washington Post* and *The Herald News* among many other daily newspapers. Before joining The Post, he wrote for *The New York Times* as a foreign correspondent in Rome, Paris and Beirut.

Education
Local Fall River Catholic schools, Portsmouth (Priory) Abbey School, Harvard College '73 and a Rhodes Scholar at Oxford in 1982.

Skills
Dionne has written five books and been a frequent guest on ABC's "This Week" and NBC's "Meet The Press," as well as on National Public Radio.

Also of Note
Dionne is also a columnist for *Commonweal*, a liberal Catholic publication.

His book, *Why Americans Hate Politics*, won the Los Angeles Times Book Prize and was a National Book Award nominee. He has also won the Annual Political Science Association Award and an Empathy Award from Volunteers of America, as well as a National Human Services Assembly Award for Excellence by a member of the media.

He is also a Senior Fellow in Governance Studies at the Brookings Institute, a University Professor in the Foundations of Democracy and Culture at Georgetown Public Policy Institute, a Senior Research Fellow at Saint Anselm College, and an NPR, MSNBC, and PBS commentator.

MARGERY EAGAN
Journalist

Profile
Born in 1954 in Fall River to Margaret Manning and Daniel Eagan, Margery Eagan and her sister grew up near North Park on Rock Street. Formerly married, she has three children.

Experience
Margery Eagan began her writing career at The *Herald News* in Fall River followed by a stint at the *Standard Times* of New Bedford. Her writing style was developed by Miss Burns at Durfee who encouraged weekly short essays and demanded "revise and rewrite." "Succinct, never verbose," were Miss Burns's directions. Being a teenage room attendant at a Cape Cod motel did not influence her career choice but has stood her well in life as a mother.

Eagan became a correspondent for the *Boston Globe* before joining the Burlington, *Vermont Free Press* and then returning to the area working again for the *Standard Times*. She moved on to a position with *The Boston Herald* as a general assignment reporter before spending three years with *Boston Magazine*. She has been columnist with the paper since 1988.

Education
Westall School, Morton Junior High and B.M.C. Durfee High School. Eagan attended Smith College and graduated from Stanford University.

Skills
Besides being a writer, Eagan is also a broadcast journalist and has enjoyed a radio career as a talk show host in the Boston market since 1999. She currently anchors a noon to 2 p.m. time slot at WBGH-FM with longtime sidekick, Jim Braude.

Information gathered from Ms. Eagan—photo courtesy of Ms. Eagan

LESTER KRETMAN
NBC News Producer, White House

Profile
Lester Kretman is the son of Charles and Sarah Kretman. He had a younger sister, Linda, who passed away in 1973. Kretman grew up on Shawmut Street in a neighborhood he describes as "right out of a sitcom." Surrounded by triple deckers, "we played in the street and we lived on the top floor for $15 a month," he said. Kretman currently lives in the Watergate in Washington, D.C. He and his wife, Kathy Postel, have two sons.

Experience
Kretman's earliest work experience was bagging potatoes and sweeping floors at his uncle's at Pleasant Street Supermarket, but it was Durfee journalism teacher John Crowley and drama coach Barbara Wellington who guided and inspired the *Durfee Hilltop* editor and National Honor Society member to realize his childhood dream in news broadcasting. Kretman was another native son whom WALE owner George Sisson (included herein) influenced. It might have been Dr. Irving Fradkin (also included herein) and Kretman's mother who had the greatest influence on him.

Before landing his lifelong dream job, Kretman was an assistant news director for WBZ-TV in Boston and then executive producer at WHDH-TV and WCVB-TV, also in Boston. He was the NBC Deputy Bureau Chief in Washington, D.C., and was also a producer assigned to the NBC bureau in Frankfurt, Germany.

Class never mattered to Kretman, a value he learned in Fall River and applied at the highest levels of power—in the White House, with Presidents, on Air Force One as well as at state dinners. His principal responsibility was covering the President all over the world.

Education
Local Fall River schools—Connell School, Highland School, Morton Junior High and B.M.C. Durfee High School. He graduated from Boston University in 1963.

Skills
Before moving to NBC, Kretman was an education reporter for the *Providence Journal.*

Kretman taught journalism classes at Georgetown University and seminars at the Brookings Institute as well as serving on the advisory board of Citizens Scholarship Foundation of America, launched in Fall River by Irving Fradkin, now known as Scholarship America.

Also of Note
Kretman won two national Emmys for NBC News, one for covering national elections and the other for his coverage of the funeral of President Ronald Reagan. He was nominated for his coverage from the White House on 9-11. Kretman has also been recognized by United Press International, Ohio State and the American Heart Association.

Information gathered from Mr. Kretman and the *Fall River Herald News*—photo courtesy of Mr. Kretman

MYRON MAGNET, PH.D.
Magazine Editor and Author

Magnet, left, with President Bush at awards ceremony

Profile
Born in Fall River in 1944 to Edith and Harry I. Magnet, M.D. an ear, nose and throat specialist, Myron Magnet lived on Weetamoe Street in the Highland section of the city as a youth. He and his wife have two children.

Experience
Magnet served as editor from 1994 to 2007, and still holds the position of editor-at-large, of the *City Journal,* a quarterly magazine created to communicate to a broad and influential audience innovative ideas about restoring the quality of life to America's cities. He has also served as a member of the Board of Editors of *Fortune* magazine.

Magnet has written for a variety of publications including *Commentary, The Wall Street Journal, National Review, The American Spectator,* and *The New York Times,* among others. He has contributed multiple articles and op-eds for various national publications on a wide variety of subject matter from American society, social policy, economics and corporate management to intellectual history, literature, architecture and the founding of America.

Education
Tansey and Highland Schools, Philips Exeter Academy, Columbia University for both bachelor and doctorates and a masters degree from Cambridge University in the U.K.

Skills
Magnet has appeared on numerous television and radio programs. His book, *The Dream and the Nightmare: The Sixties' Legacy to the Underclass,* was one of the most important books read by President George H.W. Bush. He has written five books, including, *The Founders at Home: The Building of America 1735-1817* and his most recent, *Dickens and the Social Order,* in 2004.

Also of Note
President Bush awarded him the National Humanities Medal in 2008 for "scholarship and visionary influence in renewing our national culture of compassion."

Information gathered from Dr. Magnet, *Wikipedia* and the Manhattan Institute—photo courtesy of *Wikipedia*

WAVERLY ROOT
Journalist, Author and Radio News Analysis

Profile
Born in 1903 in Providence, Rhode Island, Waverly Root was raised in Fall River between 1910 and 1920. Root was the son of Florence May Lewis and Francis Solomon Root. He had four siblings. Waverley Lewis Root was married twice; his last wife was named Colette and he had a daughter, Diane Lane Root, by his first wife. He died in 1982 in Paris of a heart attack.

Experience
Root spent the early days of his career as a news correspondent as well as an editor and advertising copy writer while living in Greenwich Village. He moved to Paris in 1927 and began writing for *The Chicago Tribune*, then for *United Press International, Time Magazine*, and finally, *The Chicago Times*.

During WWII, Root returned to the States and landed editorial jobs in New York at the *Daily Mirror*, then moved to Vermont. Root returned to Paris from 1957 to 1967 as a correspondent for *The Washington Post* under his pen name, "Unshakably American."

It was not until 1958 that Root's writings focused on food, especially French and Italian. His last book, *Food,* was an encyclopedia for the food industry.

Education
Local Fall River schools, B.M.C. Durfee High School and Tufts University.

Skills
Root worked for a time in radio for The Mutual Broadcasting System.

Also of Note
Root was president of the Anglo-American Press Association of Paris, vice president of the Overseas Press Club and an officer in the Legion of Honor.

Information gathered from Tufts University, the *Fall River Herald News* and the *New York Times*
—photos courtesy of *Wikipedia*

GEORGE L. SISSON, JR.
Radio Station Owner and
Cable Television Pioneer

Profile
George L. Sisson, Jr., and his wife, Mary Pat Doyle Sisson, were married more than fifty years until his death in 2009 at age eighty-nine. He was born in Fall River to Attorney George L. and Mary Corcoran Sisson. He, his two brothers and his sister were born on a farm in Portsmouth, Rhode Island, later moving to Fall River. They lived on Phillips Street off New Boston Road. He and his wife Pat, have a son, Mark.

Experience
Sisson founded radio station WALE and provided air time to many young and future successful broadcasters including Morton Dean and Lester Kretman. Subsequently, he served as director of public affairs for a newly granted licensee television station in the area, WLNE Channel 6 in New Bedford.

Sisson was a pioneer. He saw beyond commercial television and founded the first cable system in Westerly, Rhode Island. He moved on to larger markets with cable systems in New England, New York, Pennsylvania and Florida. He was also instrumental in the founding of C-Span.

Education
Spencer Borden School, Morton Junior High and B.M.C. Durfee High School in 1938 and the College of William and Mary in Virginia.

Skills
George Sisson remained extremely active in his home town of Bristol, Rhode Island, and the state in general. He was a delegate to the Rhode Island Constitutional Convention in 1986 and wrote an article that guaranteed citizen rights and lateral access to the shoreline. A past chair of Save The Bay, he lent his expertise to multiple organizations from preservation and history to environmental causes as well as the East Bay Bike Path.

Also of Note
Sisson was part of the Greatest Generation, spending five years in the Navy, including time at Pearl Harbor. He was a member of the R.I. Heritage Hall of Fame and a recipient of both the WJAR Jefferson Award and Hattie Brown Award.

Information gathered from *East Bay Newspapers* and Mrs. Sisson—photo courtesy of Mrs. Sisson

1926-Present

Military

The Charles Braga, Jr., Bridge from Fall River to Somerset was built between 1959 and 1966 at a cost of $25 million, spans 1.2 miles over the Taunton River. The U.S.S. *Massachusetts* is shown here at her berth. The span honors a Fall River sailor who died at Pearl Harbor.

Built Together

There are parts of a ship, which taken by themselves would sink.

The engine would sink. The propeller would sink.

But when the parts of the ship are built together, they float.

So with the events of life.

Some have been tragic. Some have been happy.

But when they are built together, they form a craft that floats

and is going someplace. And I am comforted.

RALPH W. STOCKMAN

REVEREND WILLIAM HENRY BELL, PH.D.
United States Navy Captain, Chaplain and Educator

Profile

William H. Bell, born in 1935, was the son of Thomas H. and Audrey Partington Bell. He and his four siblings were brought up on Stafford Road near the Tiverton border. He married Eleanor Wilson and they had six children. Reverend Dr. Bell died in 1996 and is buried in Quantico National Cemetery in Virginia.

Experience

As a youngster Bell was greatly influenced by Rev. Williamson of the Presbyterian Church and Miss Daley, his French teacher. He also credits his involvement in church clubs and DeMolay International–an international organization for young men ages twelve to twenty-one dedicated to teaching young men to be better persons and leaders. Bell became both a better person and a leader. He decided to become a minister and then joined the military to become a Navy chaplain. He advanced up the ranks, retiring after serving in Vietnam as part of the "Brown Water Navy" on the same boat as his Marine son.

Bell was assigned as a regimental chaplain with the 9th Marines, 3rd Marine Division in Okinawa, Japan. He later served at the Marine Corps Development and Education Command in Quantico, Virginia.

Education

Letourneau School, Henry Lord Junior High, B.M.C. Durfee High School, Westminster College, Pittsburgh Theological Seminary, University of New Hampshire and a doctorate from Andover Newton Seminary.

Skills

Music was always a major part of Bell's life. He played in a band with his high school buddies that was managed by one of the boys father. He went on to play in bands both in high school and college. Faust Fiore, his Durfee music teacher, was instrumental in his continued interest in music.

Also of Note

When Bell retired from the military as a captain his years of active duty did not end. His second career was as a history teacher in public schools. Bell also served on the Board of the Newport, Rhode Island, Chapter of the American Red Cross and Newport County Child and Family Services and played in the clarinet section of the Newport Concert Band.

Information gathered from family—photo courtesy of family

JOHN V. "JACK" BRENNAN
Marine Colonel and Aide to the President

Profile
Jack Brennan is the son of John M. Brennan and Olympia Magieri and the oldest of four children. The family lived in the Maplewood section of the city. Born in 1937 and formerly married to a Fall River girl, they had three children. He divides his time between Southern California and southern Rhode Island.

Experience
In 1969, Brennan was appointed the first Marine Corps aide to President Richard M. Nixon and accompanied Nixon to China, he was the first Marine to set foot in that country. He met Mao Zedong, Soviet General Secretary Leonid Brezhnev and Pope Paul VI. Brennan remained with Nixon and returned with him to California. He retired from duty as an active Marine after 16 years to became Nixon's civilian chief of staff, golfing partner and confidant in San Clemente, California. He remained in the Marine Reserves until full retirement after twenty years.

During his tenure in the White House, in a civilian capacity, he worked for five presidents. Journalist Diane Sawyer called the Fall River Marine "the funniest guy you ever met in your life; an irreverent, wonderful guy," just as his inspirational fourth grade teacher, Miss Lenahan, had told his parents long ago.

In 1977, Brennan negotiated the Nixon Interviews with British journalist David Frost. The interview drew the largest television audience for a political interview in history, inspiring the play, *Frost/Nixon,* and an Academy-award nominated film of the same title. Brennan served as a consultant for the film version but disagreed with many aspects of the portrayal of his former boss, saying they were created for dramatic rather than factual purposes.

Education
Local Fall River schools including Henry Lord Junior High. He graduated from Monsignor Coyle High School and Providence College.

Skills
Brennan's first job was delivering groceries in his wagon for a local small grocery store but being in the food and/or delivery business was not his life's ambition. He dreamed of being a sportscaster but his ultimate motivators were his parents, who provided influence and discipline.

Also of Note
Brennan served with the Marine Corps during the war in Vietnam earning both a Bronze Star and Purple Heart at the Battle of Khe Sanh.

Information gathered from Col. Brennan and *Wikipedia*—photo courtesy of Col. Brennan

DONALD T. CORRIGAN
*United States Navy Rear Admiral
and Bank President*

Profile
Donald Corrigan was born in Fall River in 1930, the son
of Phyllis Plunkett and John M. Corrigan. He, his brother
and sister grew up on Prospect Street near Union Hospital.
Corrigan and his first wife, Elizabeth Ann Welch, were the
parents of a son, two daughters and seven grandchildren. He
married Elizabeth McNamara after his first wife died. He
died in 2003 and is buried in St. Patrick's Cemetery.

Experience
Corrigan was an experienced businessman, serving as a
Texaco Oil real estate representative after the Korean War,
where he first served his country. He went on to work for the
General Adjustment Bureau in Fall River. In 1959, he helped

Rear Admiral Corrigan with
his wife, Elizabeth, when he
retired from the Navy.

found and eventually became the president and CEO of Slade's Ferry Bank in Somerset,
Massachusetts.

During those years he stayed active in the military. He was active on the PC 1243 off the
North Korean coast and in the Cuban Missile Crisis in 1962. Corrigan was promoted
over the years and retired from the Naval Reserve as an Admiral. Corrigan was influenced
by his family, his religion and his city. He never forgot from where he came, which he
felt kept him grounded.

Education
Sacred Heart School, Monsignor Coyle High School and Providence College. He was
bestowed an honorary degree from Providence College in 1981.

Skills
Corrigan joined other local businesspeople in 1959 to form the Slade's Ferry Trust Company, headquartered in Somerset but soon with branch banks throughout the area. He
was elected a vice president and director until he was named CEO in 1969. He remained
as chair of the board until his death.

Also of Note
His leadership skills manifested themselves in both the military and in banking. He
served on many local nonprofit boards including the United Way and Chamber of Commerce in Fall River.

*"I was trained and disciplined by the nuns, educated at Coyle and
humanized by the Order of Preachers at PC,"*

DONALD CORRIGAN

Information gathered from his son, Michael and *The Herald News*—photo courtesy of Admiral Corrigan's son, Michael

BARRY S. DIRUZZA
Colonel, United States Army

Profile
Barry DiRuzza is the son of Lieutenant Commander Santi DiRuzza, U.S. Army Retired, and Natalie Silvia DiRuzza. Brought up in Fall River with his sister, he is married to Jo Dee Buchan and they have three children.

Experience
After being commissioned in 1986 as a second lieutenant, DiRuzza served in command and staff positions within field artillery, infantry, armor and airborne during his twenty-eight-year career, earning the rank of colonel.

He began his career with the 82nd Airborne Division, deploying with B Company 1st Battalion 504th Parachute Infantry Regiment during Operation Golden Pheasant to Honduras, on the Nicaraguan border.

He was then assigned to the 210th Field Artillery Brigade as part of the 2nd Armored Cavalry Regimental Battle Group during Operation Desert Storm and later was assigned to the National Training Center from 1995 to 1998. From 1998 to 2003, Colonel DiRuzza returned to the 82nd Airborne Division as Executive Officer of the Division Artillery; he deployed to Saudi Arabia and Iraq as a Liaison Officer to Special Operations Forces for his first tour in support of Operation Iraqi Freedom. As commanding officer of 1st Battalion 319th Airborne Field Artillery Regiment, DiRuzza trained, prepared and led his battalion to fight in Iraq for 15 months as part of the 3rd Brigade Combat team, 82nd Airborne Division, during Operation Iraqi Freedom in 2006 to 2007.

Education
Local Fall River schools, B.M.C. Durfee High School and the United States Military Academy at West Point. He received master's degrees from both the Command and General Staff College and the U.S. Naval War College.

Skills
DiRuzza's awards and decorations include the Bronze Star Medal (2 Oak Leaf Clusters), the Defense Meritorious Service Medal, and the Meritorious Service Medal (4 Oak Leaf Clusters). He is a Master Parachutist who is authorized to wear both German and Chilean jump wings and who proudly wears the Ranger Tab and Combat Action Badge.

Also of Note
He is currently stationed at the U.S. Army War College in Pennsylvania where he serves as Chief, Strategic Leader Development Division, for the U.S. Army War College's Center for Strategic Leadership and Development.

Information gathered from Col. DiRuzza—photo courtesy of Col. DiRuzza

DAVID W. GAVIGAN
Colonel, United States Army
and Terrorism Expert

Profile
David Gavigan was born in Fall River in 1938, the son of Doris Martineau and James T. Gavigan. He is the oldest of four children, raised on Mount Pleasant Street near St. Patrick's Cemetery. He married Sue Palavachi, a Truesdale Hospital nurse, and they have four children and six grandchildren.

Experience
Gavigan is an international expert in terrorism. He has served his country for more than 42 years and is a former Assistant Adjutant in the Army National Guard. He was the commander of a military police battalion of more than 500 personnel in the "Blizzard of 1978" and for the papal visit to Boston in 1979. He trained special forces in Lithuania in anti-terrorism.

Gavigan was the Commander of the Bristol County Special Operations Unit at Ground Zero after the World Trade Center bombings and is a former member of the FBI Joint Terrorism Task Force.

Education
St. Mary's School, Morton Junior High and B.M.C. Durfee High School. A graduate of the University of Massachusetts Dartmouth and Bridgewater State University, he has taken advanced classes at Northeastern University, the Army War College and received special training in multiple Army training schools, including Special Forces Terrorism School.

Skills
As a teacher and guidance counselor at both Durfee High School and Silver Lake Regional High School, Gavigan later taught antiterrorism classes at Northeastern and Roger Williams Universities as well as Rhode Island and Anna Maria Colleges.

Also of Note
Gavigan has said his father was "the smartest man who guided me and taught me to respect all people." But Gavigan was also particularly motivated by his wife, who convinced him to become a teacher like some of his idols, Luke Urban (highlighted herein), Tom Hammond, Vin Fitzgerald and Bob Nagle as well as farmer and businessman Gilbert Guimond.

Gavigan is one of nearly fifty Durfee graduates to receive the Distinguished Alumni Award. He was presented the award in 2008.

Information gathered from Col.Gavigan—photo courtesy of Col.Gavigan

ELTON WATTERS GRENFELL
Vice Admiral, United States Navy

Profile
Elton (Jumpin' Joe) Grenfell was born in Fall River in 1903, died in 1980 at age seventy-six and is buried in Arlington National Cemetery. He married and was divorced from Eleanor Cook, sister of Florence Brigham (also highlighted in this book). Remarried to a Navy widow, they had three children and thirteen grandchildren.

Experience
After graduating and being commissioned an ensign in 1926, Grenfell spent the next seven years receiving higher education and serving short duty on various ships. From 1937 to 1939 he served aboard the USS *Pickerel*. After more time spent in Washington, D.C., at the Department of the Navy, Captain Grenfell assumed command of the USS *Gudgeon*, the first submarine to go on war patrol from Pearl Harbor, for a bit more than a year. He was injured in a plane crash, he was detached and eventually reassigned to command the USS *Tunny*.

Admiral Grenfell, center, taking command of the submarine USS Gudgeon.

Grenfell then reported for duty as a Strategic Planning Officer on the staff of the Commander Submarine Force, Pacific Fleet. Following that, he held various command positions in submarine squadrons and then held various positions in the Navy Department Office of Naval Operations. During the 1950s, the Durfee graduate held personnel oversight positions until 1956 when he assumed duty as Commander Submarine Force, U.S. Pacific Fleet.

Education
Local Fall River schools, B.M.C. Durfee High School and the U.S. Naval Academy in 1926. Multiple education opportunities in submarines and torpedoes, post graduate studies in Mechanical Engineering in Maryland and a master's degree from the University of California in 1936.

Skills
There are only two ranks higher than Vice Admiral in the Navy. Elton Watters Grenfell was the second-highest ranking military officer from Fall River and served his city and country proudly during his tour of duty.

Also of Note
In 1942, President Franklin D. Roosevelt presented the Navy Cross to Lieutenant Commander Grenfell for extraordinary heroism as commanding officer of the USS *Gudgeon*, which attacked and sank Japanese war ships. Shortly thereafter he received the Silver Star for attacking the enemy.

Grenfell was awarded the Navy Distinguished Service Medal in 1964 as the Commander of the Submarine Force, United States Atlantic Fleet, between 1960 and 1964 and advisor for Polaris operations to the Commander in Chief Atlantic Fleet. The only man to command the nation's submarine fleet on both the Atlantic and Pacific coasts, he was part of the Greatest Generation.

He was recognized by Durfee High School with its Distinguished Alumni Award in 1960.

Information gathered from Arlington National Cemetery and *Military Times*
—photos courtesy of the Fall River Historical Society

PAUL B. GROZEN
Captain, United States Navy Commander,
Nuclear Attack Submarine

Profile
Paul Grozen was born in 1932 to Julius Grozen and Miriam Taft Feitelberg Grozen. He was an only child of seven years of age when his mother died. He also has a half-sister. He lived in various neighborhoods of the city as he was raised by his grandparents as well as his parents. He is married to Phyllis Zelko and they have two children, and seven grandchildren, including a Navy lieutenant, and a great-grandchild.

Experience
Grozen's early experience digging ditches for the Fall River Gas Company and packing sweaters in a mill were two occupations that he did not want to pursue. Interested in engineering as a youth, he was motivated to join the Navy by his father who served during WW II and in the reserves for twenty years more.

He credits his father as the biggest influence in his life while growing up like many, many individuals who are highlighted on these pages.

Grozen was also influenced by Mary McDonald, a Durfee High math teacher, and Congressperson Joseph W. Martin, Jr., Speaker of the House of Representatives, who appointed him to the Naval Academy, and most significantly by his journalist spouse who was recognized by the Dutch government and the Department of Defense.

Grozen saw service on five different submarines, including a term as commanding officer of the nuclear-powered attack submarine *Haddock* and *Simon Bolivar,* a Polaris-missile-carrying submarine. He then spent two years training officers en route to command Pacific Fleet submarines. Grozen spent two and one half years as Deputy Director for Chief of Naval Operations on Undersea Warfare Research and Development. He also served as the United States representative to NATO meetings in Brussels.

Education
Grozen attended local Fall River schools, Morton Junior High and B.M.C. Durfee High School, University of Massachusetts Amherst and graduated from the U.S. Naval Academy and Massachusetts Institute of Technology. He credits his math and science classes at Durfee High School with his academic success at the Academy.

Skills
He served as the Defense and Naval Attaché to the Netherlands for three years, assigned to the US Embassy in The Hague.

Also of Note
He was the recipient of The Legion of Merit, Navy Commendation and Meritorious Service medals as well as the Defense Superior Medal and The Order of Oranje Nassau from Queen Beatrix of the Netherlands.

Information gathered from Captain Grozen and *Wikipedia*—photos courtesy of Commander Grozen and Collection of Bernard A.G. Taradash

ISADORE P. HORVITZ
Captain, United States Navy

Profile
Isidore P. Horvitz was born in Fall River in 1917 to Soloman and Clara Katz Horvitz. They had three children and lived in the East end section of the city. He married Lillian Joblon and they had three children, six grandchildren and one great-grandchild. He is buried in the Jewish Cemetery in the South End of Fall River.

Experience
As a member of the Greatest Generation, Horvitz served his country in the Navy during WW II. He was an officer on the *Earl V. Johnson* in the Pacific and then commanded a British corvette ship in the North Atlantic, retiring as a full captain after twenty-five more years in the Naval Reserves.

Education
B.M.C. Durfee High School and Harvard College and Bristol Community College.

Skills
Horvitz headed the family business, Modern Furniture, with showrooms in Fall River and Middletown, Rhode Island, for more than fifty years from 1945 to 1998.

Also of Note
Horvitz had a love of learning and enrolled in every credit course offered by Bristol Community College for twenty years between seventy-four and ninety-four years of age.

Horvitz had a saying that he was fond of repeating often, " I had one wife...one job... one house." He also only had one kind of car, a blue Chrysler.

Information gathered from and photo courtesy of the Horvitz family

THOMAS J. "LOU" HUDNER, JR.
United States Navy Captain and
Medal of Honor Recipient

Profile
Born in 1924, Tom Hudner grew up in Fall River with his three brothers and a sister in the Highlands. They are the children of Mary Brown and Thomas J. Hudner. He married widow Georgea Smith who had three children and they had a son together.

Experience
Hudner enrolled in the U.S. Naval Academy in 1943. By the time he graduated, WWII had ended but within a few short years the North Koreans invaded the South and China joined the conflict. Hudner was flying from the USS *Leyte* in the Mediterranean and his ship was rerouted to Korea at the direction of the United Nations Security Council. Before that time, he had served on various surface ships but flying had gotten in his blood. He piloted the F4U Corsair and flew

Hudner with his family in the background, receiving the Medal of Honor from President Harry S. Truman.

more than 27 different combat missions in Korea. One, however, was more memorable than the others. On December 4, 1950, Hudner was supporting Marines on the ground who were trapped by Chinese forces near the Chosin Reservoir as part of a six flight group. Ensign Jesse Brown, the first black Navy pilot killed in the war and Hudner's wingman, was not notified that his plane was trailing smoke as a result of ground fire. He lost control and crashed. Hudner crash-landed his plane to try to save his squadron mate, whose legs were crushed in the cockpit. Hudner tried to extricate the ensign, but was unsuccessful despite aid from a Navy helicopter pilot who came to assist both servicemen. Hudner was forced to leave a dying Brown with the promise that he would return. While the Navy bombed the site two days later with napalm to cremate Brown the pilots recited the Lord's Prayer over the radio.

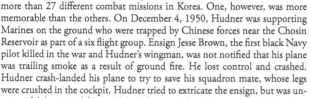

The story has not ended. On July 20, 2013, at age eighty-eight, Hudner embarked on a trip to North Korea to fulfill a promise to Brown to return. This trip would be to return Brown's remains to his family. Unfortunately, due to inclement weather the trip was unsuccessful. This is not just a story of heroism, but also desegregation. Thomas Hudner demonstrated in 1950 and again in 2013 that race does not matter.

Education
Highland School, Morton Junior High, Coyle High School and Phillips Academy Andover. Hudner graduated from the U.S. Naval Academy and became a naval aviator after training in Pensacola, Florida, and Corpus Christi Naval Air Station.

Skills
Hudner became a training pilot after the Korean Conflict but soon was named executive officer of the carrier USS *Kitty Hawk* during the Vietnam War. Before retirement, he was on the staff of the Joint Chiefs of Staff. In 1973, after retirement from the military, he participated in the ceremony with Jessie Brown's widow in the naming of the frigate USS *Jessie Brown*. He became the commissioner of the Massachusetts Department of Veterans Services.

Also of Note
The retired Navy captain with the twenty-four-year career has been honored many times over the years including a baseball field in the Highlands named in his honor. His greatest honor was the Medal of Honor, the only one presented to a Navy Aviator during the Korean Conflict, awarded to him by President Harry S. Truman. Another is soon to come—the Navy has commissioned the construction of a new Arleigh Burke class guided missile destroyer war ship named for Hudner, a rare honor for a living person. The USS *Thomas J. Hudner* is under construction in Bath, Maine. He was recognized by his present home town of Concord, Massachusetts, in 2010 as an Outstanding Citizen.

Information gathered from family, *Wikipedia*, the *Fall River Herald News* and the *Boston Globe*
—photos courtesy of the Hudner family

MAYOR JOHN F. KANE
Brigadier General, United States Army

Profile
John F. Kane was born in Fall River in 1914, the son of James and Ann Mulligan Kane. He had a sister, Mary. He married Mary Leddy Kane and they had two daughters, five grandchildren and three great-grandchildren. He died in 2007 and is buried in St. Patrick's Cemetery.

Experience
Kane is probably best recalled for his run for Mayor of Fall River in 1951 when he bested incumbent Mayor William P. Grant, Esq., by only eight votes. When the ballots were recounted, Grant won by a single vote. This dictated another recount under the watchful eye of the Massachusetts Supreme Court, which certified that John Kane was the winner by 30 votes.

Brigadier General Kane is listed here not because of his political victory or prior years as a Fall River bus driver or succeeding years serving as mayor but rather as a military leader. He served as a part of the Greatest Generation as a World War II Army soldier and after his term as mayor he held the position of the U.S. Property and Fiscal Officer for the Commonwealth of Massachusetts for 16 years.

Education
Local Fall River schools.

Skills
Kane was also an inventor, accomplished pianist and song writer.

Also of Note
Kane was a member of The Artillery Veterans Association.

Information gathered from the *Fall River Herald News*
—photos from City of Fall River and Collection of Bernard A.G. Taradash

ROBERT L. KIRKWOOD
Lieutenant Commander, United States Navy

Profile
Bob Kirkwood was born in 1931. He was the son of Irene Lapointe and Liston Kirkwood and lived on Mount Hope Avenue overlooking the Taunton River with his widowed mother and two sisters. Kirkwood married Barbara Craigie; they had six children and eleven grandchildren over their nearly sixty-year marriage.

Experience
Commander Kirkwood served in the Navy for thirty years, enlisting at age seventeen. Eight years later he entered Officers Candidate School, received his commission and began flight training. He became a fighter pilot, the fulfillment of his lifelong dream. Engaging in air fights with the enemy, Lieutenant Commander Kirkwood successfully fired Sidewinder missiles at enemy aircraft, watching them explode and enemy pilots ejecting. He shot down a Russian MIG 17 with only his guns mounted on his F-8 Crusader.

Education
Kirkwood attended local Fall River schools and B.M.C. Durfee High School, Officer's Candidate School and Naval Post Graduate School with a degree in Political Science.

Skills
In 1973, Kirkwood was assigned to the Center for War Gaming in Newport, Rhode Island. Developing war games at the center, Kirkwood brought these skills to the Naval War College.

Also of Note
During the Vietnam War, he was awarded the Silver Star and Navy Flight Medal. As his wife and family said after his death,

"He was a wonderful man, a gentleman, honorable, the best. We are very proud of him."

Information gathered from Mrs. Kirkwood, the *Fall River Herald News* and Crusader *Flight Report*
—photos courtesy of Mrs. Kirkwood

JOHN J. LISET
Brigadier General, United States Air Force

Profile
John Liset was born in Boston in 1918, but made and called Fall River home. He was the son of Frederick and Kathryn Muldoon Liset. He had a sister and married Mary Louise McGrath. They had three children and two grandchildren. He died in 2010 in Fairfield, Ohio, and is buried in Arlington National Cemetery.

Experience
Liset entered the Air Force in 1942, received his pilot wings and was commissioned as a second lieutenant in 1944. He was a commander and instructor pilot on the B-17 and the B-24 in Army Air Corps Gunnery School. Brigadier General Liset was also a B-29 commander. Involved in the material assistance program for more than fifteen years, General Liset became chief of the U.S. Air Force Section, Joint Brazil-United States Military Commission in 1971.

Education
Local Fall River schools and B.M.C. Durfee High School, Bradford Durfee College of Technology (UMass. Dartmouth) and the University of Maryland.

Skills
His duties after World War II required knowledge of the air forces of nearly every country with which the United States government had or has had military assistance programs throughout the world. In 1970, he served for a time as chair of a special task force to plan a profile for a defense logistics system between 1975 and 1980.

Also of Note
Liset was awarded the Legion of Merit with oak leaf cluster, Air Force Commendation Medal, Army Commendation Medal and Good Conduct Medal. His classification is as a command pilot.

He was also a recipient of the Durfee Distinguished Alumni Award in 1993.

Information gathered from the *Fall River Herald News* and U.S. Air Force
—photo courtesy of the Fall River Historical Society

HELEN MASLANKA, R.N.
Colonel, United States Air Force

Profile
Helen Maslanka is the youngest of five children of Hendryka Wewiorski Maslanka and Andrew Maslanka. They lived in the neighborhood known as "Below the Hill" in Fall River.

Experience
Maslanka's first military assignment was to Westover Air Base followed quickly by a transfer to Carswell Strategic Air Command in Fort Worth, Texas. During her four-year stint at Carswell, Maslanka was sent to Gunter Air Base in Alabama for officer training. While there, she attended flight school as the Air Force had just introduced a new idea of care for wounded soldiers: medical personnel treated the wounded in flight and Helen Maslanka was promoted to captain.

By 1955, Captain Maslanka had a new assignment in England. She spent eleven months of duty with the 3rd Air Medical Evacuation Squadron, then moved to Germany for seventeen months at 1st AME Squadron at Rhein-Main.

Her longest assignment was for two years at Tachikaawa Air Force Base in Japan, where she changed to administrative work in the Air Force Nursing Corps. Her desire to help others and travel the world had been met before she returned to Lackland Air Base in Texas in 1963, when she was promoted to major. It was off again to a foreign land and more promotions—lieutenant colonel and head nurse at a hospital in Turkey.

Helen Maslanka returned home to Scott Air Base in Illinois for four years and a promotion to full Colonel. She was one of more than 4,000 nurses in the corps and only one rank short of the highest rank as a Brigadier General.

Education
Local Fall River schools, B.M.C. Durfee High School, St. Luke's Nursing School and Air Force Flight School.

Skills
Maslanka was also a grocery store clerk, as her first job was working in her father's store, but she always knew she wanted to become a nurse.

Also of Note
Maslanka and her sister, Domka Maslanka Stys, created scholarships at the Durfee High School Alumni Scholarship Fund to benefit graduating Durfee High School students.

Information gathered from the *Fall River Herald News*—photo courtesy of Col. Maslanka

WILLIAM T. NELSON
Rear Admiral, United States Navy

Profile
Bill Nelson was born in Fall River in 1908. He died in Virginia in 1994 and is buried in Arlington National Cemetery. He was the son of Rear Admiral J.T. Nelson and Minnie Turner. Nelson married Lillian Moore and they had two daughters and two grandsons.

Experience
In 1940, the U.S. Navy, through its Bureau of Ships, contracted with the Manitowoc Shipbuilding Company to build 10 U.S. Fleet submarines of the Gato-class. After the outbreak of WWII, the contract was expanded to 41. The majority, 28, were completed before the war's end. Some of the more famous subs were the USS *Rasher*, USS *Hawkbill*, USS *Lagarto* and USS *Ray*. After construction, the subs were taken down the narrow stretches of the Mississippi out to sea.

USS *Petco* commissions in 1942. Left is Rear Admiral J.T. Nelson, USNR (Ret.) father of Lt. Commander William T. Nelson, right and Mrs. Nelson, wife of the submarine C.O.

During WWII Commander Nelson was the skipper of two of these subs. As captain of the *Petco*, Admiral Nelson sank two Japanese ships. After the war, he joined others in the field of logistics. Admiral Nelson also served as commanding officer of the USS *Lamprey*. He retired in 1965.

Education
Local Fall River schools, B.M.C. Durfee High School and the United States Naval Academy.

Skills
Even after retirement, the Admiral served another six years on the Military Board of Logistic Management Institute.

Also of Note
Admiral Nelson is the author of the book, *Fresh Water Submarines: The Manitowoc Story*. It is a book about submarines built by the Manitowoc Shipbuilding Company in the town by the same name in Wisconsin. The book is considered to be an interesting piece of Great Lakes history.

Information gathered from *Wikipedia* and the *Fall River Herald News*
—photos courtesy of the Fall River Historical Society

EDWARD A. "TED" RODGERS
Captain, Rear Admiral and Pilot, United States Navy
Superintendent of Maine Maritime Academy

Profile
Ted Rodgers is the son of Ella Walsh Rodgers and Thomas A. Rodgers. He was born in Fall River in 1916. There were three children in the family and he was the middle son. (His brother Tom, is also highlighted in this book.) They grew up in the Maplewood section of Fall River. He lives today with his wife, Marguerite, in Florida. They have five children and seven grandchildren.

Experience
Like many of the others whose names appear in this book, Rodgers grew up in a three-family tenement with his grandparents living on the first floor and his family above. Like others, Rodgers termed his neighborhood a good one with hardworking people. Rodgers played in the streets or at nearby parks. He also got his start as a delivery boy for a local market, while many others began their careers as paper carriers for the *Fall River Herald News*. Rodgers'

mother urged a good education and strong values, which provided great motivation for success.

Rodgers sailed from Pearl Harbor on the carrier USS *Lexington* on December 5, 1941, for Midway with a Marine air group. They searched for a Japanese target for a week. When they returned to Pearl Harbor they found the USS *Utah* "bottoms up" in the Lexington's berth. That moved Rodgers toward aviation for the next twenty years. He finished the war years as commanding officer of an antisubmarine squadron.

Education
St. Peter and Paul's School, B.M.C. Durfee High School, Bradford Durfee College of Technology, The United States Naval Academy, Massachusetts Institute of Technology and Harvard University.

Skills
He advanced to the rank of Navy captain and held four commands during his years in the service. He was a Navy pilot for twenty-two years, retiring with the rank of captain followed by twenty years as Superintendent (President) of Maine Maritime Academy, where he earned the rank of rear admiral.

Also of Note
After a first plan to become a state police officer, Rodgers saw the movie *Shipmates Forever* with Dick Powell and Ruby Keeler, that was enough to set him on a lifelong career path in the Navy.

Information gathered from Mr. Rodgers and *The Ellsworth American*—photo courtesy of Admiral Rodgers and Collection of Bernard A.G. Taradash

MELVIN ZAIS
Commanding General, United States Army
Third Army

Profile
Born in Fall River in 1916, Melvin Zais died in 1981 at age six-ty-four and is buried in Arlington National Cemetery. He is the son of Ginny Kaufman and Abraham Zais, who had five children and lived in the East End of Fall River. He had two sons, both West Point graduates and paratroopers like their father. Zais's first wife, Eileen Emert, had a stroke when their son Mick was only two and was left incapacitated. They also had four grandchildren. Zais married a military widow, Patricia Light, and retired to South Carolina.

Experience
In 1937, Zais was commissioned a second lieutenant in the U.S. Army Reserves. After serving for two years he joined the faculty of the Tennessee Military Institute where he taught military tactics. During WWII he fought in southern France and at the Battle of the Bulge, as a battalion commander of the 517th Parachute Infantry Regimental Combat Team. Called the Father of the Airborne, Zais was first to join the 501st Air Borne Infantry Battalion. He subsequently fought in Korea and Vietnam as well.

Zais remained in the service to become a career soldier, fighting in Vietnam and serving as commander of the 101st Airborne Division. He was promoted to brigadier general in 1964, major general in 1967 and lieutenant general in 1969. Under his command of the 101st Airborne Division, U.S. Army, Vietnam, the soldiers fought the Battle of Hamburger Hill. In 1973, General Zais was named Commanding General, Allied Land Forces, Southeast Europe, Turkey. A few months later he was promoted to four-star general.

Education
Local Fall River schools, B.M.C. Durfee High School, Louisiana State University, the University of New Hampshire, Harvard Business School for Senior Leaders, Command and General Staff College and the National War College.

Skills
General Zais was the Commanding General, XXIV Corps, U.S. Army Vietnam, then became the commanding general of the Third United States Army from 1972-1973.

Also of Note
The ROTC building at the University of New Hampshire is named after the four-star general, as is a ROTC scholarship at the university and a park at Fort Leavenworth, Kansas. A member of the Greatest Generation and the recipient of the Durfee Distinguished Alumni Award in 1977, Zais received five Distinguished Service Medals, two Silver Stars, four Legions of Merit medals, two Distinguished Flying Crosses, the Bronze Star and Purple Heart. Zais was the only Jewish four-star general in the Army's history.

"The Army fanned into flames the smoldering embers of my ambition,"

GENERAL MELVIN ZAIS

Information gathered from *Wikipedia* and the Zais family—photos courtesy of the Zais family

HEROES WHO DIED IN WORLD WAR II

Adams, Henry A.

Albernaz, Antone, Jr.

Alden, Frederick B.

Alpert, Stanley A.

Alves, Albert

Alves, Edward

Amaral, Alvaro Oliver

Amaral, Domingos

Amaral, Joseph

Amarello, Manuel C.

Andrade, Arthur

Andrade, Arthur C.

Andrews, J. Stephen

Andrewseski, Theodore

Araujo, Manuel, Jr.

Archer, Thomas A.

Audette, Rene N.

August, David

Avilla, Manuel

Banville, Joseph Albert

Barnaby, Alexandre E.

Beaudry, Joseph A.

Beaulieu, Paul L.

Bedard, Hormidas

Belanger, Ernest J.

Benoit, Henry

Benton, Charles F.

Bernier, Edward J.

Berube, Alfred J.

Biello, Johsn W.

Bigos, Frank

Bigos, Walter F.

Bochenski, Matthew

Boisvert, George A.

Bollos, George P.

Bonin, Vincent O. *

Borden, Robert R., Jr.

Borges, Antonio S.

Botelho, Alfred

Botelho, Antone

Botelho, Eugene V.

Bouchard, Joseph G. *

Bouchard, Roland N.

Boucher, Hector E.

Boulay, Arthur E.

Boulay, Francis A.

Boynton, William L.

Braga, Charles, Jr.

Brilliant, George

Brisson, Raymond J.

Brouillard, Arthur H.

Brown, Frederick A., Jr.

Brown, Silas H.

Brzostek, Walter E.

Burdett, Thomas W.

Butler, Joseph T.

Cabral, Herman

Cabral, Manuel

Cadrin, George T.

Campos, William

Cardin, Fleurian P.

Cardin, Joseph R.

Carey, William T.

Carpano, Pasquale

Carrier, John B.

Cartier, Edgar N.

Carvalho, Antone

Carvalho, Joseph

Chagnon, Oscar O.

Champion, Mark

Chase, William B.

Chasse, Armand J.

Chaves, William M., Jr.

Chenard, Roland R.

Chouinard, Leo A.

Chouinard, Robert J.

Claudio, Manel F.

Clement, Melvin J.

Coady, James J.

Connolly, James Bernard *

Connors, James E.

HEROES WHO DIED IN WORLD WAR II

Conroy, James W.

Collette, Fredreick S.

Cordeiro, Francisco

Correia, Antone T.

Correia, Edward *

Correiro, Manuel

Costa, Abel

Costa, Antone

Costa, Arthur

Costa, Edmond

Costa, Joseph

Cote, Roger G.

Couto, John O.

Cox, Thomas

Crapo, Andrew

Croteau, Armand *

Cushman, Henry, I.

Cybert, Stanley

Cyr, Emile

Darcy, Edward J.

Darcy, Thomas D.

Dean, Holgate Joseph

DeOliveira, Alfred

Desforge, Louis N.

Desrochers, Rodolphe A.

Dickenson, Joseph E.

Dionne, Lucien E.

Dozois, Robert N. *

Drapeau, Roland L.

Dumoulin Henry Dorant

Dupont, Joseh H.

Dupras, Edmond E.

Duquette, Ernest J.

Duquette, Donat G., Jr.

Faria, George B.

Ferguson, Paul

Ferreira, Michael

Fielden, Edward A.

Fissette, Daniel

Fish, Charles A.

Fitzler, William E.

Fitzpatrick, John

Flanagan, Thomas E.

Flores, Adelino D.

Flores, Joseph

Flores, Lionel

Flynn, Joseph P.

Foley, James J.

Fontes, Thomas W.

Fournier, Leo D.

Francisco, Joseph

Francoeur, Roland

Freitas, Victor S.

Fuller, Edward K.

Furtado, Alfred P.

Furtado, Manuel R. *

Gaboys, Edward A.

Gadsby, Paul

Gage, John

Gagne, Arthur J.

Gagnon, Napoleon R.

Gagnon, Roland J.

Garant, Normand J.

Gardella, William M.

Garron, Henry C.

Gaskill, Russell D.

Gaudreau, Paul E.

Gauvin, Bertrand M.

Gesner, Edward H.

Gibeau, Wilfred Joseph

Gignac, Norman J. *

Ginsberg, Erwin

Glyn, Hugh

Golding, Lawrence H.

Gonsalves, John

Gorman, David H.

Grandfield, John

Grandfield, John G.

Granoff, Harry

Giffin, James T.

Griffin, Oswald J.

HEROES WHO DIED IN WORLD WAR II

Grise, Edward A.

Gromada, Frank J.

Guay, Joseph R.

Guerette, Ernest

Hamel, Y. Rene

Hardy, Leopold

Harrington, Daniel J., Jr.

Harrington, Thomas

Hathaway, James D.

Healy, Milton *

Hebert, Rene O.

Heddy, Alfred

Heneghan, John

Henry, William F.

Higgins, John T.,

Holden, Richard J.

Holt, Leo

Jarabek, John

Jobin, Joseph E.

Johnson, Allen C.

Joncas, Joseph W.

Jusseaume, Joseph E.

Kafel, Stanley

Kaliff, Sabba A.

Kaminski, Frank W.

Kapitan, Peter

Kaplan, George

Kaplan, Max

Katzman, Gerald

Keavy, Thomas E. *

Kelley, Christopher E.

Kelley, Ralph E.

Kelly, Hugh C.

Kennedy, Leo J.

Kocor, Herny G.

Kokaszka, Walter

Koohy, Samuel

Kot, Kasimer

Kravif, Harry

Krupa, Theodore

Kuss, Walter M.

Labbe, Normand L.

Lachance, Adelard R.

Lachance, Norman B.

Lafleur, Joseph A.

Lafleur, Roger J.

Lambert, Norman

Lapka, Michael N.

Lapointe, Francis H.

Lariviere, Normand O.

Larrivee, Leo O.

Larson, Laurence Everett

Lavallee, Napoleon T. (Paul)

Lavoie, Ernest

Lavoie, Gerard

Lavoie, Joseph A.

Lavoie, Roland J.

Lavoie, Wilfred J.

Lee, William A.

Leeming, Albert W.

Legault, Normand

Lekakis, Peter L.

Lemay, Alfred F.

Lemay, Sylvio

Lemerise, Edward, Jr.

Lenaghan, Arthur C. (Rev.)

Lescault, Dominique D.

Lessard, Paul O.

Levesque, Albert P.

Levesque, George R.

Levesque, Marcel E.

Levesque, Wilfred J.

Lewis, Cyrus A.

L'Homme, Lionel

Liggett, Guy W.

Lord, Vincent G. *

Lopes, George P.

Lynch, Francis P.

HEROES WHO DIED IN WORLD WAR II

Luz, Joseph C.

Macedo, Joao

Macomber, Robert L.

Macri, Francis A.

Maher, Edward L., Jr.

Maia, Manuel S.

Manchester, John K.

Manning, Alan S.

Marchington, William E.

Marciarille, Charles

Margarido, Arthur S.

Martel, Leo

Martin, Manuel L.

Martini, Armand J.

Maynard, Roger R.

Mayo, Frederick L., Jr.

McCann, Thomas E., Jr.

McCarthy, Eugene F.

McCarthy, George E., Jr.

McCarthy, John J.

McDonald, James T.

McMullen, Joseph E.

Medeiros, Alfred

Medeiros, Charles *

Medeiros, Edward

Medeiros, Lewis V.

Melancon, Edmont J.

Mello, Arthur R.

Mello, Frank

Mello, Leonel P.

Mello, Lionel F.

Mello, William

Mercier, Leopold A.

Metras, Albert *

Michaud, Alfred J.

Michaud, Henry P.

Michaud, Rene O.J.

Miller, David L.

Miller, John L.

Miller John M., Jr.

Mirman, Alexander N.

Mis, Edward A.

Moniz, George T.

Monsour, Abdallah

Montgomery, Charles F.

Moore, Albert S.

Moreau, Arthur J.

Morin, Raymond J.

Morneau, Henry

Morrow, Claude L.

Muir, Charles R.

Mulcahy, William P.

Mulrooney, Joseph T.

Nasser, Henry A.

Newbury, Robert E.

Nickerson, Harold *

Nicolau, Manuel R.

Nofal, Charles A.

O'Hearn, WIlliam F.

Olancin, Stephen

Oliveria, Edward

Oliveira, James

Ormerod, George

Ouellette, Joseph N.H.

Pacheco, Edwin G.

Pacheco, Fernando

Pacheco, George M., Jr.

Pacheco, John

Pacheco, Manuel

Patten, Louis

Paul, Wilfred A.

Pavao, Edward

Pavao, Gilbert

Pavao, John

Pedro, John, Jr.

Pelletier, Joseph A.

Pelletier, Joseph G.

Pelletier, Paul R.

Pempek, Stanley

Pencak, Henry

Pereira, Alberty C.

HEROES WHO DIED IN WORLD WAR II

Pereira, Joseph C.

Perrault, Roland H.

Perreira, Daniel

Perreira, Leo

Perry, James

Perry, Manuel J.

Pescarino, Joseph A.

Piela, Milton W.

Pimental, Daniel R.

Pineault, Leo J.

Pirkle, Willis S.

Plamandon, Jean M.

Pond, Edwin M., Jr.

Pontes, Edward

Portella, Antoinio R.

Porter, Edward A., Jr.

Proulx, Armand J.

Radovsky, Joseph H.

Raposa, James

Raposa, Joseph M.

Rapoza, Daniel

Rapoza, John

Rapoza, Manuel, Jr.

Rapoza, Thomas S.

Ratcliffe, Everett

Ray, Howard

Reed, Edward

Rego, Arthur M.

Reis, George H., Jr.

Rivers, Herbert P.

Roach, Richard *

Robidoux, Adjutor

Robin, Joseph E. W.

Rogers, Francis J.

Rogers, William

Rose, Gerard

Ross, J. Maurice

Rousseau, Henry R.

Roy, Charles E.

Ryan, James T.

Ryan, Thomas J.

Ryley, Francis J.

Rzasa, John I.

Sabra, Philip F.

St. Denis, Leopold

St. Denis, Richard J.

St. Laurent, Leo A.

Santos, Adelino M. L.

Santos, George F.

Santos, Rudolfo S.

Saucier, Octave J. B.

Saulnier, Roland G.

Savoie, J. Raymond

Schraer, George

Schwartz, Albert

Scrivo, Ferdinand J.

Searil, Elmer

Senay, Joseph C.

Shea, Daniel

Sheehan, John F.

Shelley, Joseph E., Jr.

Shengarn, George

Shoesmith, George W.

Shovelton, Raymond L.

Silva, Antero

Silva, Manuel M.

Silva, Manuel M., Jr.

Simister, William H.

Simonetti, Alfred R.

Simonin, Louis E.

Silwa, Edward

Smith, Mason W.

Smith, Thomas Jr.

Snyder, William*

Soroka, Stephen

Souza, Henry

Souza, John F.

Souza, Manuel

Souza, Romeo V.

Spellman, Thomas L.

Stabila, WIlliam

Stachura, John A.

Staffa, Henry J.

Standish, Thomas G., Jr.

HEROES WHO DIED IN WORLD WAR II

Steele, William, Jr.

Stefanik, Joseph R.

Stubbs, Walter N., Jr.

Sullivan, Jeremiah J., Jr.

Sullivan, Timothy R.

Sullivan, William S.

Sweet, George L.

Tavares, Joseph

Tavares, William J.

Taylor, James E.

Teixeira, Jose S.

Teixeira, Joseph, Jr.

Thomas, Daniel

Thompson, George

Thompson, Russell

Treholme, Alvin E.

Troup, Alexander J.

Twersky, Jacob A.

Tyrrell, James W.

Uchman, Michael V.

Valton, Antone *

Varanese, Louis G.

Vasconcellos, Adeline C.

Vasconcellos, Alfred V.

Vezina, Thomas J.

Viens, William

Vietri, Anthony J.

Waite, Raymond F.

Walkden, Francis G. *

Ward, John A., Jr.

Warrener, Charles F.

Whalley, Alvin E.

Wheadon, Elmer D.

Wilson, Clarence

Wisz, Bronsislaus J.

Wolowiec, Walter S.

Wood, Milton J.

Wordell, Arthur J.

Woytaszek, John

Wrigley, Joseph, Jr.

Yokel, Arthur A. *

Young, Arthur

* The Kerr Mill Boys
The American Thread Company housed at the Kerr Mill was one of the state's largest employers with 1,600 on staff. From this number, 565 entered the war and 20 died in action.

Information gathered from the City of Fall River Veteran Affairs Office-Ray Hague—photos courtesy of *Wikipedia*

HEROES WHO DIED IN THE KOREAN CONFLICT

Almeida, Joseph

Anctil, Gerard R.

Beaulieu, Joseph

Boardman, Stuart A.

Botelho, Alfred M.

Brissette, Norman

Byron, Thomas

Cochrane, Charles W.

Correia, Daniel

Costa, George

Dennis, Charles M.

Duperre, Robert

Fernandes, John A.

Fragoza, Joseph

Garcia, John R., Jr.

Harrop, Joseph

Hennecke, Ralph S.

Hession, Mary M.

Kneen, John J.

Lapointe, John N.

Leite, Dennis

Lohnes, Glenn L., Jr.

Marsland, Richard E.

Minkin, J. Robert

Moran, Jr., Edward F.

Moss, William R.

Nolan, John

O'Leary, James P.

Oliveira, Daniel Ponce

Oliveira, Robert G.

Ouellet, George

Phillips, John F.

Raposa, Raoul

Reagan, John Kevin

Richardson, Arthur

Roberts, Joseph A.

Rochefort, John R.

Romano, Aime

Sampson, Orrie D. W., Jr.

Senay, John F.

Silvia, Joseph M., Jr.

Smith, Bertram H.

Smith, Douglas Edwin

Souza, Lawrence

Sullivan, Charles R., Jr.

Valcourt, Arthur L.

Woodward, Francis W.

Information gathered from City of Fall River Veteran Affairs Office-Ray Hague—photos courtesy of *Wikipedia*

HEROES WHO DIED IN THE VIETNAM WAR

Almeida, Richard Henry

Carvalho, Gilbert

Constantine, Michael Eugene

Derosier, Thomas Albert

Dufault, Paul

Dupere, Edward Joseph

Furtado, Edward, Jr.

Gagne, Donald

Gagne, Louis Phillip, Jr.

Gaspar, Alfred John

Guilmette, Joseph, Jr.

Johansen, Donald Charles

Lake, Ronald Francis

Lawrence, John Lauzon

Medeiros, Michael John

Peixoto, Gilbert Coroa

Perry, Daniel

Rago, Stephen Joseph

Rodrigues, Richard

Santos, Albert Willard

Soares, Manuel Aguiar

Tavares, Charles Albert

Viera, Joseph

Information gathered from City of Fall River Veteran Affairs Office-Ray Hague—photos courtesy of *Wikipedia*

HEROES WHO DIED IN THE MIDDLE EAST WARS

PERSIAN GULF WAR
Perry, Kenneth James
Smith, Russell G., Jr.

IRAQ
Bouthot, Michael

AFGHANISTAN
Andrews, Scott
Barrett, Robert
Fagundes, Paul
Goncalo, Ethan
Pool, Jason

Information gathered from City of Fall River Veteran Affairs Office-Ray Hague—photos courtesy of *Wikipedia*

1926-Present
Others with Ties*

"Those who want respect, give respect."

TONY SOPRANO

* Despite not having attended school in Fall River,
the following eight individuals in the category are so
closely associated with Fall River that they deserve inclusion
in this book.

EARLE P. CHARLTON
Merchant and Philanthropist

Profile
Earle P. Charlton was born in Chester, Connecticut, in 1863 and died in 1930 at his summer home in Westport Harbor, Massachusetts. He married Ida Stein and had three children and several grandchildren. He is buried in Oak Grove Cemetery in the family mausoleum.

Experience
Charlton began his life and career in Connecticut as a traveling salesperson selling inexpensive household items out of the trunk of his automobile. He turned that $7 per week profit into a fortune and Fall River has long been one of the major beneficiaries of his success.

What began with the E.P. Charlton Five-and-Ten-Cent Store on South Main Street grew throughout New England to the West Coast and into Canada. Charlton later merged with the Woolworth brothers to become a company vice president.

Charlton's business acumen earned him money, but it was his benevolence that earned him his reputation. His generosity to his adopted hometown is legendary. It took him forty years of hard work to amass his wealth—none of it was inherited. His support of Charlton Memorial Hospital and the Charlton College of Business at UMass Dartmouth as well as the United Way and Boys and Girls Club among many other health and human service agencies demonstrate his legacy.

Education
Charlton was a self-made man and did not attend school in Fall River.

Skills
Although not from Fall River, he left his indelible mark on the area through his incredible generosity.

Also of Note
During WWI, he was appointed by President Wilson to the War Industry Board and was awarded a decoration by the French for his services.

Information gathered from Charlton Health System: *Our Story, The Charlton Story*
—photo courtesy of *The Charlton Story*

DR. IRVING A. FRADKIN
Scholarship Founder

Profile
Born in 1921 in Chelsea, Massachusetts, Irving Fradkin is still at it in Fall River at age ninety-two. Married to Charlotte, they are the parents of three, grandparents to four and great-grandparents to nine.

Experience
Called "Dollars for Scholars" when he formed the first chapter of Citizens Scholarship Foundation in 1958, his idea was simple: Everyone in the community can give a dollar to send children to college. Three years later, he took the program national and formed the Citizens Scholarship of America. Today, it is known as Scholarship America. The idea took off but not without the determination of Fradkin in the forefront and behind the scenes. Today, there are 1,100 chapters in 3,500 communities.

Education
He attended Chelsea schools and graduated from the New England College of Optometry, which also awarded him an honorary degree.

Also of Note
Fradkin has received various honors including the Schow-Donnelly Service Before Self Award and the Presidential Task Force on Private Initiatives. On May 15, 2013, he was awarded the Congressional Service Before Self Award. He was named Fall River's Outstanding Citizen in 1995 by the Greater Fall River Chamber of Commerce. He was featured on the 2013 Thanksgiving day show of *Katie-Talk That Matters* with Katie Couric.

Information gathered from the *Fall River Herald News*—photo courtesy of Dr. Fradkin

DANIEL GITTELMAN
Entertainment Agent and Concert Producer

Profile
Daniel Gittelman was born in Brooklyn in 1924, the son of Sophie and Rubin Gittelman; he has lived in this area nearly all his life. Married to Sheila Kausman Gittelman, they are the parents of a son and daughter.

Experience
Gittelman is best known for managing the early career of pop legend, Whitney Houston. After Gittelman turned his young star over to his friend Clive Davis of Columbia Records, he continued to manage the business end of her career until 1992 when the movie hit, *The Bodyguard*, was released.

Gittelman with a young Whitney Houston at his daughter's wedding.

John Houston, Whitney's dad, then became her agent but offered the position back to Gittelman a year later. It did not work out.

Gittelman maintained an office on the third floor at Ten North Main Street, which looked like a Las Vegas suite complete with gold and platinum records albums adorning the walls.

Education
He graduated from Hope High School in Providence, Rhode Island, but never attended college. He became a medic in the Army.

Skills
Gittelman founded U.S. Records in 1958 and co-owned the Music Box, a retail store, in downtown Fall River. U.S. Records employed hundreds for years in the area.

Information gathered from the *Fall River Herald News*—photo courtesy of Mr. Gittelman

THOMAS B. GRABOYS, M.D.
Cardiologist and Harvard Medical Professor
Nobel Peace Prize Recipient

Profile
Tom Graboys is the youngest child of Lewis M. and Rebecca Sobiloff Graboys and brother of George (also featured in this book) and two other siblings. He was born in Fall River in 1943. The family lived on Doherty Street and then moved to Highland Avenue. Married, he has two daughters.

Experience
At age forty-nine, the renowned Boston cardiologist was diagnosed with an aggressive form of Parkinson disease, which has prevented him from seeing or administering to patients for more than twenty years. At Brigham and Women's Hospital, his research revolved around cardiac arrhythmia and sudden death. He was part of "The Medical Dream Team" that treated Boston Celtics star Reggie Lewis in and after 1993.

Education
Graboys attended Friends Academy and Tabor Academy, going on to Cornell University and New York Medical College. He received an Honorary Degree from University of Massachusetts Dartmouth and a teaching faculty award from Harvard University.

Skills
Graboys served on the National Board of Directors of Physicians for Social Responsibility, which was awarded the Nobel Peace Prize, along with fellow Fall River physician David Greer (whose story follows).

Information gathered from *Life in the Balance*—photos courtesy of Dr. Graboys

DAVID S. GREER, M.D.
Brown Medical School Dean
Nobel Peace Prize Recipient

Profile
Married to Marion Clarich for more than sixty years, the Greers had two children and two grandchildren and have lived in Fall River for more than fifty years. Greer was born and raised in Brooklyn, New York, but relocated to Fall River four years after graduating from medical school.

Experience
A Truesdale Clinic internal medicine physician, Greer was also the chief of staff at the former Fall River General Hospital. He was a senior clinical instructor in medicine at Tufts University before joining the medical school at Brown University, where he founded and chaired the Department of Family Medicine, the International Health Institute, the Center for Gerontology and Health Care Research and finally, as Dean of Medicine at Brown University. He continued to see patients at his offices over the years.

Education
University of Notre Dame (1948) and University of Chicago School of Medicine (1953).

Skills
During the 1980s and 1990s, Greer worked with AIDS patients when many physicians refused to treat them. He also helped form the Family Medical Center at SSTAR to assist patients without insurance and developed Cardinal Medeiros Towers in Fall River as a prototype for assisted living residents. He was named Fall River's Outstanding Citizen in 2003 by the Chamber of Commerce.

He and fellow former Fall River resident Dr. Thomas Graboys (also included herein), along with other American and Soviet Union physicians, established Physicians for the Prevention of Nuclear War and were awarded the Nobel Peace Prize in 1985.

Greer received the Massachusetts Medical Lifetime Achievement Award in 2007.

Information gathered from the Massachusetts Medical Society, the *Fall River Herald News*
—photo courtesy of Dr. Greer

THE LECOMTE FAMILY
Quality Bakery Products

Profile

Auguste LeComte, the founder of Quality Bakery Products, was born in 1912 and died in 1936. His sons Roland and Leo who have since passed and Roland's sons, Roland and Jean who died in 2004, were all part of the family that created the business. Leo LeComte married Georgette Boulay and they had three children, none of whom entered the business.

Experience

After the death of the founder at a young age in 1936, Roland and Leo set the wheels in motion for the success the Gold Medal Bakery still enjoys today. Producing 4,500 loaves of bread per week with nine employees in 1912, the firm now employs hundreds and produces, packages and ships thousands of loaves of bread, rolls and muffins all over New England from the modern, expansive plant.

Education

Auguste LeComte attended local Fall River schools, Roland Sr. graduated from Mc-Gill University after graduation from B.M.C. Durfee High School. Leo LeComte also graduated from Durfee High School. Roland's two sons, Roland and Jean, graduated from Case High School in Swansea.

Skills

Expansion occurred in 1969 on Bay Street, in 1990 and again in 2000 on Penn Street, all in Fall River. Also, in 2000, the company acquired a large distribution center in West Haven, Connecticut.

Information gathered from the *Fall River Herald News* and History of Gold Medal Bakery
—photo courtesy of Gold Medal Bakery

DICK SIEBERT
Professional Baseball Player

Profile
Richard Walther Siebert was born in Fall River in 1912 and died in Minneapolis in 1978. He had a brother and sister. He was married to Marie Schoening and they had a son Paul, who also played major league baseball as a pitcher, and another son and two daughters.

Experience
Siebert made our national pasttime his life's work. At age twenty, after sandlot ball in Fall River and other communities, he played professional ball for the Brooklyn Dodgers and St. Louis Cardinals of the National League. He finished his twelve-year career with the Philadelphia Athletics of the American League. He had a lifetime batting average of .282 with 32 homers and 482 runs-batted-in and was a 1943 All-star with the Athletics.

Following his playing career, Siebert became the head baseball coach for the University of Minnesota Golden Gophers. His teams won College World Series three times in an eight-year period. "The Chief" would go on to become one of the greatest coaches in college baseball history with a winning percentage of .676 and only three losing seasons.

Education
St. Paul Concordia High School, Concordia Junior College and Concordia Seminary in St. Louis.

Skills
Among other accolades, Siebert was twice named college baseball's Coach of the Year, is a member of the College Baseball Hall of Fame and the recipient of baseball's highest honor, the Lefty Gomez Trophy. On Saturday, April 21, 1979, the University of Minnesota Baseball Stadium was officially renamed "Siebert Field," in honor of its great coach and friend.

Information gathered from Greater Fall River Baseball and Paul and Marilyn Siebert—photo courtesy of *Greater Fall River Baseball* and *Wikipedia*

GEORGE R. STEPHANOPOULOS
Political Advisor, Television Journalist and Author

Profile
George Stephanopoulos, born in Fall River in 1961, spent his preschool days living on Hood Street in Fall River. He is the son of Greek Orthodox priest Robert G. and Nickolitsa (Nikki) Chafos Stephanopoulos and attended school in Cleveland, Ohio. He married actor Alexandra Wentworth and they have two daughters.

Experience
It was the political bug that bit Stephanopolous. Starting as a congressional aide, he moved on to work on the presidential campaign of Michael Dukakis in 1988. After that unsuccessful effort, he served as the communications director for the campaign of Bill Clinton and soon after was the White House Director of Communications from 1992 to 1994.

Stephanopoulos is a television journalist with ABC News and serves as co-anchor of *Good Morning America* and is the host of *This Week* on ABC.

Education
Balliol College, Columbia University, Rhodes Scholar at Oxford University and received an honorary doctorate from St. John's University.

Skills
Stephanopoulos also has an ABC News blog, *George's Bottom Line.* He is a member of the Council on Foreign Relations and the author of *All Too Human.*

Information gathered from *Wikipedia*—photo courtesy of *Wikipedia*

1926-Present
Professional

———◦———

Fortune favors the prepared mind.

———◦———

<small>Louis Pasteur</small>

JUDGES WITH SOME EDUCATION IN FALL RIVER

The first two judges listed on this page have been designated with an individual pages due to their outstanding achievements:

Honorable Edward F. Harrington – Durfee Distinguished Alumni Award 1995

Honorable Beatrice Hancock Mullaney* – Durfee Distinguished Alumni Award 1976

United States Courts

Honorable James H. Smith ** – Magistrate – Durfee Distinguished Alumni Award 2002

Massachusetts Superior Court

Honorable William H. Carey – Durfee Distinguished Alumni Award 2006

Honorable E. Susan S. Garsh

Honorable Joseph L. Hurley*

Honorable Thomas F. McGuire, Jr.

Honorable James P. McGuire – Durfee Distinguished Alumni Award 2000

Massachusetts District Court

Honorable George F. Driscoll

Honorable Joseph I. Macy

Honorable John H. O'Neil

Honorable Milton R. Silva – Durfee Distinguished Alumni Award 1994

Honorable Roger (Roddy) F. Sullivan* **

Industrial Accident Board

Honorable William F. Long, Jr. – Durfee Distinguished Alumni Award 2000

Probate and Family Court

Honorable Colonel George F. Phelan

*There are scholarships in their memories at Durfee High School.

** Elected members of the Durfee High School Sports Hall of Fame.

WESLEY J. FASTIFF, ESQUIRE
Chair, Littler Worldwide Law Firm

Profile
Wesley J. Fastiff was born in 1932, the second born in his family, he lived on Valentine Street. His parents were Ida Bertman and Jacob Fastiff. He married Bonnie Barmon and they have two children and four grandchildren.

Experience
A Navy veteran, Fastiff always wanted to be a lawyer. Motivated centrally by his mother, he was the first in his family to go to college. Fastiff is nationally recognized as one of the leading labor and employment attorneys in the nation. He provides advice to employers dealing with union representation and recognition, contract negotiations and arbitrations. He once represented a small trucking company in a contested union matter where Jimmy Hoffa was on the opposite side of the table. He found Hoffa to be a respectful adversary.

His legal career after Harvard Law School began at the National Labor Relations Board in Washington, D.C., but he soon moved to San Francisco, where he has spent the rest of his life.

Fastiff's other legal specialties include transportation, discrimination and harassment. He has argued cases before the National Labor Relations Board, U.S. Court of Appeals and the U.S. District Court and most significantly the U.S. Supreme Court. After joining the firm in the 1960s, he helped build the firm by handling landmark transportation cases. It is now the largest law firm in the United States representing management in employment, employment benefits and labor law.

Education
Highland School, Morton Junior High School and B.M.C. Durfee High School. He graduated from Tufts University and Harvard Law School.

Skills
Fastiff is presently Chair Emeritus of the Board of the Littler Law Firm, which is more than seventy years old and maintains 55 offices across the nation and six foreign countries. There are 1,050 lawyers in the firm. He often speaks before professional and business organization throughout the country.

Also of Note
Fastiff is a member of the California and Massachusetts State Bar Association and was named a Best Lawyer in America and Super Lawyer in San Francisco.

Information gathered from Mr. Fastiff and Littler Law—photo courtesy of Littler Law

EDWARD B. HANIFY, ESQUIRE
Partner, Ropes & Gray Law Firm

Profile
Edward B. Hanify was the son of Judge Edward F. Hanify (also highlighted herein) and Mary Brodkorb. He was born and raised in Fall River, the oldest of three children. He was married to Jane Dillon for sixty years and they had two sons and a daughter as well as eleven grandchildren and ten great-grandchildren. He died in Boston in 2000 and is buried in St. Patrick's Cemetery.

Experience
After graduating summa cum laude and valedictorian from College of the Holy Cross and then Harvard Law in 1936, Hanify was admitted to the Massachusetts Bar in 1936. During his years in the service, he assisted Admiral Husband E. Kimmel in the Pearl Harbor investigation. His efforts that began in 1942 to vindicate Kimmel at Pearl Harbor were successful in 2000 when Congress passed and the President signed a resolution that posthumously allowed the promotion of Kimmel.

In 1962, President John F. Kennedy consulted with Hanify regarding plans to create a presidential library. Hanify was a trustee, secretary and director of the Kennedy Library Foundation. He served for many years as a partner in the prestigious Boston law firm of Ropes & Gray.

Education
Local Fall River schools, B.M.C. Durfee High School, College of the Holy Cross and Harvard Law. He received honorary degrees from University of Massachusetts Lowell and Dartmouth as well as College of the Holy Cross, Suffolk University, and Tufts University.

Skills
Hanify was active in many civic and charitable endeavors in Massachusetts, including the Greater Boston Community Fund Campaign (United Way), advisory board of the Massachusetts Welfare Department and the President's Council at College of the Holy Cross. He was president, trustee or director of numerous judicial, educational and religious organizations. He was responsible for reorganizing the state court system in 1956.

Referrals
Hanify was part of the Greatest Generation and served in WWII as a Navy lieutenant in the JAG Corps.

He is a recipient of the Distinguished Alumni Award from Durfee High School in 1964 among many other awards including The Catholic Lawyers' Guild Thomas More Award and the Gold Medal from the Eire Society of Boston. He was President of the Boston Clover Club.

Information gathered from *Wikipedia*, College of the Holy Cross, the *Fall River Herald News* and HighBeam Research
—photo courtesy of College of the Holy Cross

JO A. HANNAFIN, M.D., PH.D.
Orthopaedic Surgeon

Profile
Jo A. Hannafin was born in Fall River 1955 and brought up on High Street and Lincoln Avenue between Morton Junior High and Durfee High School with her sister and brother. They are the children of Arthur C. and Helen Hannafin. She is married to John Brisson and they have three children.

Experience
Hannafin is a board certified orthopedic surgeon and sports medicine physician, as well as Director of Orthopedic Research at Hospital for Special Surgery in New York City. She is also a professor of Orthopaedic Surgery at Weill Cornell Medical College. Hannafin was a 2004 Olympic Games Physician in Athens and the Pan Am Games in 2003.

Hannifin was the first clinician-scientist at the Hospital for Special Surgery and maintains an active research program in the area of ligament physiology. Her subspecialties include knee, shoulder, elbow and sports medicine with special expertise for female athletes. She was the co-founder of the Women's Sports Medicine Center at HSS.

Hannafin is in the top of the photo during the Head of the Charles regatta in the Alumni 8.

Education
St. Joseph's School, Mount St. Mary's and Bishop Gerard High School, the successor school to Mount Saint Mary's Academy. She graduated from Brown University with a BS and Yeshiva University. She has both a medical degree and Ph.D.

Skills
She is presently the vice president of the Board of Trustees of the National Rowing Foundation and is the president of the American Orthopedic Society for Sports Medicine.

Also of Note
Repeatedly honored as one of the Best Doctors in America, Hannafin was a silver medalist in the lightweight double at the 1984 Rowing World Championships and a three-time gold medalist at the U.S. National Rowing Championships. She began her rowing career at Brown University, where her swimming coach persuaded her to try a new sport. Hannafin serves on the FISA Medical Commission and was the FISA physician for the 2012 Olympic Games in London. She is also a steward of the Brown Rowing Association.

Information gathered from Brown University, Hospital for Special Surgery, Dr. Hannafin and Charlton Hospital Radiology—photos courtesy of Dr. Hannafin

HONORABLE EDWARD F. HARRINGTON
United States District Court Judge
Naval Officer, JAG Corps

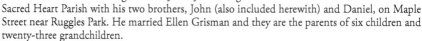

Profile
Edward F. Harrington was born in Fall River in 1933, the son of
Elizabeth C. Tolan Harrington and John J. Harrington. He lived in
Sacred Heart Parish with his two brothers, John (also included herewith) and Daniel, on Maple
Street near Ruggles Park. He married Ellen Grisman and they are the parents of six children and
twenty-three grandchildren.

Experience
A trial attorney with the U.S. Department of Criminal Justice from 1961 to 1965, Harrington
was part of a group conducting a nationwide probe of the Teamster Union (the Hoffa Squad).
He credits his selection to that task force to former Fall Riverite and attorney Robert Peloquin
(also included in this book). He was then assigned by Attorney General Robert Kennedy to pro-
tect civil rights workers in Mississippi who were conducting voter registration.

From 1965 to 1969, Harrington was an Assistant United States Attorney for the District of
Massachusetts. He assisted the FBI in the successful prosecution of Raymond L.S. Patriarca, the
alleged boss of New England organized crime, for interstate racketeering. From 1969 through
1973, Harrington was a major player in the Justice Department Organized Crime Strike Force.
He served in the Dukakis Administration as chair of the Alcoholic Beverage Commission.

Appointed by President Jimmy Carter as United States Attorney for the district of Massachusetts,
Harrington concentrated on public corruption and the conviction of members of the Winter
Hill gang in the famous "horse fix case." From 1981 to 1988, he engaged in private practice until
President Ronald W. Reagan named him a United States District Court Judge, assuming senior
status in 2001.

Harrington helped coordinate security for the Pope John Paul II's visit to Boston. Special people
in his life beside his family were Durfee teachers Helena Withrow and Anna G. McCarthy and
of course, Luke Urban, whose motivation of young men proved invaluable in life. (Urban is
highlighted herein.)

Education
Sacred Heart School, B.M.C. Durfee High School, College of the Holy Cross and Boston College Law School.

Skills
In 1974, Harrington ran unsuccessfully for Massachusetts Attorney General against Francis X.
Bellotti. The party persuaded him to run for political office again in 1986, but he lost to James
Shannon.

A child of the Depression who grew up during WWII, Harrington's life (like many others in Fall
River at the time) centered on the church and family. His neighborhood was composed of three
family homes near a park. Everyone knew each other and traditional values, along with love of
city and church, were ingrained.

Also of Note
Harrington was a Naval ROTC member during his college days and was on active duty as a
lieutenant in the JAG Corps from 1955 to 1957. He was a recipient of the Durfee Distinguished
Alumni Award in 1995.

Information gathered from Judge Harrington and *Wikipedia*—photo courtesy of Judge Harrington

JOHN T. HARRINGTON, M.D.
Dean of Tufts Medical School
Senior Nephrologist Tufts Medical Center

Profile
John Harrington is the son of John J. and Elizabeth Tolan Harrington. He lived in Sacred Heart Parish with his two brothers, Ted (also included herewith) and fellow physician Daniel, on Maple Street near Ruggles Park. His wife Gertrude (Trudy) Hargraves was a fellow Durfee graduate. They have seven children and twenty-one grandchildren.

Experience
Working summers in banking during school vacations convinced Harrington he was not cut out for the business world. Unable to play sports because of a heart valve murmur resulting from contracting rheumatic fever at age eight (before penicillin), education became his primary focus. His parents were both teachers as well but it was teachers Mr. McIlwaine in chemistry, Miss McCarthy in Latin, Miss Withrow in English, and Dr. John Corrigan, the first Fall River cardiologist, who joined family and religion in motivating him to become a world-class physician.

Harrington was a renal fellow between 1965 and 1968 at Tufts Medical Center, with emphasis on acid base and salt and water disorders. He became a world-renowned expert in nephrology and initiated a kidney transplant program at Tufts. With his colleagues at Tufts, he published the premier Acid-Base text in the early 1980s.

Education
Sacred Heart School, B.M.C. Durfee High School, College of the Holy Cross (magna cum laude), Yale Medical School (cum laude). Medical resident from 1962 to 1965 at University of North Carolina at Chapel Hill.

Skills
Harrington has been a professor of medicine at Tufts since 1979 and was the Dean of Tufts Medical School from 1996 to 2002. He was the co-chair of the Tufts Health Care Institute for a decade. He published approximately 90 to 100 scientific and clinical papers in medical literature.

In 1993, he wrote, "My Three Valves," which appeared in the *New England Journal of Medicine*. His first valve was impaired by rheumatic fever and the second valve was replaced in 1984 and lasted until 1992 when one cusp of his valve had torn and produced a searing pain in his chest. He now has a mechanical valve—a St. Jude valve, perhaps appropriate for a religious, Catholic physician. The article tells his story of the Fall River educated physician dealing with heart issues while helping to cure kidney patients.

Also of Note
Harrington, like his brother, Ted, received the Durfee High Distinguished Alumni Award in 1999. He is an honorary fellow at Royal College of Physicians in Ireland. He received the Distinguished Faculty Award from Tufts Medical School and the Outstanding Physician Award from the National Kidney Foundation of Massachusetts and Rhode Island. He was also listed in *Who's Who in the World* and received the Sanctae Crucis Alumni Award from Holy Cross.

Information gathered from Dr. Harrington, Tufts Medical Center and The Massachusetts Medical Society
—photo courtesy of Dr. Harrington

JEREMIAH J. LOWNEY, JR., D.D.S., MS, MPH
Founder and President of the Haitian Health Foundation

Profile
Jeremiah Lowney is the oldest of eleven children of Jeremiah and
Auxilia Lowney. He and his siblings were all born in Fall River
and raised in the Corky Row section of the city. He married a
Fall River girl, Virginia Winiarski, more than fifty-two years ago.
They have three daughters, a son who is a practicing physician in
Fall River at this time, and ten grandchildren.

Experience
Lowney, a retired orthodontist in Norwich, Connecticut, has practiced since 1966, retiring several years ago to devote his time to work
with the charity that he founded in Haiti. He began the outreach to
Haiti in 1982 and worked for three years as a dentist in Port au Prince,

returning every three months for the past thirty-two years. The first three years were spent with
Mother Teresa's Missionaries of Charity in Port au Prince. He established a friendship with
Mother Teresa and she asked him to move his small group of volunteers to Jeremie, a town of
600,000 people with no access to health care except a small, ill-equipped government hospital.

Dr. Lowney now spends his time raising money for Haiti–writing grants and doing public speaking. The Haitian Health Foundation has 230,000 people under its umbrella of care, serving not
only the city of Jeremie but also 105 rural mountain villages. This work employs 210 full-time
employees, primarily Haitian. The Haitian Health Foundation provides outpatient and inpa-
tient medical care and dental care, and feeds thousands of malnourished children and pre and
postnatal women.

Education
St. Mary's School, Monsignor Coyle High School, Tufts and Temple University. Other graduate
degrees were earned at the University of Connecticut and SUNY at Buffalo. He has also received
four honorary degrees.

Skills
Lowney's first jobs in Fall River were like many others in this book. He worked in a small
restaurant, at the A&P grocery store and at the Berkshire Hathaway mills. He was a lieutenant
commander in the Navy Dental Corps during the Cuban Missile Crisis.

He is also the author of *But to Serve*. His "Ten Ways to Make A Difference" provides options
for those who want to help support the HHF with operating support, housing, family support,
a center for hope, feeding children and assistance for a health agent. It also allows donors to
provide a family with a goat for food, adopt a village or provide an ambulance to the people in
the community.

Also of Note
Lowney has been awarded the Humanitarian of the Year Award from both the American Dental
Association and the American Association of Orthodontists. He is a member of the Knights of
Malta and was recently recognized at the White House as a Champion of Change, one of twelve
Rotary International members so named.

Information gathered from Dr. Lowney and the Haitian Health Foundation
—photos courtesy of the Haitian Health Foundation

BAYLESS A. MANNING, ESQUIRE
Stanford University Law School Dean

Profile
Bayless Manning was born in 1923 in Bristol, Oklahoma, and brought up in Washington, D.C. and Fall River. He was the son of Helen and Rafael A. Manning. His father started the local Social Security office in Fall River. At the time of his death he was married to Alexandra Zekovic. He had five children and six grandchildren. He died in Boise, Idaho, at home in 2011 at age eighty-eight.

Experience
A leading authority on corporate law, Manning began his career as a clerk for Associate Justice of the Supreme Court, Stanley Reed. From 1956 to 1964 as a law professor at his alma mater Yale University, Manning helped organize the Peace Corps and did research for the CIA. He also helped draft the 1962 Trade Extension Act and worked for NATO on the problems of a multinational nuclear force.

From 1964 to 1971 at Stanford University, Manning made groundbreaking changes to the curriculum. He founded the *Stanford Lawyer Magazine* in 1966. He was well-known for saving law students' careers by arranging scholarships for them courtesy of various law firms in California.

Manning left Stanford to serve as the first full-time president of the Council on Foreign Relations. In 1998, he joined the board of a startup technology company call Keynetics. He is credited today with its move to Boise, Idaho, where it is still a privately owned technology company.

Education
Local Fall River schools, B.M.C. Durfee High School, Yale University and Yale Law School.

Skills
Manning was the co-founder of the Peace Corps in South America and at age nineteen was an army cryptanalyst. He is credited with breaking the Japanese naval code in WWII, helping the U.S. to victory at Midway.

Also of Note
Manning graduated first in his law school class at Yale and was editor-in-chief of the *Law Review*. The U.S. Office of Government Ethics for the Executive Branch honored him in 2001 for his work as a member of a 1962 study review panel that led to government reform legislation.

Manning was the 1983 recipient of the Durfee High School Distinguished Alumni Award.

Information gathered from *Wikipedia*, the *Idaho Statesman* and Stanford Law School—photo courtesy of Stanford Law

HONORABLE BEATRICE HANCOCK MULLANEY
First Woman Probate Court Judge in Massachusetts

Profile
Married to Joseph E. Mullaney who died in 1961, Beatrice Hancock Mullaney had five children including Joe, Jr. (also highlighted in this book). She died in 1990 at age eighty-four while attending her beloved Durfee High School 67th reunion in a Tiverton, Rhode Island restaurant. Mullaney was the daughter of Fred Hancock and Margaret O'Loughlin Hancock. She and her brother grew up on North Main Street in the Steep Brook section of the city.

Experience
Beatrice Hancock was the top-ranking member of her class at St. Joseph School, the beginning of many "firsts" in her illustrious career. Soon after, she was named the top girl in her class at Durfee High School. Her most important first was as the first woman ever appointed as a probate judge in Massachusetts. They kept coming. Mullaney was the first chair of the Stonehill College Board of Advisors and followed that as the first chair of the Marine Museum in Fall River. She was first listed in *Who's Who in American Women* in 1950 and represented the International Federation of Women Lawyers at the United Nations.

Mullaney was an Assistant Attorney General for the state from 1949 to 1950 and then entered private practice until Governor Christian Herter appointed her a judge in 1955.

Her unsuccessful candidacy for Massachusetts Secretary of State in 1952 garnered over 1 million votes. For nearly twenty years after she quipped, "I may not have the wisdom of Solomon but I have the patience of Job." Judge Mullaney presided over 10,000 divorces, separations, custody, equity, will and land cases. An exceptional debater at both Durfee High and Boston University, Mullaney returned to BU to help coach the debate team. Mullaney also served as the debate team coach at Sacred Hearts Academy and Stonehill College. She was the first female Boston University debating team member and was the first female captain of an international debating team.

Education
St. Joseph's School and B.M.C. Durfee High School. She graduated from Boston University and Boston University Law School. Honorary degrees were presented to her by Stonehill College and the University of Massachusetts Dartmouth.

Skills
Mullaney not only served as a full time justice, she maintained a home with five children and advised a multitude of civic and charitable organizations and dug her permitted share of shell fish from the Westport River each summer.

Also of Note
She was the first woman in the Fall River Diocese to be invested as a Lady of the Equestrian Order of the Holy Sepulchre by Cardinal Spellman. A founding member of the Junior Foresters, Mullaney was a Durfee Distinguished Alumni recipient in 1976. There are multiple scholarships in her name awarded from Durfee High School.

Information gathered from her family and the *Fall River Herald News*—photo courtesy of her family

ROBERT D. PELOQUIN, ESQUIRE
U.S. Justice Department
Naval Commander and Intertel President

Profile
Robert Dolan Peloquin was the son of Charles G. and Loretta Harpin Peloquin. His father owned Peloquin's Market on Linden Street and his mother was a school teacher. He was born in Fall River in 1929 and lived on Ray Street with his sister, Beth, who was the longtime principal of the Highland School. He and Margaret "Peggy" Sheridan were married fifty-nine years and they had six children. He died in 2011 in his sleep from heart failure.

Experience
Peloquin served as a naval officer during the Korean Conflict until 1955. He retired from the Naval Reserves as a commander in 1975. After law school at Georgetown in 1955, Peloquin worked as Deputy Chief at the National Security Agency. From 1957 to 1967, he remained in government service as an attorney with the Justice Department. He was a trial attorney with the Organized Crime and Racketeering Division and eventually as Chief of Organized Crime Special Task Forces. He was instrumental in placing young attorney Ted Harrington (included in this section) as a member of the Task Force. They both worked for Attorney General Robert Kennedy.

In 1970, Peloquin became a full-fledged sleuth. He founded Intertel, a private international intelligence agency composed of former government investigators with a global clientele list. He remained president from 1970 until he joined Resorts International in 1985. He continued to practice law with a concentration on casino regulations until 2011.

Education
Highland School, Mount Saint Charles School, Georgetown University and Georgetown Law School.

Skills
His client list included the Shah of Iran, Howard Hughes and ITT. In 1973, *Readers Digest* magazine featured Peloquin in an article, calling him a "Super Sleuth." He busted some of the most untouchable Mafia bosses. His Washington-based Intertel, with offices around the world and 35 associates, has been involved in protecting businesses from fraud. As a result of his international investigation into Clifford Irving's book about Howard Hughes, and proving the work to be a fraud, the publishing firm of McGraw-Hill never published it.

Also of Note
In 1967, Peloquin joined the National Football League as Commissioners Associate Counsel, advising the league on security issues. Peloquin retired as chair of Resorts International in 1990, after five years with the casino firm.

Information gathered from the Peloquin family and *Readers Digest*

IRVING H. PICARD, ESQUIRE
Securities Investor Act (SIPA) Trustee
for Liquidation of Bernard L. Madoff
Securities Investment LLC (BLMIS)

Profile
Irving Picard, son of Claire Dryfus Picard and Dr. Julius
Picard, was brought up in Fall River on Walnut Street and
Cherry Street with his two brothers, Hans and Ernest. The
family came to the United States after fleeing Nazi Germany. Today Picard lives in New
York with his wife, Sharon, and their son.

Experience
Picard has had a long and distinguished career in bankruptcy law, much as his father did
in medicine in Fall River. After graduating from the Wharton School of Economics at
the University of Pennsylvania, Picard returned to Boston University Law School where
he received a J.D. and he then on to New York University Law School where he received
an LL.M.

A bankruptcy lawyer since 1972, Picard has been a court-appointed trustee in more than
ten security brokerage house liquidations. He has also served as Assistant General Counsel for the Securities and Exchange Commission and spent time working as a lawyer on
Wall Street. From 1982 to the present, Picard has been in private practice and is now a
partner in the firm of Baker Hostetler in its New York City office.

Since 2008, when he was appointed SIPA Trustee for the liquidation of Bernard L. Madoff Investment Securities LLC, Picard has recovered more than $9.501 billion and re-
turned more than $5 billion to defrauded BLMIS customers with allowed claims. He has
been called the hardest-working man in the collection business. He is quoted as saying,
"You don't take this job if you are thin-skinned," when faced with criticism for returning
recovered funds more slowly than some had hoped. Upon accepting the appointment as
SIPA Trustee, Picard projected it would take more than five years to complete.

Education
Westall School, Morton Junior High, B.M.C. Durfee High School and an undergradu-
ate degree at University of Pennsylvania. He received law degrees from both New York
University and Boston University.

Skills
He is a member of both the New York and American Bar Associations, the American
Bankruptcy Institute and the National Association of Bankruptcy Trustees among other
professional affiliations.

Also of Note
Picard is the 2012 recipient of the Durfee High School Distinguished Alumni Award.
He is a sought-after panelist and contributing author to professional publications.

Information gathered from *Durfee Chimes, Fall River Herald News*, Baker Law, and *Wikipedia*
—photo courtesy of Mr. Picard

DAVID R. POKROSS, ESQUIRE
Managing Partner Boston Law Firm
Naval Commander

Profile
David Pokross was the son of Jennie Lucksniansky and Israel Pokross. He was born in 1906 and raised in Fall River on Harrison and Second Streets with his three surviving sisters. He was married to Muriel Kohn for sixty-seven years and they had three children. He died in 2003 at age ninety-six.

Experience
Pokross signed on with the Boston law firm of Gaston Snow in 1930. A mere two years later he joined the firm Peabody, Brown, Rowley & Story (now Nixon Peabody) and remained with that firm for another seventy years. He became the firm's managing senior partner. His specialty was general corporate law, electric public utility law and estate planning.

It was not only law in which Pokross excelled. He was committed to helping his fellow citizens. He was involved in and honored by dozens of charities and created the David R. Pokross Fund for Children in Need at the Boston Foundation.

Pokross believed strongly in giving back. He provided his expertise to many nonprofit organizations in Greater Boston over the years, including the United Way, Combined Jewish Philanthropies, Beth Israel Hospital, the United Planning Corporation and Heller Graduate School at Brandeis University. In addition he served on the boards of other non-profits including the Boston Symphony Orchestra and Buckingham, Browne and Nichols School.

Education
Davis and Spencer Borden Schools and B.M.C. Durfee High School. He graduated from Harvard (1927) and Harvard Law School (1930).

Skills
From age seven, with the urging of Miss Peters at Davis School, Pokross's lifelong ambition was to be a lawyer. He was called the "ultimate gentleman" by former Harvard Law Dean Robert Clark.

Also of Note
Part of the Greatest Generation, Pokross served in the JAG Corps from 1943 to 1946 during which time he ascended to the rank of Naval lieutenant commander.

JOSEPH F. SABIK III, M.D.
Thoracic and Cardiovascular Surgeon

Profile
Joe Sabik, the son of Grace Sabra and Joseph Sabik, was born in Fall River in 1961. He and his two siblings were brought up in the East End of Fall River. He is married to fellow physician, Ellen Mayer, and they have two children.

Experience
One of Sabik's early jobs in high school was as a tax preparer for H & R Block. His motivation for medicine and surgery in particular came from his uncle, Dr. James Sabra, a Fall River surgeon.

Sabik completed his surgical residency at Massachusetts General Hospital and was named Chief Resident in Surgery. From MGH, he moved on to the Cleveland Clinic and became Department Chair of Thoracic and Cardiovascular Surgery in 2008. He is a world-renowned physician. Frequently operating on patients in the Middle East, Sabik travels with his team to Saudi Arabia to treat members of the royal family in a surgical center built there for him. He is also Director of the Cardiothoracic Residency Training Program in the Sydell and Arnold Miller Heart and Vascular Institute. He has performed more than 7,000 surgeries.

Education
Sabik attended local elementary schools and graduated from B.M.C. Durfee High School. He earned his BS at Massachusetts Institute of Technology and his medical degree from Harvard.

Skills
Sabik is widely published in leading professional journals, including the *Journal of American Medicine Association*, the *Journal of Thoracic and Cardiovascular Surgery* and the *Annals of Thoracic Surgery*, and he is the author of many chapters on cardiac surgery for medical textbooks. He is a frequent lecturer at national and international conferences, speaking on the latest innovations in heart disease management and cardiac surgery, such as minimally invasive techniques.

His international speaking engagements have included the 54th Annual Meeting Kansai Thoracic Surgeon Association (Takamatsu, Japan), 30th Anniversary of Cardiac Surgery at Epworth Hospital (Melbourne, Australia) and the 2009 Salzburg Medical Seminar in Cardiac Surgery.

Also of Note
Sabik received the Durfee High School Distinguished Alumni Award in 2012.

Information gathered from *The Durfee Chimes* and the Sabik family—photos courtesy of Durfee *Chimes*

RUSSELL P. SENECA, M.D., SURGEON
VCU Medical School Associate Dean

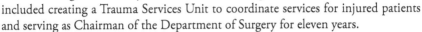

Profile
Russell Seneca was the son of Delia Pereira and Henry Seneca. He and his two sisters were brought up on Chaveneson Street. He has been married twice and has five children and fourteen grandchildren.

Experience
After serving in the military as an Army surgeon, Seneca settled in Virginia. His days at Inova Fairfax Hospital included creating a Trauma Services Unit to coordinate services for injured patients and serving as Chairman of the Department of Surgery for eleven years.

He helped establish a branch campus for third-and fourth-year medical students from Virginia Commonwealth School of Medicine at the Inova Campus.

Education
Sacred Heart School, Monsignor Coyle High School, Providence College, M.D. from Georgetown University and EMBA from George Mason University.

Skills
At Coyle, Seneca was a varsity baseball player after gaining experience at Lafayette Park. He was also coeditor of the yearbook. He served his country as a lieutenant colonel in the Army from 1973 to 1976. While in the Army, Seneca was Chief of Surgery at Wuerzburg, Germany.

Also of Note
Seneca's father, Henry, was his great motivator. Street-smart and as the owner of Delia's Driving School, Henry Seneca knew education was key to success. He pushed his son toward medicine since the youngster was unsure of his career path.

Although Fall River was not the place Seneca wanted to spend his life, he has a soft spot for it, as do most in this book. Seneca still remains in contact with many good Fall River friends and fondly recalls and uses the line, *"I didn't just get off the turnip truck."*

Information gathered from and photo courtesy of Dr. Seneca

JOEL TEPPER, M.D.
Professor of Cancer Research

Profile
Joel Tepper was born in 1947 and was brought up in Fall River, the son of Ira and Alice Tepper. He and his sisters lived on Highcrest Road near St. Patrick's Cemetery. He is married and he and his wife have two children and six grandchildren.

Experience
After graduating from M.I.T. with a degree in electrical engineering, Tepper moved west to attend medical school at Washington University in St. Louis, followed by residency at Massachusetts General Hospital. He joined the University of North Carolina School of Medicine as the chair of the Department of Radiation Oncology.

Twenty years later, Tepper stepped down to spend more time on research activities including working on the Gastro Intestinal SPORE grant for which he is the Principal Investigator. Active for years in GI Research, Tepper also spends time in the work of The Cancer Genome Atlas related to GI malignancies.

Education
Local Fall River schools and graduated from B.M.C. Durfee High School. He went on to Massachusetts Institute of Technology and received his medical degree from the University of Washington.

Skills
Tepper is presently The Hector McLean Distinguished Professor of Cancer Research.

Also of Note
He served as president and then board chair of the American Society of Clinical Oncology (ASTRO). He received the ASTRO Gold Medal of in 2008.

Information gathered from the Carolina Center of Nanotechnology Excellence and Fall River City Directory
—photo courtesy of Dr. Tepper

WILLIAM D. TOMPKINS, M.D.
Thoracic Surgeon
Tuskegee Airman

Profile
William D. "Sonny" Tompkins was born in Fall River
in 1921. His aunt was his legal guardian. He married
Claire MacDonald and they had four children and
seven grandchildren. Tompkins died in Falmouth in
2011 and was buried with Military Honors at the Massachusetts National Cemetery
in Bourne.

Experience
Tompkins is one of the many individuals who could qualify in more than one category, either Professional or Military.

He was a Hood Milk 18-wheel delivery truck driver after graduating from high
school but Durfee Vice Principal Herbert Pickup encouraged him to attend college.
After one year at South Carolina State College, Tompkins enrolled at the University
of Michigan. After three semesters at the Big Ten School, he was drafted into service
during WWII. After the war, he returned to Michigan and received a degree in Biology before returning to Massachusetts and Tufts Medical School.

After years as a resident at Boston City Hospital, Tompkins moved on to Whidden
Memorial Hospital in Everett, Faulkner Hospital, Longwood Hospital and Santa
Maria Hospital in Cambridge.

Education
Wixon School, Henry Lord Junior High and B.M.C. Durfee High School. Tompkins
enrolled in South Carolina State College, Tuskegee College and transferred to the
University of Michigan, followed by Tufts Medical School.

Skills
Tompkins was a member of the Greatest Generation and he was a member of the
Army Air Force Tuskegee Air Men, an all-black squadron of pilots. The Airmen received the Congressional Gold Medal for their service and were cited for not losing
any bombers in more than 200 missions.

Also of Note
Tompkins was the recipient of the Durfee High School Distinguished Alumni Award
in 2008.

Information gathered from *The Durfee Chimes* and the Tompkins family—photo courtesy of the Durfee *Chimes*

1926-Present

Religion

———•◆•———

"The years I was blessed to serve as Bishop of the Diocese of Fall River stand as a bright light among my decades of ministry as a priest and bishop. The faith of the people of Fall River, particularly the devotion of the Portuguese Catholic population to the Blessed Mother, Our Lady of Fatima, was and continues to be a source of strength and inspiration. I often recall and give thanks for the Diocese's tremendous success in bringing young people together for the March for Life in Washington and the celebrations of World Youth Day. Also, I continue to be grateful for the generous support diocesan leaders provide for the St. Mary's Education Fund, securing the presence of Catholic Schools as a means of building for the future. May the Lord's blessings be upon the Diocese of Fall River as the faithful go forward, building on the foundations of a proud history."

———•◆•———

CARDINAL SEAN P. O'MALLEY, OFM, CAP.
ARCHBISHOP OF BOSTON

WILLIAM O. BRADY, S.T.D.
Archbishop of Saint Paul, Minnesota

Profile
Born in Fall River in 1899, William Otterwell Brady was the son of John J. and Gladys Davol Brady. He had an older brother and younger sister. Archbishop Brady died of a heart attack in Rome in 1961.

Experience
During his days in the seminary in Washington, Brady was offered an opportunity by Archbishop Dowling to join the Archdiocese of St. Paul, Minnesota.

Ordained a priest in 1923, Brady went to the Archdiocese of Saint Paul in 1924. He was consecrated a bishop and served the diocese of Sioux Falls, South Dakota, from 1936 to 1956. During that period he taught theology at Saint Paul Seminary and recruited another young Fall River priest, James L. Connolly (highlighted in this book), to join him in Minnesota. The bishop was elevated to the position of archbishop in 1956 and served in that capacity for five years until he passed in Rome just before the start of the Second Vatican Council.

Education
Local Fall River schools, B.M.C. Durfee High School and St. Charles College. Brady continued his studies at St. Mary's Seminary and later at Catholic University. Brady went on to the Pontifical University in Rome and earned his doctorate in Sacred Theology, summa cum laude.

Skills
The Archbishop was responsible for reviving the diocesan newspaper, building four new Catholic high schools and supporting efforts to recruit new priests and vocations in the diocese.

Also of Note
To commemorate his tenure, the diocese named a high school in West Saint Paul in his honor, Archbishop Brady High School. It has since closed.

Information gathered from *Wikipedia* and the Archdiocese of Saint Paul—photo courtesy of the Archdiocese of Saint Paul

MOST REVEREND JAMES LOUIS CONNOLLY, SC.H.D.
Bishop of the Fall River Diocese

Profile
James L. Connolly was born in Fall River, one of two
children of Francis and Agnes McBride Connolly. He
died in Fall River in 1986 at age ninety-one and is laid
to rest in the crypt at St. Mary's Cathedral.

Experience
Connolly studied at the seminary in Washington, D.C.,
before ordination in 1923. He was assigned to a Cape
Cod area church until he went to Europe to further his
studies where he earned a doctorate, summa cum laude,
in 1928. Connolly returned to America and was one
of three priests from Fall River requested to go to the
St. Paul Diocese in Minnesota. At St. Paul's Seminary
he served as a professor, spiritual director and then as
rector.

Connolly returned to Fall River as Coadjutor Bishop in 1945 after his appointment by Pope
Pius XII. Bishop Brady served as one of his consecrators at the time. He was named fourth
Bishop of Fall River in 1951 after the death of Bishop James Cassidy. Connolly served in
that capacity for two decades, ministering to more than 300,000 Catholics in Bristol and
Barnstable Counties, as well as the islands of Martha's Vineyard and Nantucket.

During his tenure as bishop, Connolly was instrumental in erecting fifteen new parishes as well
as constructing new churches and schools. In particular he was responsible for the building
of new high schools throughout the diocese—Bishop Stang in Dartmouth, Bishop Feehan
in Attleboro, Bishop Cassidy in Taunton and one named after him, Bishop Connolly, in Fall
River. All are currently educating young people in the area.

Education
Local Fall River schools, B.M.C. Durfee High School, Saint Charles College and the Sulpician
Seminary. Connolly also studied at the Catholic University of Leuven in Belgium and
participated in all four sessions of the Second Vatican Council.

Skills
Connolly, like one of his colleagues Bishop Brady (also featured herein), founded the *Anchor,*
the diocesan newspaper. He also encouraged vocations and built seventeen schools and thirty-
three new churches.

Also of Note
After nineteen years as bishop, Connolly retired in 1970 but not before creating three Nazareth
Hall institutions in various cities of the diocese to aid the mentally challenged as well as
expanding sites for the elderly. The diocese also built a new Catholic Youth Center in New
Bedford. Connolly received the Durfee Distinguished Alumni Award in 1962.

Information gathered from *Wikipedia* and the Roman Catholic Diocese of Fall River—photo courtesy of the
Roman Catholic Diocese of Fall River

MOST REVEREND JOSEPH PATRICK DELANEY, S.T.L.
Bishop of Fort Worth, Texas

Profile
Born in Fall River in 1934, Joseph Patrick Delaney was the son of Joseph and Jane Burke Delaney and was the oldest of five children. He died in his Fort Worth, Texas, home in his sleep after a long bout with cancer at age seventy. He is buried in Fort Worth.

Experience
Delaney was motivated by family, his religion and his teachers, including Mother Anna Gertrude, SUSC, principal of Sacred Heart School. Several of his siblings also spent time in religious communities.

After his ordination in Rome in 1960 for the Diocese of Fall River, Delaney returned to his roots and was a teacher at Monsignor Coyle High School, including educating his youngest brother in class. While at Coyle High School, he was also an assistant pastor at a Taunton parish and assistant superintendent of schools for the Diocese of Fall River.

In 1966, at the request of the Bishop of Brownsville, Texas, former chancellor of the Fall River Diocese and soon to be named Cardinal, Humberto Medeiros (also highlighted in this book), Delaney moved to Texas to become a pastor, superintendent of schools, editor of the diocesan newspaper and co-chancellor.

In 1981, Father Delaney was named the second Bishop of Fort Worth, Texas, by Pope John Paul II. During his tenure, Delaney greatly expanded diocesan services to the faithful until he died in 2005.

Education
Sacred Heart School, Monsignor Coyle High School, Cardinal O'Connell Seminary, the Theological College in Washington and North American College in Rome.

Skills
Delaney was chair of, and later consultant to, the U.S. Bishops Subcommittee on Lay Ministry.

Also of Note
His ordination took place before 7,000 people at the Fort Worth Convention Center, including the U.S. Speaker of the House of Representatives Jim Wright.

Information gathered from Ann Delaney Carruth and *Today's Catholic* and Boston.com—photo courtesy of the Roman Catholic Diocese of Fort Worth

MOST REVEREND NORMAN J. FERRIS
Chorbishop of the Eparchy of Saint Maron

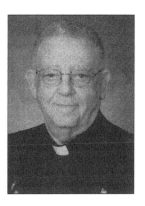

Profile
Norman J. Ferris was the son of John and Rose Ferris and had six siblings who all grew up on Flint Street (his brother, Monsour, and nephews, Ron and Monte, are also highlighted in this book). He died at St. Anne's Hospital in 2006 and is buried in St. Patrick's Cemetery in Fall River.

Experience
It was no secret to family, friends and educators that young Norman Ferris wanted to be a priest. When asked in school to draw a picture of himself as an adult, he drew himself as a priest. It was God who had the greatest influence on Ferris.

Ordained in 1953 by Bishop Connolly (also included herewith), he was assigned to a parish, school and ministering to the sick in the Taunton area for seventeen years. In 1970, after a brief time in Fall River at Immaculate Conception Church, he was named administrator of St. Anthony of the Desert Church in the Flint section of his hometown near where he grew up.

Father Ferris was ordained a Chorbishop for the Eparchy of Saint Maron of Brooklyn, New York, in 2002. He became extremely active in all affairs of the Maronite Church.

Education
Aldrich, Davis and Notre Dame elementary schools, B.M.C. Durfee High School, Prevost High School and St. Charles High School in Maryland, St. Mary's Seminary and Sacred Heart Seminary for advanced degrees.

Skills
He was responsible for the construction of the St. Anthony of the Desert Church and Parish Hall on Eastern Avenue in Fall River. He and close family and friends also formed the Order of St. Sharbel to help educate seminarians and assist retired priests.

Also of Note
Not only did he serve his parishioners but also ministered to the sick in area hospitals and was the chaplain at the Massachusetts Maritime Academy for many years.

Information gathered from *The Durfee Chimes* and the Tompkins family—photo courtesy of the Durfee *Chimes*

HUMBERTO CARDINAL SOUSA MEDEIROS, S.T.D.
Archbishop of Boston

Profile
Humberto S. Medeiros was born in 1916 in the Azores and died during open heart surgery in Boston in 1983. He is buried in St. Patrick's Cemetery in Fall River. He was the son of Antonio and Maria de Jesus Sousa Mass Flor Medeiros.

Experience
When his parents emigrated to Fall River in 1931, the young Medeiros knew no English. He swept floors in the mills and studied his new language in his spare time. After graduating from high school in 1937, he obtained a scholarship from the Fall River High School Alumni Scholarship Fund to attend Catholic University of America in Washington, D.C., where he went on to obtain both his master's and doctorate degrees.

Medeiros was ordained in Fall River in 1946 but returned to Rome for another degree. He served parishes in Somerset and Fall River and was named assistant chancellor in 1953. He served in various positions in the diocese including chancellor before being named a monsignor in 1958 and pastor of St. Michael's Church in 1960.

In 1966, Medeiros was appointed Bishop of Brownsville, Texas. The multilingual Medeiros became an advocate for Mexican migrant farm workers looking to be paid a minimum wage of $1.25 per hour at the time. It was during this period that Father Joseph Patrick Delaney (featured herein) transferred from Fall River to assist his friend.

The humble Fall Riverite took steps similar to the current sitting Pope Francis. He sold the episcopal limousine and converted all but one room in the Episcopal Residency into a dormitory for visiting priests.

In 1970, he was elevated to Archbishop of Boston. A mere three years later, Pope Paul VI appointed him a cardinal, a position he held until his untimely death.

Education
B.M.C. Durfee High School and Catholic University of America followed by a master's degree and a Licentiate of Sacred Theology at the Pontifical Gregorian University in Rome in 1952.

Skills
Medeiros was an elector in the conclaves to elect both Pope John Paul I and Pope John Paul II in 1978.

Also of Note
He is one of many in this book who is a recipient of the Durfee Distinguished Alumni Award. The award was presented to him in 1972. There is a scholarship in his memory at Durfee High School to benefit graduates.

Information gathered from *Wikipedia* and the *Fall River Herald News*—photo courtesy of the Roman Catholic Archdiocese of Boston

CAROL REGAN, S.U.S.C.
Congregation Leader of the Holy Sisters

Profile
Carol Regan is the daughter of Francis W. and Eleanor Duclos Regan, the older of their two daughters. She was born in Fall River in 1942 and lived on Linden Street between the two schools of her youth, Sacred Heart Elementary School and Sacred Hearts Academy.

Experience
Following four years at Sacred Hearts Academy on Prospect Street, Regan joined the Holy Union Sisters, a congregation of Catholic women who trace their origins to France. The sisters are an international congregation with a presence on four continents. They were banished from France around 1905 and relocated in Belgium. The Sisters were also welcomed locally by Bishop William Stang in 1886 to Fall River with a convent and school on Prospect and Linden Streets.

Sister Carol with Pope Benedict XVI.

As a young woman, she worked as a neighborhood babysitter then as a clerk for the Boland family at Fall River News Company during school vacations. As the saying goes, "It takes a village to raise a child." In this case, the village of Linden Street and the family she was part of provided the safe and secure environment that many in this book felt was an integral part of growing up in Fall River. In Regan's case, that also included nuns and priests.

Regan's short-term objectives and accomplishments within her order were to lead her congregation to membership in UNANIMA, a non-governmental organization (NGO) accredited to the United Nations. The objective of this organization is to work with others toward a more just world and in particular against the practice of human trafficking. Regan has also been able to establish mechanisms that share personnel and financial resources across the congregation.

Education
Sacred Heart School, Sacred Hearts Academy, Hunter College, Loyola College in Maryland and Washington Theological Union in Washington, D.C.

Skills
Regan lives the life of a Catholic woman and she hopes to enjoy holiness as her greatest accomplishment someday. Her order has presence in nine states and thirteen countries.

Also of Note
As a young teacher, Regan was sent to New York to teach as well as study at Hunter College, where she majored in political science. Wearing an enormous religious habit, she was thrust amid people from all backgrounds and religions from all over the world to debate and learn. She learned there is more than only one right way to do things or think.

Upon completion of her second term as leader of the Holy Union Sisters, Regan returned to the United States in 2012. She continues her service to members of the religious congregations as an Associate Director of the Religious Formation Conference in Washington, D.C.

Information gathered from Sister Carol and the Holy Union Sisters and
Victorian Vistas 1901-1911—photos courtesy of Sister Carol

1926-Present
Sports

— ✦ —

It ain't over 'til it's over.

— ✦ —

Yogi Berra

JOSEPH ANDREWS, JR.
Professional Baseball Player
Who Fought Racism

Andrews, right, with his longtime friend, Hank Aaron.

Profile
Joseph Andrews was born in 1932 in Fall River and died unexpectedly at home in Swansea at age sixty-eight in 2001. He was one of three children of Joe Andrews, Sr., and Ida St. John. Divorced twice, he was married to Linda Bettencourt and he had four daughters and a son.

Experience
Andrews was a protegé of Durfee coach Luke Urban on the gridiron and hardwood and in the field. After a brief college stint on the West coast, the homesick Andrews returned to Fall River and signed a contract to play professional baseball with the Milwaukee Braves. In 1953, he headed to the Braves farm team in Jacksonville, Florida.

In Florida, Andrews met Hank Aaron and the two developed a lifelong friendship. Aaron was one of few black players in baseball then and was subjected to racial abuse and slurs, especially in the South, where most of the team's games were played. When restaurants refused to serve Aaron and other black players, Andrews brought them food and ate with them on the bus.

When leaving Jacksonville or other Southern stadiums, Andrews would say to Aaron, "Stick close." He would carry a Louisville Slugger bat to intimidate those who would attack them on the streets. While becoming lifelong friends, the two would play together for only one year. Andrews drank himself out of baseball.

Education
Local Fall River schools and B.M.C. Durfee High School followed by the University of Washington on scholarship to play football. Andrews was offered scholarships at Boston College and Notre Dame and was contacted by 52 colleges.

Skills
After his playing days were over, Andrews dedicated his life to helping local people fight alcohol and substance abuse. He also owned an auto dealership and served as a Durfee High School baseball hitting coach in 1995 when the team won the Division 1 State Championship under coach Ray Medeiros (also highlighted herewith).

Also of Note
Many called him Fall River's greatest athlete. Hank Aaron termed him one of Eastern Massachusetts's finest athletes and best baseball player he had ever seen. Andrew's jersey, number 44 (which Aaron also wore), was the first ever retired at Durfee High School.

Information gathered from *The New Bedford Standard Times*, the *Fall River Herald News*, the *Los Angeles Times*
—photo courtesy of *Wikipedia*

MARK V. BOMBACK
Professional Baseball Player

MARK BOMBACK
PITCHER

Profile
Born in 1953 in Virginia, Mark V. Bomback moved to Fall River with his brother, Herman, and sister at a young age. They were the children of Mabel L. Conway and Raymond H. Bomback and were brought up in the South End of Fall River. Formerly married to Susan DeMoura, he has a son and daughter.

Experience
His baseball career started in the Bayside Little League in the South End of Fall River. Leaving Fall River to live in Texas with his family, Bomback returned to the Spindle City in time to play in the Maplewood Babe Ruth circuit. He pitched for Coach Skip Lewis (also highlighted herein) at Durfee High, leading the 1971 team to the Division 1 State Championship. In the summers he pitched with the Stafford Post team in the Legion Baseball League.

Following the state title victory, Bomback signed a contract to play for the Red Sox, every Fall River kid's dream. After some time with Red Sox minor league clubs, the organization traded him to Milwaukee in 1977.

Bomback pitched in the junior circuit for two years and his career hit its stride in 1979 when he was named Minor League Player of the Year for Pacific Coast League Vancouver. That performance of 22 wins catapulted him to the New York Mets in the majors, where he won 10 of 18 games in 1980. From the Mets, he was traded to the Toronto Blue Jays and was the Opening Day Pitcher in 1982.

Education
Local Fall River schools and B.M.C. Durfee High School.

Skills
The big right-hander had a career-earned run average of 4.47, struck out 124, and had a career 16-18 won-loss record over four years in the major leagues.

Also of Note
Bomback and his brother, Herman, made up one of the top pitching staffs in Massachusetts high school baseball in the late 1960s and the early 1970s. While pitching in 1979 in Vancouver, British Columbia, Mark recorded 22 wins, the most ever in one year by a minor league pitcher. It earned him a spot in the Baseball Hall of Fame in Cooperstown, New York.

He is an elected member of the Durfee High School Sports Hall of Fame.

Information gathered from family, *Wikipedia*, *Greater Fall River Baseball* and *Durfee Chimes*—photo courtesy of Herman Bomback

THOMAS E. GASTALL
Professional Baseball Player

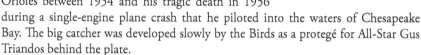

Profile

Thomas E. Gastall was born in 1932 in Fall River and died in a plane crash in 1956 in Maryland while a member of the Baltimore Orioles. At the time, he was married to Rosemary and was the father of one son, Thomas.

Experience

Gastall only got to play in 52 games for the Baltimore Orioles between 1954 and his tragic death in 1956 during a single-engine plane crash that he piloted into the waters of Chesapeake Bay. The big catcher was developed slowly by the Birds as a protegé for All-Star Gus Triandos behind the plate.

He had 15 hits including three doubles during his 83 at-bats and batted a career .181 with four runs batted in.

Education

Local Fall River schools, B.M.C. Durfee High School and Boston University.

Skills

Gastall was not only a professional baseball player but was one of Durfee's three-sports phenomena coached by Luke Urban. Gastall went from Durfee to the playing fields of Boston University, where he was selected to play in the North-South Football game when he threw four touchdown passes against a Syracuse University team starring the great Cleveland Brown Jimmy Brown. Gastall was drafted to play football for the Detroit Lions after he quarterbacked the Terriers to their most successful season ever up to that point. His basketball performances were more of the same. It was baseball Gastall loved best, though, and he was courted by fourteen of the then sixteen teams in Major League Baseball.

Also of Note

Gastall was named an Outstanding Scholar Athlete and athlete of the year by Boston University, where he was the captain of both baseball and basketball teams in his senior year. He is also a member of the Durfee High School Athletic Hall Of Fame.

Information gathered from *Wikipedia, Greater Fall River Baseball* and *Baseball Almanac*—photo courtesy of *Greater Fall River Baseball*

JOHN RUSSELL GIBSON
Professional Baseball Player

Profile
John Russell Gibson was born in Fall River in 1939 and died in 2008 at age sixty-nine, on the same day his Red Sox major league manager Dick Williams was inducted into the Baseball Hall of Fame. He and his two brothers grew up in the Maplewood section of Fall River. He was married to Virgie Ann Johnson and they were the parents of two sons and four grandchildren.

Gibson, far right, enjoying a road victory with teammates from left Mike Ryan, Ken Harrelson and George Thomas.

Experience
Gibson played on the Red Sox Impossible Dream team of 1967, but his dream could have ended in a nightmare if it was not for skill, dedication and perseverance. Another three-sport player for Durfee coach Luke Urban, Gibson started in the Federal Little League and played for the St. Williams CYO team in the Maplewood Park area.

After high school, the eventual major league catcher spent ten long years traveling in the junior circuit until 1965 when he met up with manager Dick Williams in Toronto, Canada. In 1967, Williams reached the big leagues and brought Gibson with him to Boston. He played on a team with Yaz, Tony C., Rico, Boomer, and his pal, The Pipster, Mike Andrews. Andrews and Gibson became best friends. They played Triple A together in Toronto and then moved to the Sox together. Andrews recalls how Fall River gave Gibson "A Day" at Fenway in that first year and how Yaz commented in jest that he had been playing for several years and he never had "A Day" or been given a new car like the catcher from Fall River.

Gibson and former Yankee great Elston Howard shared the duties behind the plate for pitchers including Doctor "Gentleman Jim" Lonborg. After winning the American Division title, the Sox played the St. Louis Cardinals and Gibson was behind the plate for the first game.

Education
Local Fall River schools and B.M.C. Durfee High School. He was offered scholarships at Rollins College, Boston College, Boston University and College of the Holy Cross. He elected to sign with the Boston Red Sox right after graduation instead of attending college.

Skills
In six seasons in the majors, three with both the Sox and San Francisco Giants, Gibson batted .228 with eight home runs and 78 runs batted in 264 games, including 34 doubles, 4 triples and 2 stolen bases.

Also of Note
The 28-year-old major league rookie is a member of the Durfee High Sports Hall of Fame and the only baseball player from Fall River to ever play in a World Series.

Information gathered from *Wikipedia*, Mike Andrews and The Baseball Bio Project—photos courtesy of the Gibson family

BRANDON PAUL GOMES
Professional Baseball Player

Profile
The only child of Paul and Lynette Gomes, Brandon Paul Gomes was born in Fall River in 1984 and lived on Varley and North Ogden Streets. He married his wife, Blair, in 2011.

Experience
Gomes always wanted to be a baseball player and unlike some other highly successful locals who did not achieve their sports dreams, he did. His parents emphasized education but also provided him with baseball opportunities in leagues and camps to strengthen his skills.

After a poor pitching outing in the minors, Gomes began questioning his career choice. Being a dedicated young twenty-six-year-old, he decided his motion needed some adjustments. On came the sidearm delivery and into the major leagues the kid from the Flint jumped. He landed in Tampa with the Rays at age twenty-seven and threw from the right side in his May 2011 debut, which also gave him the opportunity to throw in the 2011 playoffs for the Rays.

Education
Small Elementary School and Talbot Middle School, followed by B.M.C. Durfee High School and Tulane University.

Skills
It was not just baseball that interested Gomes at Durfee. He played basketball for two years and was highly motivated by his English and AP English instructor at Durfee, James Tavares, who also was cited by others who succeeded in the arts.

Also of Note
His life philosophy mirrors that of residents of his hometown:

"Work hard, grind things out and be an honest and loyal person/ teammate."

Information gathered from Mr. Gomes—photos courtesy of Mr. Gomes

GEORGETTE "JETTE" VINCENT MOONEY
Professional Baseball Player

Profile
Georgette Vincent Mooney was born in Fall River in 1928 and died in 1980. She was the daughter of Evelyn Dufresne and Robert Vincent, and lived "Below the Hill." She married Robert Mooney and moved to South Bend, Indiana. She leaves a daughter in South Bend, Indiana.

Experience
Vincent's professional baseball career began in 1947 and lasted seven years, two with the Racine Belles and five with the South Bend Blue Sox. She was a pitcher who threw right and batted right as well.

In her first season in 1948, she pitched in only four games for the Belles. The following year she won three and lost five with a 3.66 earned run average over 15 games through 59 innings. In 1949, playing with the Sox, she enjoyed a winning 3-2 season with an improved 3.50 ERA working 36 innings in 11 relief appearances.

By 1950, she often pitched the second game of all double headers and still finished the year with an 8-12 record over 153 innings.

Vincent's most productive year came in 1951 when she helped her team win the pennant and the title game. She finished the year with a 13-9 record and an impressive 2.42 ERA. She pitched in game four of a best-of-five championship series, winning to tie the series. (Mooney's team took the title handily in the final game 10-2.) In the 1952 season she had an 8-8 record and had a career-best 2.36 ERA to help South Bend win another title. Due to a player shortage, she played second base in the playoffs.

Education
Local Fall River schools.

Skills
Married in the 1953 season, she missed most of the year but completed the season as Georgette Mooney.

Also of Note
Vincent-Mooney is part of Women in Baseball, a permanent display at the Baseball Hall of Fame and Museum which honors the All-American Girls Professional Baseball League. Her league was featured in a 1992 film, *A League Of Their Own*, which starred Madonna.

Victory Song
Batter up! Hear that call!
The time has come for one and all
To play ball.

We are the members of the All-American League.
We come from cities near and far.
We've got Canadians, Irishmen and Swedes,
We're all for one, we're one for all
We're All-Americans!

Each girl stands, her head so proudly high,
Her motto 'Do or Die.'
She's not the one to use or need an alibi.

Our chaperones are not too soft,
They're not too tough,
Our managers are on the ball.
We've got a president who really knows his stuff,
We're all for one, we're one for all,
We're All-Americans!

The "Victory Song" was the official Song of the All-American Girls Baseball League and was co-written by Lavonne "Pepper" Paire Davis and Nalda "Bird" Phillips.

Information gathered from *Wikipedia* and the *Fall River Herald News*—photo courtesy of *Wikipedia*

AMBROSE J. "AMBY" MURRAY
Professional Baseball Player

Profile

Ambrose J. Murray was born in 1913 in Fall River to Sadie Bagslaw and Raymond Murray. He grew up in Somerset with his sister and died in Port Salerno, Florida, in 1997. He was married to a Fall River woman, Ruth Rudd, whose contractor father built some of the city's mills. They had two children and four grandchildren.

Experience

Murray became a baseball player at Durfee High School and continued playing at Tabor Academy. He was an outstanding hurler at Brown University, competing in the Ivy League.

Murray became a professional baseball player for the Boston Bees (later the Boston Braves) and pitched for the team when he was 23 years old during the 1936 season. Murray had one of the shortest major league careers of any big leaguer from the Spindle City. He only pitched in four games and had no decisions on his record but he did suffer an earned run average of 4.09. He gave up 15 hits and five runs, one home run and struck out two while giving up three bases on balls.

Education

Local Fall River schools, B.M.C. Durfee High School, Tabor Academy and Brown University.

Skills

While Murray never made it big, he did make it. He was offered the position of batting practice pitcher for the 1937 Bees but rather than accept that position he retired and moved on to the business world.

Also of Note

At Durfee High School Murray was a hard-throwing lefty who also excelled in tennis.

Information gathered from *Greater Fall River Baseball* and *Baseball Almanac*—photo courtesy of *Greater Fall River Baseball*

JOHN REDER
Professional Baseball Player

Profile
Reder was born in 1909 in Poland. He migrated to Fall River with his family and died in Fall River at age eighty in 1989. He is buried in St. Patrick's Cemetery. He is survived by his son, John J. Reder.

Experience
Reder is another one of those individuals who could be listed in two sections of this book, soccer and baseball. He was a soccer All-American as well as a first baseman with the Boston Red Sox.

His soccer career came first. He played in the National Cup as a goalie and set a new standard for net minders. Because of his baseball background he developed a unique (for those days) ball clearing technique: he threw the ball down field to his forwards rather than kick the ball in a less than direct fashion. His style of goal keeping drew the attention of Sam Mark, owner of the Marksmen in 1929, who is included in this book.

In August 1930, before he sold his team, Mark traded Reder to New Bedford because he had started to play baseball and the two competed with each other for time. By March 1932, Reder was bound for Red Sox spring training as a hurler. He was quickly moved to first base and showed great promise. He lasted in baseball for seven years until retirement in 1939. Johnny Reder was at first base in April 1932 when the Sox were playing the Yankees before 66,000 fans. His first guest at first base was none other than the immortal Babe Ruth who told him, "Don't let the crowd get ya."

Education
St. Stanislaus School and B.M.C. Durfee High School.

Skills
Reder became the chief engineer with the J.J. Corrugated Box Company in Fall River.

Also of Note
He became friendly with some of the greats of the game including Jimmy Foxx and Lefty Grove. He overheard rookie Ted Williams, who was being sent to the minors, tell Foxx he would be back soon and make more money than him.

Information gathered from *Greater Fall River Baseball*, *Wikipedia* and Baseball Reference.com—photos courtesy of *Greater Fall River Baseball*

CHARLES INIGO "BUTCH" SUTCLIFFE
Professional Baseball Player

Profile
Born in Fall River in 1915, Charles Inigo Sutcliffe died in 1994. He was the son of James and Annie Jones Sutcliffe. He had a sister Ruth as well as numerous nieces and nephews. He spent nearly his entire life in Fall River and is buried in Oak Grove Cemetery.

Experience
Excelling in three sports in high school, Sutcliffe pursued a career in baseball. Following high school, he played a year of baseball in the Fall River North End League. The Boston Braves signed him in 1937. He spent two years in the minor leagues before the Braves called him up to Boston.

The Spindle City catcher suffered a shoulder injury in 1939 and played in only four games. He was at the plate four times with one hit for a lifetime batting average of .250. For the next few years, Sutcliffe played minor league ball but joined the service and concluded his military career after the bombing of Pearl Harbor.

Education
Local Fall River schools, B.M.C. Durfee High School and attended University of Miami to play football.

Skills
Sutcliffe worked as a route salesperson for the Fall River News Company after his major league baseball days and military career.

Also of Note
Sutcliffe is a member of the Durfee High Athletic Hall of Fame in football, basketball and baseball. He was awarded eleven varsity letters in those three sports.

He was a member of the Greatest Generation, serving his country from 1944 to 1946 in the U.S. Army.

Information gathered from *Greater Fall River Baseball, Wikipedia* and *Baseball Almanac*—photos courtesy of *Greater Fall River Baseball* and *Wikipedia*

CHRISTOPHER ALBERT HERREN
Professional Basketball Player

Profile
Chris Herren was born in 1975 in Fall River. He and his brother, Michael, are the sons of Albert and the late Cynthia Carey Herren. Herren married his high school sweetheart, Heather Gray. They have three children.

Experience
Despite being from a basketball town, Herren is the only resident of Fall River to ever make it to the National Basketball Association. Drafted by the Denver Nuggets right out of college in the second round at number 33 overall, the 6'2" guard played with the Nuggets from 1999 to 2001 and then joined the Boston Celtics.

Herren's life has been chronicled in two highly successful books, *Fall River Dreams* and *Basketball Junkie: A Memoir* by *Providence Journal* sportswriter Bill Reynolds. He has also been the subject of an ESPN documentary, *Unguarded*. Herren played professional basketball in various foreign countries and during the time he was also under the influence of various forms of substances.

Herren getting off a pass while a member of the Denver Nuggets.

While he was basketball savvy, Herren struggled with substance abuse for much of his basketball career. At Denver during the 1999-2000 season, he played in 45 games, for the Celtics he played in only 25 games in the 2000-01 season. He averaged a bit over 14 minutes per game in his career and his three-point shooting percentage almost equalled his overall shooting percentage of .336.

Education
Local Fall River schools, B.M.C. Durfee High School, Boston College and California State University at Fresno.

Skills
Conquering substance abuse is most likely Herren's greatest achievement. He has been drug-free and sober since the summer of 2008. Herren today is a motivational speaker and travels across the country speaking about substance abuse.

Also of Note
Herren launched "Hoop Dreams with Chris Herren," a basketball player development firm, to mentor players on and off the court. In 2011, he founded the Herren Project, a nonprofit organization dedicated to providing assistance to families touched by addiction. He is a member of the Durfee High Sports Hall of Fame.

Information gathered from *Wikipedia*—photos courtesy of Hoop Dreams with Chris Herren

EVERETT SINDEROFF
Body Building Champion

Profile
Everett Sinderoff was born in Fall River in 1921, son of Benjamin and Leah Sinderoff. He had a sister and they lived in the Flint section of the city on Albion Street. He was married to Maxine Clasky and they had a son, a daughter and a grandchild.

Experience
Sinderoff took on a personal challenge when he was in school in Fall River. No one was going to throw sand in his face at the beach. He trained at the Boys Club on Pocassett Street in the weight section off the basketball court. While pumping iron he retrieved errant basketballs that came into the weightlifting area from the courts.

He represented the club starting at thirteen years old at various invitational meets in New England. In 1945 and 1946, Sinderoff entered the Junior Mr. America contest and he won. At twenty-five, Sinderoff was declared Mr. New England, setting his record-breaking weight lifting performance of 335 pounds for the clean and jerk at the New England AAU event in Woonsocket, Rhode Island. The previous record was 318.5 pounds.

Education
Local Fall River schools and B.M.C. Durfee High School.

Skills
Sinderoff served in the Navy as a physical training instructor for two years after high school. When not weight lifting, he sold used cars and trucks.

Also of Note
In 1972, Sinderoff went to Holyoke, Massachusetts, to serve as a judge for the National Weight Lifting Championship. To his surprise, there were not enough contestants in the 181-pound category to hold the event. He was now forty-eight years old but reluctantly agreed to participate after he was egged on by friends. The results were based upon physical strength and endurance with three lifts the test. He competed against much younger men and to their chagrin, he won again!

In 1947, Sinderoff appeared in *Muscle Power* and *Your Physique* magazines.

When attempting to sell a used car or truck, Everett was known to confidently say to a prospective buyer while standing near the rear end,

"I stand behind every vehicle I sell!"

Information gathered from the *Fall River Herald News* and Classic Bodybuilders.com—photo courtesy of Classic Bodybuilders.com

NERO FARIAS
Professional Boxer

Profile
Nero Farias was born in Fall River in 1930 and lived on Pitman Street with his twenty-one siblings. Yes, you read that right! Twenty-two children were born to Marianna and Augostinho Farias and Nero was the baby. He had a daughter with his first wife, and has a son with his current spouse Grace, and has three grandchildren.

Experience
Growing up in such a large family and influenced by his older brother George, Farias always wanted to be a police officer—especially after spending part of his youth working in the mills.

Farias began his boxing career under the name of Nero Ferry in the late 1940s in the fly, bantam and featherweight divisions with his brother, John, as his manager. From 1948 to the end of 1952, Farias won 26 fights and only lost three. The majority of his victories were knockouts. He was the undefeated New England Amateur Champion in the 118 pound class.

He worked with matchmaker Sam Silverman, and lived for some time in Boston where his winnings were shared with his manager brother and sent home to his father. Farias was undefeated in his first 17 bouts and finished his career with four straight wins. Some of the highlights of his career were meeting legends Jack Sharkey, Sugar Ray Robinson, Joe Louis and Rocky Marciano.

Education
Watson School and B.M.C. Durfee High School. He had to leave Durfee after two years to work and help support the family.

Skills
Farias joined the Fall River Police Department and served in various capacities during his career, including detective and the city police safety officer, speaking to school children throughout the city.

Also of Note
Farias founded the Police Athletic League in Fall River while he was a detective on the Fall River police force. He oversaw the police auxiliary and served as president of the Safety Officers League. He also served on the Board of Police Commissioners in Fall River, he was a director of the Fall River Municipal Credit Union and the Battleship Massachusetts Memorial Committee.

Information provided by Mr. Farias and his son—photo courtesy of Mr. Farias

1926-Present
Coaches and Trainers

———•◆•———

Show me a thoroughly satisfied man,

and I will show you a failure.

———•◆•———

THOMAS A. EDISON

THOMAS "SKIP" KARAM
Hall of Fame Basketball Coach and Educator

Skip, left, congratulates his grandson Matt Medeiros, on scoring 1,000 points for the Westport High School Wildcats. Matt is also the grandson of baseball coach Ray Medeiros, who is also highlighted herein.

Profile
Thomas "Skip" Karam was the oldest of three sons (all are included herein) of Tanous (Thomas) and Barbara Karam. He was raised on Flint Street and married fellow Fall Riverite Elizabeth DeFusco. They have three children and three grandchildren.

Experience
Karam was a protege of legendary coach Luke Urban on and off the basketball floor. He was Durfee's fourth highest scorer in the 1950s. His first job was at Westport High School as a teacher and coach. Basketball was always his first and greatest love and he had his eyes set on a professional career.

Karam began his stellar coaching career in 1961. He won five state championships during his thirty-two years and won 659 games and 32 trips to postseason tournaments. In 1988, he was highlighted in *Sports Illustrated* for recording 500 wins in only twenty-one years of coaching.

Karam was not only widely known for his coaching talents but also his vocal intimidation skills with referees. He was one of the finest basketball strategists in New England Boys High School ranks for more than three decades. He provided NBA player Chris Herren (also included herein) with the foundation to reach the professional ranks. It was Karam's parents and spouse who were his inspiration and strength over his coaching career.

Education
Davis School, B.M.C. Durfee High School, Tabor Academy, Providence College and Bridgewater State College for his master's degree.

Skills
Karam was not only coach, but an educator as well. After teaching physical education on the elementary and middle school levels, he assumed the position of vice principal at Morton Junior High and later at Durfee High School. He retired from Durfee in 1995.

Also of Note
Karam is a member of the Massachusetts Basketball Coaches Hall of Fame as well as the Durfee High School Sports Hall of Fame. The basketball court in the Durfee High School Luke Urban Field House is named in Karam's honor.

Information gathered from Mr. Karam, *Southcoast Today* and *Sports Illustrated* Vault—photo courtesy of the Karam family

JOSEPH "SKIP" LEWIS
Baseball Coach and Educator

Profile
Joe "Skip" Lewis was born in Fall River, the son of M. Bernice Wood and Joseph W. Lewis, Sr. He and his sister grew up in the Sacred Heart Parish near Ruggles Park. Lewis married Frances A. Herlihy and they had two sons, a daughter and two granddaughters. He died in Somerset in 1996 at age sixty-four.

Experience
Lewis was a standout baseball player in the Fall River parks, a record-setting pitcher at Coyle High School and later an All-American at Duke. His professional playing days were short lived when his arm failed him a during a stint in the minor leagues with the Detroit Tigers organization. He then moved to the coaching and scouting ranks for the big club. Lewis was the minor league coach for some of the 1984 World Series stars of the Tigers like Alan Tramwell, Lance Parrish and Lou Whitaker. He was also a manager of the Cape Cod League.

Lewis was the head baseball coach at Durfee High School from 1964 to 1982. He coached the Hilltoppers to a Division 1 State Championship as well as two Eastern Massachusetts and many Bristol County titles over the years. During that time, he also coached Detroit Tiger farm teams in New York and on Cape Cod.

Education
Local Fall River schools, Monsignor Coyle High School, Duke University and Elon College and a master's degree at Bridgewater State University.

Skills
Lewis was not only a great baseball coach, he was also an educator in Fall River and was named a vice principal at Henry Lord Junior High School. Lewis's son, Tim, paints a picture of Lewis as a hard-drinking, gravelly-voiced, easy-to-hold-a-grudge, sarcastic old-time baseball player and coach in his book, *A View from the Mound: My Father's Life In Baseball*. Lewis retired from the Fall River School system in 1992.

Also of Note
Lewis served in the Army during the Korean Conflict and played baseball on the All-Army Championship team. The baseball field at Durfee High School was named in Lewis's honor.

He is an elected member of the Durfee High School Sports Hall of Fame.

Information gathered from the *Fall River Herald News*—photo courtesy of Baseball Reference.com

SAM MARK
*Professional Soccer Team
Owner and Promoter*

Profile
Born in Fall River in 1897 to Annie Cohen and Mendell Markelevitch as Sam Markelevitch, Sam shortened his name to Mark. He had a brother, Shawkey. He died in Westport in 1980. He never married but was survived by two nieces.

Mark, front left, with his great team from 1926.

Experience
Mark was considered to be one of the country's finest basketball players. At Durfee High and then at Lehigh University in Pennsylvania he starred in football, basketball and baseball. He promoted basketball by bringing the New York Celtics to the area for games against local players including himself, his brother and the great Luke Urban (who is also highlighted in this book).

During the 1920s, Mark became involved in soccer. He'd never played the sport but Fall River was a hot bed for the game and the American Soccer League was interested in enrolling another team. Mark, ever the promoter, needed a field so he arranged for one in Tiverton, Rhode Island, where, unlike in Massachusetts, Sunday sporting games were allowed.

Mark put his money where his mouth was and during the first contest, 14,000 fans looked on as his team, The Marksmen, defeated J.P. Coates of Pawtucket, Rhode Island, in the National Challenge Cup game. His team was extremely successful and played at Big Berry Stadium off Pleasant Street (now Britland Park) in Fall River.

Mark sold his team in 1930 and moved on to promote other local events.

Education
Mark attended local Fall River schools, graduated from B.M.C. Durfee High School and attended Lehigh University.

Skills
As well as being a topnotch athlete, Sam Mark was a first-class promoter. After soccer he moved into the entertainment field and bought the Highway Casino in Westport, located on U.S. Route 6 between Fall River and New Bedford. Patrons there were entertained by Don Rickles, Totie Fields and Gerry Vale among others. Mark also owned the Picadilly Lounge in New Bedford and Big Berry stadium in Fall River.

Also of Note
During college, Mark joined the U.S. Army and served in France during WWI. He is an elected member of the Durfee High School Sports Hall of Fame.

Information gathered from *Wikipedia* and the *Fall River Herald News*—photos courtesy of *Wikipedia*

RAYMOND MEDEIROS
Baseball Hall of Fame Coach
and Educator

Profile
Raymond Medeiros is the son of John and Adele Beaulieu Medeiros and the oldest of four children. Born in Fall River in 1936, Medeiros married Eileen Galego and they had four sons. He grew up on lower Locust Street and is a lifelong resident of the Spindle City.

Ray notifies the umpires of a lineup change.

Experience
As a youngster, Medeiros always dreamed of being a big league baseball player. A great pitcher in his day, Medeiros was called "rubber arm" because he would pitch an afternoon game in Newport for the Newport Sunset League and head back to Ruggles Park for a night cap with the Sacred Heart team in the C.Y.O. Senior League, where he helped the team win the diocesan championship in 1953.

During his Durfee High School pitching days, Medeiros went 19-1. He also posted a 17-8 record with Bradford Durfee College of Technology during his college playing days and was voted Most Valuable Player in 1958.

After the 1998 season Medeiros retired from coaching after capturing a State Division 1 Baseball title while at Durfee in 1995. He coached at the high school level for sixteen years as a head coach.

Education
Sacred Heart School, Morton Junior High School, B.M.C. Durfee High School and Bradford Durfee College of Technology.

Skills
Medeiros was not only a great baseball coach, he was also a teacher in the Fall River school system for forty-four years, twenty years at Henry Lord Junior High School and twenty years at Durfee. He attributes his teaching career to changing his life and his parents were his major influences.

Also of Note
Medeiros is a member of the Durfee Athletic Hall of Fame and the University of Massachusetts Dartmouth Athletic Hall of Fame and the Massachusetts Baseball Coaches Hall of Fame.

Information gathered from Mr. Medeiros—photos courtesy of Mr. Medeiros

NICHOLAS OLIVIER
Prevost High Baseball Coach
and Educator

Profile
Nick Olivier was a lifelong Fall Riverite. He was born in 1909 and died in 1983 after a long illness. He was the son of Alberta Misurara and Donato Olivier. He and his sister lived in the Columbus Park area their entire lives.

Experience
Olivier was one of Fall River's great sports coaches. He spent thirteen years between 1945 and 1958 coaching the Prevost High School baseball team. He was responsible for four State Championships and two undefeated teams. The coach won 162 of 205 games and back-to-back Narry League Championships in 1950 and 1951. Olivier's first Narry title for the Maple Leafs occurred in 1945 and it was the first such title in the school's history.

From Prevost, Oliver turned his talents to Henry Lord Junior High School and served as the physical education director as well as the baseball and basketball coach for the school. He helped provide the foundation for the great Durfee High School teams thereafter.

Education
Local Fall River schools, B.M.C. Durfee High School and Providence College.

Information gathered from *Prevost High School 75th Anniversary* yearbook and the *Fall River Herald News*
—photo courtesy of *Prevost High School 75th Anniversary* yearbook

DAVID OZUG
Running Coach and Educator

Profile
David Ozug was born in Fall River in 1952 to Inurina Correia and Joseph C. Ozug. He and his five siblings grew up in the South End of the city.

Experience
Ozug's work experience started as a Youth Corps member working general maintenance at the Marine Museum at Fall River. His mother taught him right from wrong with no in-between, but his coaches Jim Wilcox during his years at Durfee High and Bob Dowd at UMass Dartmouth instilled in him his true passion: running and coaching.

Ozug began his coaching career in 1975 at Bishop Connolly High School as Assistant Boys Track Coach before moving across Elsbree Street to Durfee assisting with cross country and track for both boys and girls.

Like many others in this book, Ozug learned his strong work ethic in Fall River. It took hard work to succeed because nothing would be handed to you. He ran hard and studied hard to become a teacher and coach at Durfee High and finish third in the National Masters Mile in 2000. He was named an All-American then.

During his Durfee teaching days, Ozug created a class entitled "History of Fall River," which proved to be one of the most popular at the time as an upper class elective.

Education
St. Stanislaus School, Monsignor Coyle High and B.M.C. Durfee High School. A graduate of UMass Dartmouth, Ozug received a graduate degree from Bridgewater State University.

Skills
Ozug holds the Durfee record at 54 for the most consecutive varsity sports wins between 1987 and 1992. During that period, his 1990 team won the state cross country championship.

Information gathered from Mr. Ozug—photo courtesy of the Durfee High School 1988 yearbook

LOUIS JOHN "LUKE" URBAN
Professional Baseball and Football Player,
Coach, Athlete Extraordinaire

Profile
Luke Urban was born in Fall River in 1898. He was one of three sons and two daughters of William and Hendrica Urban. Married to Mercedes "Pat" O'Hara Urban, they were the parents of a son and a daughter and seven grandchildren. Urban died in Somerset at age eighty-two in 1980. He is buried in Notre Dame Cemetery.

Experience
If one person in this book could appear in multiple categories, it would be Urban: basketball, baseball, football and coaching.

LUKE URBAN
BOSTON BRAVES – CATCHER   1928

An All-American football player as part of the 1920 undefeated "Iron Man" team at Boston College, Urban's number is retired by the college. He was also captain of the basketball and baseball teams.

Upon graduation from BC, Urban took his talents to Canisius College in Buffalo, New York, as the football coach. During that time the New York Yankees came calling and signed him to a professional baseball contract as a catcher. He quickly became a Boston Braves for two seasons, ending his career with a .277 lifetime batting average but not before he was showered with lavish praise on his "day" in 1927. During his stay in Buffalo, Urban also played five seasons with that city's entry in the National Football League.

Upon returning to Fall River, Urban took over the coaching reins from 1940 to 1960 at his alma mater, Durfee High School, and won two New England Championships in basketball and one in baseball.

According to Tony Abraham, who played on the line at Durfee High for Urban and went on to star at center for BC, Urban ran his football practices like the military. "On the first day of Durfee practice at Alumni Field the prospects would line up, receive equipment and start trotting around the track for four laps (one mile)—no water was permitted—very few guys made it," said Abraham, the team center and sometime fullback.

Education
Local Fall River schools, B.M.C. Durfee High School and Boston College.

Skills
Urban was a mentor to many, many student athletes at Durfee who excelled in life and are included in this book. Urban began his coaching career in 1941 and after his coaching days concluded, he remained the school's athletic director until he retired in 1967 at seventy years old.

Also of Note
Urban was one of only four people to earn a varsity letter in four sports (he was also the hockey team goalie) at Boston College, was elected to the all-time all-star football team and was a charter member of the Boston College Varsity Hall of Fame. His jersey is retired in the end zone of Alumni Field at BC. Urban was also elected to the Athletic Halls of Fame at Canisius and Durfee High for his coaching success and talents and to the Massachusetts Baseball and Basketball Halls of Fame. The Durfee High School Field House is named in his honor.

Information gathered from *Greater Fall River Baseball*, Data Base Football, *Baseball Almanac*
—photos courtesy of *Wikipedia*

STANLEY WONG
Olympic Ice Hockey, NHL and NFL Trainer

Profile
Stan Wong was born in 1959 in Fall River to Albert T. and Barbara J. Wong. He is the third oldest of six children and the family lived in the Maplewood section of Fall River.

Experience
Wong loved sports growing up, which was the prelude to his life's work. Playing ball in the yard or driveway, at Maplewood Park or during class breaks initiated by teacher Ron Boulay, Wong was at his happiest. In middle school, Coach Ray Medeiros (also highlighted in this book) taught him baseball fundamentals and at Durfee High School, Stan Kupiec provided another level of direction.

Absent a professional baseball contract, it all came together for Wong at Northeastern University, where his interest in sports turned to athletic training for football and hockey players.

Wong, right, with Jack Johnson

Wong's list of accomplishments is exciting for anyone who loves sports: ten USA junior ice hockey teams, six USA Men's National Ice Hockey Teams, sixteen years as an NFL Head Trainer, two NHL All-Star Games, one Stanley Cup Final, five years as a NFL Trainer and one Super Bowl ring with the Eagles in Super Bowl XV.

Education
Letourneau School, Henry Lord Junior High and B.M.C. Durfee High School. Wong graduated from Northeastern University in 1981.

Skills
Wong has an NFL Championship ring from the 1980 Philadelphia Eagles as well as Olympic rings in hockey. He was honored to be selected to his third Winter Olympic Games as an athletic trainer for the men's ice hockey team participating in Sochi, Russia.

Also of Note
Wong's hardworking family (also highlighted in this book) set an example for his success. Long days for everyone at the Oriental Chow Mein Company produced an example of why details matter, why self-respect is so important and teamwork is so vital.

Wong was a member of the National Honor Society while a student at Durfee High School.

Information gathered from Mr. Wong and the *Fall River Herald News*—photos courtesy of Mr. Wong

FREDERICK ALBERT DAGATA
Professional Football Player and Educator

Profile
Fred Dagata was born in Fall River in 1908 and died here in 1989 and is buried in St. Patrick's Cemetery. He was the son of Albert and Coceta Graziano Dagata and the fourth of six children. He married Anelita "Reggie" Regoli they had a daughter, Barbara, five grandchildren and thirteen great-grandchildren.

Experience
After college, Dagata played professional football for the Providence Steamrollers, an NFL team at the time. He was a fullback in high school, college and in the pros. The 5'10" 187 pound star, after one season with the Rollers, hung up his cleats to coach and teach.

Education
Davis School and B.M.C. Durfee High School. He received a full scholarship to Boston College but transferred to Providence College with another football scholarship.

Fred is middle right with Luke Urban, middle left and Principal Charles Carroll far right, with Vice Principal Ralph Small, left.

Skills
Not only was Dagata a great athlete, he was also a great coach and humanitarian. For a number of years, he served as principal of the former Ruggles School where he mentored troubled students from broken homes. He was an assistant coach of both football and basketball for his friend Luke Urban.

Also of Note
President of his senior class at Durfee, he is a member of the Durfee High Sports Hall of Fame.

Information provided by the *Fall River Herald News*, Barbara Dagata Jackson and Fantasy Football Challenge
—photos courtesy of the Dagata Family

MARC MEGNA
Professional Football Player

Profile
Marc Megna was born in Fall River in 1976 to Mike and Pauline Lambert Megna. He and his older brother lived in the North End of the city.

Experience
He wanted to be the first in his family with a college degree and become one of the top football players in the country. His mother always told him he could do it. He accomplished both his goals with his mother's influence and that of Durfee teachers Vin Fitzgerald and Sandra Curtis.

Whatever aggression Megna had, he took it out on the football field with the Richmond Spiders team. His objective was to help his single mom have a better life.

He started professionally with the New York Jets in 1999 right out of Richmond. The big linebacker and defensive end had a seven-year professional career. He is now a training coach, NFL skills coach and writes articles about health for two publications.

Education
Local Fall River schools, Morton Junior High, B.M.C. Durfee High School and the University of Richmond.

Skills
Megna played in the American National Football League, European NFL and Canadian Football League as a 6'2" 245-pounder. Drafted by the New York Jets, he played under Bill Parcells with the Jets, Dick Lebeau with the Bengals, and Pete Carroll and Bill Belichick with the New England Patriots.

Also of Note
A member of both the Durfee High School Hall of Fame and the University of Richmond Hall of Fame, Megna received the Dudley Award in 1998 (Virginia's top college football player) and was also as a two-time All-American at the University of Richmond. He still holds the record for career sacks at Richmond with 32 1/2. While playing in Canada, he garnered Canadian Eastern League All-star status in 2002 as well as a member of the Grey Cup Championship team when he played for Montreal Alouettes.

Information gathered from Mr. Megna, Bomarito and *Wikipedia*—photos courtesy of Mr. Megna

ART LESIEUR
Professional Hockey Player

Profile

Born in Fall River in 1907, Arthur Lesieur was the son of Charles and Rosilda Lesieur. He was one of four siblings and was married to Matilda Henry. He died in 1967.

Experience

Lesieur played professional hockey for nearly twenty years in four different leagues. He began in 1927 as a defenseman with the American Hockey League Providence Reds. Shortly after, he moved on to the National Hockey League with the Chicago Black Hawks and the Montreal Canadians. In 1931, the 5'10" 195-pound skater won the Stanley Cup with his Canadian teammates.

Lesieur is the only Fall River-educated person to ever play professional hockey. He played with the Pittsburgh Hornets as well as the Minnesota Millers and the Reds. Lesieur played in not only the American and National Hockey Leagues but also the Canadian and US Hockey Leagues.

Education

Attended Fall River schools.

Skills

When his playing days ended, the Fall Riverite served as coach of the Millers and then had a stint as the coach of the Reds.

Information provided by Hockey Reference.com and NHL.com—photo courtesy of NHL.com

JOSEPH REGO-COSTA
Professional and Hall of Fame
Soccer Player

Profile
Joseph Rego-Costa was born in Fall River in 1919 and died in Fall River in 2002. He had three brothers and three sisters and they were the children of Mary Souza Cabral Rego-Costa and Manuel Rego-Costa. Rego-Costa married Mary Jo Moniz; they had two sons and one daughter, three grandchildren and six great-grandchildren during their fifty-eight years of marriage.

Experience
Rego-Costa was a U.S. soccer right halfback who earned four caps* and was named the captain of the U.S.A. 1948 Olympic soccer team in London for the summer games. He earned the right to play when Ponta Delgada S.C. won the 1947 National Challenge Cup and National Amateur Cup. After those victories the team was selected by the Federation to represent the country in the NAFC Championships. The U.S. lost two games but Rego-Costa was named captain for the 1948 Olympic team. Unfortunately, the team never had the chance to practice together before the London games.

Education
Local Fall River schools.

Skills
Rego-Costa played in two more international events after losing in the Olympics to a powerful Italian team 9-0.

Also of Note
He was inducted into the New England Soccer Hall of Fame in 1988.

*A player is "capped" for each international match played. A player who has played in 50 international matches has 50 caps.

Information gathered from *Wikipedia* and the *Fall River Herald News*—photo courtesy of *Wikipedia*

ADELINO "BILLY" GONSALVES
Professional and Hall of Fame Soccer Player

Profile
Adelino "Billy" Gonsalves was born in Portsmouth, Rhode Island, in 1908 and died in Kearny, New Jersey, in 1977. He grew up in Fall River and was one of seven children of Augustine and Rose Gonsalves.

Experience
Gonsalves began his soccer career at age 14 playing amateur soccer on the local pitch in Fall River. His teams included the Pioneers, Charlton Mill and Liberal. While still a teenager, "Billy" Gonsalves, a nickname given to him by fellow players, joined with the Cambridge, Massachusetts-based Lusitania Recreation Club. In 1927, his team won the Boston City and District League titles.

Gonsalves, left, with Bert Patenaude, on ship board on their way to London for the 1948 Olympic Games.

The following year, Gonsalves signed with the professional Boston Soccer Club of the American Soccer League. Due to a depth of talent on the team, Gonsalves didn't play his first game until Christmas Eve, when the teenager scored his first of what was to be many goals with the Boston Wonder Workers.

Gonsalves, bottom row 2nd left, with his teammates from the National Team in 1930.

He played with 14 different teams from 1929 to 1952, including the Fall River Marksmen, where he scored 49 goals in 75 games.

Education
Local Fall River schools.

Skills
Not only was Gonsalves a topnotch soccer player, he was also an excellent boxer and baseball player. He played on the United States National Team from 1930 to 1934 and scored one goal in six games.

Also of Note
Gonsalves was inducted into the first class of the United States Soccer Hall of Fame in 1950. It was reported that he was the ultimate gentleman on the pitch and he was never cautioned or ejected from any match.

Information gathered from *Wikipedia*—photos courtesy of *Wikipedia*

MANUEL O. "YOUNGIE" MARTIN
Professional and Olympic Hall of Fame
Soccer Player

Profile
Manuel "Youngie" Martin was born in Bristol, Rhode Island, in 1917 and died in Fall River in 1997 and he is buried in St. Patrick's Cemetery. The son of Mary Massa and John Martin, he and his wife, Rita Rainone, had two children and six grandchildren.

Experience
Martin began his athletic career not on the pitch but on the football field. His football career, though, was short lived. After a Durfee High School football practice, his mother, Mary, took his uniform and set it afire. She thought the game was too dangerous for her son to play so she told him to continue to try soccer. That set him on a lifelong career path that took him to the 1948 Summer Olympics in London and the New England Soccer Hall of Fame.

As a member of the Ponta Delgada S.C. team chosen by the United States Soccer Federation to represent the U.S. at the 1947 NAFC Championship, Martin traveled to Cuba with the team in July, 1947. He played again in 1948 but the team came up short in its four matches over that two-year period. In a game against Norway, he served as team captain.

Martin was selected for and joined the 1948 Olympic team that lost to Italy, but he continued to be a stalwart for the U.S. team during five more games in the 1949 NAFC tournament. The team earned a spot in the 1950 FIFA World Cup based upon that performance.

Education
Fall River schools, Henry Lord Junior High and B.M.C. Durfee High School.

Skills
After retiring as an active player, the personable Martin stayed in the game as a coach. He coached young people at Bradford Durfee College of Technology. He also coached at Diman Regional Vocational School and held the position of supply clerk there as well.

Also of Note
Between 1947 and 1949, he earned seven caps* with the U.S. National team. He was a member of Fall River's "Fab Four" during the 1948 Olympics.

*A player is "capped" for each international match played. A player who has played in 50 international matches has 50 caps.

Information provided by *Wikipedia*, the *Fall River Herald News* and Mr. Martin's family—photo courtesy of *Wikipedia*

BERTRAND PATENAUDE
Professional and Hall of Fame Soccer Player

Profile
Bertrand Patenaude was born in 1909 in Fall River and died on his 65th birthday in 1974. He was one of eight children of Wilfred and Roseanna Mailloux Patenaude. Bert had a son, Bert, and three grandchildren. He is buried in Notre Dame Cemetery in Fall River.

Experience
In 1928 while still a teenager, Patenaude began his professional soccer career with the Philadelphia Field Club of the American Soccer League. He scored 6 goals in 8 games before returning to Fall River as a member of the Marksmen, which won the National Challenge Cup in 1930. Patenaude moved to another team but returned to the Marksmen, which merged with the New York Soccer Club to create the New York Yankees. The combined team went on to win the National Cup, and he scored five of the six

Patenaude moving the ball down the pitch.

goals in the final game over the Chicago Bricklayers and Mason, F.C.

Patenaude moved to other clubs in the early 1930s and was part of the winning National Challenge Cup team in 1935.

Education
Local Fall River schools.

Skills
In only seven seasons, Patenaude scored 119 goals and an additional 6 in 4 games on the 1930 U.S. National Team. He scored four goals in one World Cup, an 80-m year record he held until 2010.

Also of Note
A member of the United States Soccer Hall of Fame since 1971, Patenaude is officially credited with the first hat-trick in World Cup history.

Information gathered from the *Fall River Herald News* and *Wikipedia*—photos courtesy of *Wikipedia*

WALTER ROMANOWICZ
National Soccer Player

Profile
Walter Romanowicz was the son of Eliaz and Anastasia Demko Romanowicz. He was the third from the youngest of eight children and grew up in Fall River. He married Rita (Pat) Robert and they had two daughters and five grandchildren. He died of an apparent heart attack while driving his car in Fall River in 1986 at age sixty-eight. He is buried in Notre Dame Cemetery.

Experience
Romanowicz, unlike his fellow Fall River soccer stars, was not a scorer but a goalkeeper. He played for Ponta Delgada S.C. and won the 1947 National Challenge Cup and National Amateur Cup. As a result of those wins, the team played Cuba in the North American Soccer Championship and Romanowicz earned two caps* with the U.S. National Team.

Education
Local Fall River schools.

Skills
His first full time job was in the Civilian Conservation Corps (CCC) during the Great Depression, which was part of the Works Progress Administration (WPA).

Romanowicz was a Vice President of Manufacturing at Globe Manufacturing, where he was employed for thirty-eight years. Rather than go to the 1948 Olympics as a goalkeeper, he decided to take a position with the newly created Globe Manufacturing.

Also of Note
He was inducted into the New England Soccer Hall of Fame in 1986, the same year he died. In the 1960s, he served as the City of Fall River Municipal Personnel Director and a bank trustee in the 1980s.

* A player is "capped" for each international match played. A player who has played in 50 international matches has 50 caps.

Information gathered from his daughter Nancy Cook, and the *Fall River Herald News*
—photos courtesy of the Romanowicz family

JOHN "CLARKIE" SOUZA
Professional, Hall of Fame and
Olympic Soccer Player

Profile
John "Clarkie" Souza was born in Fall River in 1920 to Mary Pavao and Frank Souza and grew up in the Flint with his six siblings. He married Anita Medeiros and they had two daughters. He died at age ninety-one in 2011 and is buried in the National Cemetery in Bourne, Massachusetts.

Experience
A member of the powerhouse Ponta Delgada Club, Souza was part of the team that won the National Challenge Cup in 1947 and The National Amateur Cup in 1946 through 1948. He was a member of both the 1948 and 1952 Olympic soccer teams, which was well documented in the book and film of the same name, *The Game of Their Lives*.

Souza played in one of his earned 14 caps* when the U.S. team defeated London in the 1950 World Cup in Brazil, which remains one of the gigantic soccer upsets of all time and is arguably one of the greatest U.S. soccer victories ever.

Souza also played for the U.S. against Scotland in 1952. He was the playmaker on his teams and a true ball-control artist. He was a member of the Fall River "Fab Four" in the 1948 Olympics.

Education
Local Fall River schools.

Skills
Teammates dubbed him "Clarkie" because his youthful good looks and dark wavy hair reminded them of Clark Gable.

Also of Note
A member of the Greatest Generation, Souza served in WWII in the U.S. Navy in the South Pacific, working on a supply ship as a Morse code man.

He and fellow World Cup teammates were inducted together into the National Soccer Hall of Fame. He was also selected to the World Cup All-star team and remained the only U.S. soccer player ever so named until 2002.

* A player is "capped" for each international match played. A player who has played in 50 international matches has 50 caps

Information gathered from the *Fall River Herald News* and *Wikipedia*—photo courtesy of *Wikipedia*

EDWARD "WOLFANG" SOUZA-NETO
Professional, Hall Of Fame and
Olympic Soccer Player

Profile
Edward Souza-Neto was born in Fall River in 1921 and died in Warren, Rhode Island, in 1979 at age fifty-eight. He's buried in Notre Dame Cemetery. "Wolfang" Souza-Neto and his brother were the sons of Manuel and Antonia Couto Souza. He had two sons and three daughters.

Experience
Souza-Neto played club soccer with the triumphant Ponta Delgada F.C. before moving up to the United States Men's National Team. He played as a forward on the team and won a 1-0 victory over England in the 1950 FIFA World Cup finals.

Education
Local Fall River schools.

Skills
A member of the U.S. team for the 1948 Olympics in London, Souza-Neto was a member of a group called "The Fab Four." All but one of the team lived in Fall River at the time.

Also of Note
He earned six caps* and is a member of the National Soccer Hall of Fame.

Information gathered from *Wikipedia* and *The Herald News*—photo courtesy of *Wikipedia*

HENRY "HANK" NOGA
Professional Soccer Player

Profile
Henry Noga was born in Fall River in 1928. He was the son of Josephine Mamulska and Peter Noga. He and his two siblings grew up in the South End of the city. He married Pauline Francoeur and they had a daughter. He died in 1992.

Experience
Noga was a U.S. soccer goalkeeper. He played with the U.S. National team in 1960 and earned two caps in World Cup qualifying games versus Mexico. The team record in those two contests was one tie and one loss.

Education
Local Fall River schools and B.M.C. Durfee High School.

Skills
It was not just soccer where the young Fall River athlete gained his reputation. In the 1940s he was the top scorer on the Durfee High School basketball teams with a 16.2 average per game. He scored 32 points in a game in 1947. He led the team in rebounding as well and to a state championship. For years he was also the city handball champion.

Also of Note
Noga is a member of the Durfee High School Sports Hall of Fame. He was captain of both football and basketball teams and played on the baseball team for four years under Coach Luke Urban.

* A player is "capped" for each international match played. A player who has played 50 international matches has 50 caps.

Information gathered from the *Fall River Herald News, The Golden Age of Durfee Basketball*—photo courtesy of Durfee High School yearbooks

1926-Present

Teams

———◆◆———

Human pride is not worth while;

there is always something lying in wait

to take the wind out of it.

———◆◆———

MARK TWAIN

MASSACHUSETTS STATE CHAMPION
or
UNDEFEATED SPORTS TEAMS

1940s

1945 Prevost Baseball Undefeated

Coach Nick Olivier

1945 Champions

1st row: George Briere, Georges Bonnafe, Paul Peloquin, Roger Mercier.
2nd row: Daniel Latendresse, Alfred Pelletier, Armand Boissonneau, Marcel Simoneau, Rene Desrochers, Edmond Levesque, Roland Gamache.
3rd row: coach Nicholas Olivier, Raymond Giasson,

Georges Levasseur, Henri Lagasse, Romeo Fortin, Samuel Ford, athletic director Bro. Francis.

1946 Prevost Baseball Undefeated

Coach Nick Olivier

1946 champs
10-0

1st row, from left: Philippe Lavoie, Edmond Pelletier, Georges LeBreux, Fernand Bonnoyer, Albert Tremblay. 2nd row: Maurice Hamel, Romeo Fortin, Armand Boissonneau, Rene Desrochers, Alfred Pelletier, Armand Routhier, Hector Dion, Edmond Valiquette, Paul Peloquin.

3rd row: coach Nick Olivier, Raymond Giasson, Earl William Wall, Daniel Latendresse, Samuel Ford, Adrien Picard, Romeo Guimond, and athletic director Brother Francis.

MASSACHUSETTS STATE CHAMPION
or
UNDEFEATED SPORTS TEAMS

1940s

1947 Durfee Boys Basketball State Champions
Coach Luke Urban

In no particular order: Joe Andrews, Andy Farrissey, Hank Noga, John Brenner, Shay Lynch, Bernie McDonald, Larry Klimka, William Farrissey, Dick Sample, Stan Sincoski and Ray Samson.

1948 Durfee Boys Basketball New England Champions
Coach Luke Urban

| J. ANDREWS | P. COLLIAS | A. FARRISSEY | J. BRENNER | S. SINCOSKI | H. FINE |
| Forward | Forward | Center | Guard | Guard | Center |

| C. BURTON | G. CHAROS | W. FARRISSEY | B. McDONALD | R. SAMSON | J. WILLIAMSON |
| Forward | Forward | Guard | Guard | Forward | Forward |

MASSACHUSETTS STATE CHAMPION
or
UNDEFEATED SPORTS TEAMS

1950s

1950 Diman Vocational Boys C Basketball State Champions

*Coach Charlie O'Keefe**

Team-Jim Carey, Ed Fernandes, Ed Schmoke, George Lelievre, Matt Burke, Armand Farias, Louis Leduc, Joe Waring, James Quinn and Len Perreira.

1952 Durfee Boys Basketball State Champions

Coach Luke Urban

Left to right - Seated - J. Borden, T. Kamm, W. McHenry, T. Burke, R. Mickool, F. Nasiff.
Standing - A. Farrissey, C. Sincoski, P. Bogan, A. Moson, R. McMahon, A. Freeman, R. Golz, J. Costa, J. Richards.

*He is an elected member of the Durfee High School Sports Hall of Fame.

MASSACHUSETTS STATE CHAMPION
or
UNDEFEATED SPORTS TEAMS

1950s

1955 Diman Vocational Boys Soccer State Champions
Coach Bill Shea

DIMAN SOCCER TEAM

Front, left to right: Ronnie Levesque, H. (Butch) Perreira, Tom Clarke, Arman Jovian, Joe Cabral, Frank Marelle, Bill Arruda, Manuel Souza, Dick Clarke, Tom Podesky.

Rear: Coach Bill Shea, Jim O'Neil (Student Mgr.), Jim Moiera, Paul Chicro, Co-Capt.; Tony Borges, Ernie Mercier, Co-Capt.; Tom Ferreira, Ron Fernandes, Andy Andrade, Ron Pereira, Bob Masseud (Trainer).

MASSACHUSETTS STATE CHAMPION
or
UNDEFEATED SPORTS TEAMS

1950s

1956 Durfee Boys Basketball New England Champions

Coach Luke Urban, Asst. Coach John J. Harrington

Captain Al Atar, Mike Drewniak, Jim Caldeira, Tom Arruda, Russ Gibson, George Darmody, George Reed, Jerry Schwartz, Luke "Topper" Urban, Jr., Gordon Andrews, Jerry Elias, Doug Baxendale, John Harty, Stan Kupiec, Ken Palmer and Ernie Mizher.

MASSACHUSETTS STATE CHAMPION
or
UNDEFEATED SPORTS TEAMS

1950s

1956 & 57 Durfee Tennis State Champions

Coach Frank Jordan

(no photos available)

Sid Poritz, Kalman Pollen, Don Oldham, Lionel Spiro (see Business section), Ken Palmer, Larry Pollen, Jay Buffington, Harvey Trieff, Don Lincoln, Jerry Hahn, Mike Mendell, Doug Salmond, Marty Cohen and Tom Coelho. Some mentioned competed on only one team.

1957 Durfee Boys Baseball State Champions-Undefeated

Coach Luke Urban

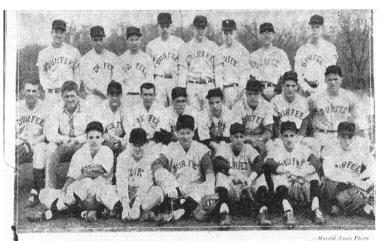

—*Herald News Photo*

HILLTOPPERS SEEK ANOTHER TITLE: Durfee High is striving to repeat as Bristol County Baseball League champion this season. Coach Luke Urban's Hilltoppers are, front, left to right—Larry Wilbur, Luke Urban Jr., Manny Sousa, John O'Brien, Tommy Arruda, Charley Carey; middle—Dick Bonalewicz, Ken Burton (manager), Frank Latessa, Charley Copley, Frank DeNardo, Ed Pereira, Stan Kupiec, Gerry Elias, Russ Gibson; rear—Don Ray, Dick Campion, Roger Alves, Jack Driscoll, Al Lavoie, Bob Hargraves, John Rini, Doug Baxendale.

MASSACHUSETTS STATE CHAMPION
or
UNDEFEATED SPORTS TEAMS

1960s

1961 Durfee Boys Soccer-Undefeated

Coach David Sullivan

Left to right, first row — J. Vianna, J. Dias, W. Holt, G. Drewniak, T. Kwan. Second row — T. Furtado, W. Hamyl, D. Botelho, R. Hipolito, P. Dutra, J. Romano. Third row — P. Trzasdel R. Bradbury, W. Arruda, M. Papoula, G. Medeiros, P. Petri, F. Reilly, Coach Sullivan.

1963 Durfee Football State Champions-Undefeated

Coach Donald Montle, Assistant Coaches Steve Nawrocki, Skip Lewis and Skip Karam.

Bill Carey, Joe Souza, Dave Bouchard, George Lavoie, Bob Greeson, Art Arruda, Jim Feijo, Dan Michael, Bob Farias, Bill Cooper, Bob Smith, Bob Klimka, Glynn Gesner, Ken Silva, Everett Correia, Mike Shaughnessy, John Mills, Bruce Isador, Don Howarth, Vin Schieri, Len Bly, Joaquim Fachada, Larry Souza, Pete Machado, Ron Franco, Joe Karam, Ron Gagnon, Charley Harrington, Art Murray, George Potts, Geoffrey Potts, Mike O'Shaughnessy, Henry Lord, Wayne Levesque, August Pimental, Dave Pacheco and Len Martin.

Front row — D. Michaels, J. Feijo, R. Greeson, A. Arruda, G. Lavoie, D. Bouchard, J. Souza, W. Carey. Standing — G. Potts, R. Smith, R. Klimka, R. Farias, W. Cooper, C. Harrington, A. Murray.

300

MASSACHUSETTS STATE CHAMPION
or
UNDEFEATED SPORTS TEAMS

1960s

1966 Durfee Boys Basketball State Champions
Coach Skip Karam, Assistant Coach Len Alves

From left, first row—M. Rebello. E. Fleming. W. Winarski. R. Dempsey. E. Seligman. Second row—C. Fitzgerald. D. August. T. Doyle. P. Barrette. Third row —J. Barry. B. Hankins. D. Carey. J. Leandro

MASSACHUSETTS STATE CHAMPION
or
UNDEFEATED SPORTS TEAMS

1970s

1971 Durfee Boys Baseball State Champions

Coach Skip Lewis and Assistant John Pontes

Eastern Massachusetts Class A champion Durfee High makes its bid for the state title Saturday at 2, at Fraser Field in Lynn. Front, from left :— Bob Murphy, Paul Oliveira, Dave Sullivan, Tom Gastall; middle — Mike Naser, Kevin Ainsworth, Bruce Vieira, Mark Bemback, Paul Silva; rear — Bob Holl, Ray Parise, Steve Winarski, George Rodrigues, Tom Chippendale, Roger Bessette. Doug Carvalho, Steve Rivest and Paul Peloquin are also squad members. Herald News Photo

1972 Durfee Girls Basketball-Undefeated

Coach Beverly Cambra.

In no particular order: Kathy and Chris Farrell, Sheila Rego, Joyce Faria, Denise Bundy, Marilyn Oliviera, Pat Murphy, Donna Mathais, Kathy Kaegael, Susan Korber, Joyce Taylor, Marianne Bonalewicz, Marge Mello.

MASSACHUSETTS STATE CHAMPION
or
UNDEFEATED SPORTS TEAMS

1970s

1976 Diman Boys Cross Country Undefeated

Coach John Cantwell

Sitting (L to R) Wayne Valcourt, Chris Carreiro, Brian Tavares, Wesley Dunham, Chris Menard, Rick Cabral, Don Proulx, Bill Tillson, Don Normandin. Kneeling: Tim Tillson, Jeff Howard, Richard Brogan, Al Carreiro, Dave Berube, Ken Cartier, John Ciullo, Phil Araujo, Tom Bergeron, Chris Julian. Standing: Coach John Cantwell, Bob Dunn, Mike Deschenes, Dave Gregory, Karl Herzier, Con Bienvenue, Steve Donnelly, Dwane Mellen, Mark Lapointe, Assistant Coach Ed Hill.
CONFERENCE ALL STAR TEAM: Phil Araujo, Karl Herzier, Chris Menard, Dwane Mellen.

1977 Durfee Boys Basketball State Champions-Undefeated

Coach Skip Karam, Assistant Coach Jack Campbell

Number One!
State Champions
An amazing basketball season has come to an end for the Hilltoppers of Durfee High School, who captured the state championship Saturday at Brockton High. In the front row, from left, are, Paul Amorin, Greg Brilhante, Steve Ogden, B.J. McDonald. Rear, Jim Donnelly, Mike Facchiano, Kevin Whiting, Capt. Ken Fiola, Rick Yarbough, Charles Woitowicz, Harvey Littman, John Powers and Jim Plaiski.

MASSACHUSETTS STATE CHAMPION
or
UNDEFEATED SPORTS TEAMS
1970s

1977 Bishop Connolly Boys Tennis State Champions
Coach Ted Pettine

Front, l-r: P. Kret, M. McGuill, P. Keating, R. Ironfield; Middle, l-r: L. Stratton, D. Bedard, J. Cummings, J. McGuill; Back, l-r: E. Pettine, Coach; D. Kaliff, M. Sheridan, K. Holden, R. Correllas.

1978 Durfee Girls Swimming State Champions
Coach Rick Swalm

In no particular order: Sharon Bogan, Katie Hudner, Ann Salois, Alison Smith, Cindy Jarabek, Karen Jarabek, Susan Kitchen, Kerry Hartnett, Melanie Pimental, Sarah Smith, Nancy Stanton, Kellyann Sullivan, Christine Dionne, Katie O'Neil, Beth Costa, Merri Cyr, and Jane Feitelberg.

MASSACHUSETTS STATE CHAMPION
or
UNDEFEATED SPORTS TEAMS

1980s

1984 Durfee Boys Basketball State Champions-Undefeated

Coach Skip Karam, Assistant Coach Jack Campbell

In no particular order: Joe Stanton, Paul Hart, Brian O'Neil, Vic Perreira, Nick Eagan, Bob Hargraves, John Carvalho, Tom and John D'Ambrosio, Skip Karam, Jr., Mike Pontes, Paul Donnelly and Mitch Lown.

1988 Durfee Girls Cross Country-Undefeated

Coach Dave Ozug

In no particular order: Megan McClosky, Lorie Branco, Sue St. Laurent, Jen Bougie, Kellie Kerkin, Lisa Travis, Kara Brogan.

MASSACHUSETTS STATE CHAMPION
or
UNDEFEATED SPORTS TEAMS

1980s

1988 Durfee Boys Basketball State Champions
Coach Skip Karam, Assistant Coach Jack Campbell

B.M.C. DURFEE HIGH SCHOOL
1987-88 DIVISION I BASKETBALL — MASSACHUSETTS STATE CHAMPIONS
Won 24 - Lost 1

Front Row (l to r): John Murray, Lamar Stevens, Kevin Galvin, Brad Pingley, Rick Dias, Jason Correira, Jay Carvalho
Back Row: Head Coach, Tom "Skip" Karam; Asst. Coach, Robert Dempsey; Allen Bernier; Jud McDonald, Chris Mears, Captain, Matt Attar; Mike Herren; Wade O'Connor; Kyle Kopec; Chris Medeiros, Student Manager; Danny Mauricio

1989 Durfee Girls Cross Country-Undefeated
Coach Dave Ozug

Left to right: Kara Brogan, Megan McCloskey, Capt.Sue St. Laurent, Marcie Poulos, Kelly Kirker, Jen Bougie, Coach Ozug and not pictured: Goretti Pacheco.

306

MASSACHUSETTS STATE CHAMPION
or
UNDEFEATED SPORTS TEAMS

1980s

1988 Durfee Boys Soccer-Undefeated

Coach John Santos

No team photo avaialable but members included: Joe Cordeeiro, Mike Dias, Ed Silva, Jeff Melo, Bret Reis, Peter Sousa, Ralph Valencia, Rui Sardinha, Michael Sousa and Ed Jacob among others.

1989 Durfee Boys Basketball State Champions-Undefeated

Coach Skip Karam and Assistant Coach Bob Dempsey

In no particular order: Co-Captains Juddy McDonald and Mike Herren; Pat Malloy, Wade O'Conner, John Murray, Chris Means, John Medeiros, Matt Kuss, Kyle Kupiec, Mark Feitelberg,Todd Majkut, Lamar Stevens and Roger Plante.

1989 Durfee Girls Winter Track-Undefeated

Coach George Moniz and Assistant Coach Tom Botelho

No team photo available but team members included: Jen Perreira, Lindsay De Farias, Danielle Machado, Amy Shovelton, Mary Jo Ferreira, Laurie Gastall, Jessica Golden, Sue St. Laurent, Jen Bougie, Megan McCloskey, Melissa Cavaco, Gorette Pacheco, Kara Brogan, Lisa Travis and Megan Daley.

MASSACHUSETTS STATE CHAMPION
or
UNDEFEATED SPORTS TEAMS

1990s

1990 Bishop Connolly Baseball State Champions

Coach Don Choiunard

Front: left to right Scott Tripp, Conrad Paquette, Matt Palma, Kevin Aguiar, Robert Clappi, Greg Harrison, Middle: Asst. Coach Bill Courville, Eric Brenner, Vinnie Paquette, Brian Lavigne, Fred Currier, Monte Perez. Rear: Luis Torres, Mike Gendreau, Bob Kennedy, Marc Rebello and Jared Owen.

1990 Durfee Girls Cross Country-Undefeated

Coach Dave Ozug

kneeling, left to right - Goretti Pacheco, Mary Murphy, Becky Masterson, Kara Brogan, Stephanie Bougie, Michelle Silvia; standing, left to right - Coach Dave Ozug, Jen Bougie, Megan McCloskey, Sue St.Laurent, Shannon Harrington, Rachel Hunt.

MASSACHUSETTS STATE CHAMPION
or
UNDEFEATED SPORTS TEAMS

1990s

1991 Durfee Girls Cross Country-Undefeated
Coach Dave Ozug

, left to right- Victoria Soares, Debbie Cabral, Rachael Hunt, Shannon Harrington, Michelle Silvia, Rochell
yster.
le, left to right- Laurie Dextraze, Mary Murphy, Keri Gibney, Jessica Sanders
om, left to right- Sheri Dube, Jennifer Powell, Kara Brogan, Becky Masterson, Sue Miranda

1991 Durfee Softball-Undefeated
Coach Jack Campbell

left to right- Jodi Pavao, Kelly Fournier, Tammy Gustafson, Kelly Monte, Michelle Fournier
m, left to right- Kathy Attar, Terry Pacheco, Jennifer Powell, Meribah Dean, Tricia Angelini, Amber Roy, Valerie Veins

MASSACHUSETTS STATE CHAMPION
or
UNDEFEATED SPORTS TEAMS

1990s

1994 Durfee Girls Cross Country-Undefeated

Coach Dave Ozug

: Janice Gagnon, Krissy Librera, Corine Givens.
: Jessica Berube, Sarah Tinsley, Michelle Porto, Katie Charette, Jen Farabini, Kerry LePage, Annie Pacheco, lexandra Porto
: Shelly Kenyon, Danielle Lima, Jocelyn Gonsalves, Melissa Souza, Nancy Medeiros, Nicole Maurer, Kendra k, Kara Maurum, Kelly Lannigan, and Melissa Silva.

1993 Bishop Connolly Boys Hockey State Champions

Coach Mike Relihan, Assistant Coaches John Senra and Dave Maurer

1992-1993 VARSITY HOCKEY TEAM
front, Craig Bettencourt, Tom Pavao, Sean Stubbert, Lenny Moniz, John Ruel, Ted Buxbaum, Danny Rego, *middle*, Trainer George Angelo, Chris Cassamas, Paul Simister, Jay Carvalho, Brian St. Pierre, John Chepren, Judd Berube, Derek Potvin, Matt Furtado, Asst. Coach Dave Maurer, *back*, Coach Mike Relihan, Justin DeMatos, Charles Walsh, Joe Aleardi, Jason Ruel, Jim D'Amiano, Mark Aguiar, DJ Moniz, John Guay, Asst. Coach John Senra, not pictured, Pat Meffert, Eric Chace,

MASSACHUSETTS STATE CHAMPION
or
UNDEFEATED SPORTS TEAMS
1990s

1994 Durfee Boys Indoor Track-Undefeated
Coach George Moniz and Assistant Coach Dave Ozug

1: Eric Alberto, Paul Teves, Ronnie Ferreira, Billy Ferreira, Bryan Nadeau, Kevin Costa, Luis Cruz, Mike
s, and Joe Goes.
2: Mike Orlowski, Shawn Skeffington, Gary Leite, Mitch Sousa, Tim Duclos, Brian Pacheco, Kevin Pearson,
Rodgers, and Ken Levesque.
3: Asst. coach Dave Ozug, Keith Fragoza, Matt Coeltho, Brian Nawroki, Kevin Teves, Matt Duarte, Ryan
ara, Mike Brodeur, Jeff Mikolavzk, Barden Castro, Andrew Ouellette, and head coach George Moniz.

1996 Durfee Girls Cross Country-Undefeated
Coach Dave Ozug

Sitting: Kendra Bullock, Mandy Cordeiro, Nicole Bullock.
Kneeling: Beth Figuredo, Jenn Cote, Alyshia Allaire, Shelly Kenyon.
Standing: Coach Dave Ozug, Jen Couto, Twylear Clear, Danielle Lima, Jessica Thompson,
Jocelyn Copely, Melanie Souza.

MASSACHUSETTS STATE CHAMPION
or
UNDEFEATED SPORTS TEAMS

1990s

1995 Durfee Baseball State Champions

Coach Ray Medeiros, Assistant Coaches Joe Andrews and Glen Chatterton

Front: Batboys Matt and Brendan Medeiros; front left to right : Ryan Sylvia, Pat Devlin, Brent Medeiros, Jessie Eaton, Eric Correia, Matt Coriarty, Ryan Mello, Shaun Skeffington, Brian Mauricio, Mark Gendreau and Coach Ray Medeiros. Second Row l to r: Hitting instructor Joe Andrews, Keith Henriques, Brian Pacheco, Adam Roy, Jamie Mitchell, Adam Guilmette, Capt.Neil Dankievitch, John Camara, Mike Silvia, Brian Nawrocki and Coach Glen Chatterton.

1996 Durfee Boys Wrestling-Undefeated

Coach Mike Perreira

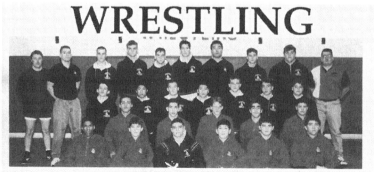

1st Row: Pat McMullen, Coach Mike Alves, Chris Bouchard, Teddy Bouchard, Derrick Correia, Michael Bertoncini Chi Chiu, Daniel LePage, Chris Martel, and Coach Mike Perreira.
2nd Row: Dave Marques, Doug Bang, Kane Vandel, Nhan Bang, Chad Cummings, Tommy Pacheco, and Dave Me
3rd Row: Ian Mullarky, Frankie Charete, Chris Jones, Keith Santos, and Ray Schofield.
4th Row: Tommy Texeira, Chad Hickman, Chris Antao, Robert Padeiro, Keith Bouchard, and John Torres.

MASSACHUSETTS STATE CHAMPION
or
UNDEFEATED SPORTS TEAMS

1990s

1998 Durfee Softball State Champions

Coach Steve Winarski

In no particular order: Jamie Fereira, Denise Souza, Paula Costa, Nicole Gendreau, Stephanie Menard, Melissa Cassavant, Amy Napert, Kelly Orton, Alysha LaFrance, Megan DeNardo, Marissa Fitzgerald, Kathy Ward, Michelle Lavoie.

VSTATE CHAMPION
or
UNDEFEATED SPORTS TEAMS

2000s

2004 Durfee Softball State Champions

AGAINST ALL ODDS, this softball team won the Division One State Championship.
Front Row: Vanessa Dias, Stephanie Bonalewicz, Jenn Fitta, Sarah Stack, Ashley Maucione
Second Row: Kayla Peixoto, Brittany Poissant, Ashley Saraiva, Caitlin Belanger, Meaghan Connor
Coaches from left to right: Bob Bonalewicz, James Swanson, Head Coach Steven Winarski

MASSACHUSETTS STATE CHAMPION
or
UNDEFEATED SPORTS TEAMS

2010s

2013 Bishop Connolly Boys Basketball
Division 4 State Champions

Coach Frank Sherman

Players: Tommy Keyes, Michael Watts, John Goncalo, Jack Santoro, Brian Quinn, Michael Sullivan, Alex Medeiros, Konrad Bradbury, Dylan Holland, Drew Keyes, Kevin Sullivan, Troy Hood, Coaches: Matt Coute, Eddy Keyes

1926-Present
Suburbs*

———•◦•———

The best executive is the one who has

sense enough to pick good men to do what he wants done,

and self-restraint enough to keep from

meddling with them while they do it.

———•◦•———

THEODORE ROOSEVELT

* Despite not having attended school in Fall River,
the following individuals from the Fall River suburbs of
Somerset, Swansea, Tiverton and Westport are so closely
associated with the city that they deserve inclusion.

PAMELA BUSTIN
Olympic Field Hockey Player and Coach

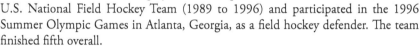

Profile
Pamela Bustin was born in 1967 and is the daughter of Joseph and Marcia Wright Bustin. She and her sister and brother grew up in Somerset.

Experience
Upon her college graduation from University of Massachusetts Amherst, she played and competed for the U.S. National Field Hockey Team (1989 to 1996) and participated in the 1996 Summer Olympic Games in Atlanta, Georgia, as a field hockey defender. The team finished fifth overall.

Bustin was a field hockey coach as an assistant at Temple University for three seasons and then five years at Michigan State. She accepted the head coaching job at Hofstra University and a year later, the head job at University of Louisville. The Cardinals were the cellar dwellers in their conference until Bustin arrived in 1998. She turned the program around, won six conference titles that included 2 Mid-American titles, three Big East Championships in four years, and multiple honors as Coach of the Year in both the Mid-American and Big East conferences.

In 2011, Bustin took over the Duke University field hockey program. The team finished sixth in the country and she earned the ACC Coach of the Year award. In 2013, Bustin took Duke to the NCAA finals before losing in the championship game.

Education
Somerset public schools and University of Massachusetts Amherst.

Skills
Bustin is now the field hockey coach at Duke University. The Somerset High graduate has also served as an Olympic assistant coach from 2005 to 2008 to the U.S. Women's Olympic Field Hockey team that competed at the Beijing games in 2008. From 2009 to 2012, Bustin has coached the US Junior teams, and in 2012, helped the U21 National team earn an eighth place finish at the Junior World Cup in Germany.

Information gathered from *Wikipedia*—photo courtesy of Ms. Bustin

MOST REVEREND GEORGE W. COLEMAN, S.T.L.
Bishop of Fall River

Profile

George W. Coleman was born in Fall River in 1939 to Beatrice Shea and George W. Coleman. He and his sister were raised in Somerset.

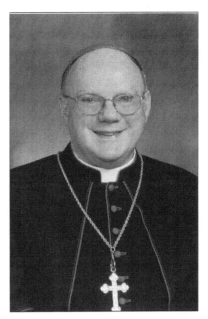

Experience

Coleman served as diocesan superintendent of schools from 1977 to 1985. In 1985, after serving as pastor of St. Patrick's Parish in Fall River, Father Coleman was transferred to Cape Cod where he served until 1994. In 1994, Bishop Sean O'Malley appointed Father Coleman as Vicar General of the Diocese. In 2003, he was appointed bishop by Pope John Paul II. He became the seventh bishop and second native son in the 100-year history of the Diocese.

Education

Village School Somerset, Coyle High School and College of the Holy Cross. Coleman studied at St. John's Seminary and the North American College in Rome, where he earned a graduate degree.

Skills

The role of the bishop is to pastor to more than 350,000 Catholics in 101 parishes in the Catholic Diocese of Fall River.

Information gathered from the Roman Catholic Diocese of Fall River—photo courtesy of the Catholic Diocese of Fall River

ALICE G. DeCAMBRA
Professional Baseball Player

Profile

Alice G. DeCambra was born in Somerset in 1921, one of ten children. She died in Somerset in 1988. She was the daughter of Antonia Chaves and William DeCambra. Her younger sister Lillian joined the league in 1947 but never played in a game.

Experience

In 1946, "Moose" DeCambra pitched for the Fort Wayne Daisies and the Peoria Redwings during her first two years in the All-American Girls Professional Baseball League. She moved on to infield duty in 1949 with Peoria before joining the Kalamazoo Lassies in 1959.

At 5'3" and 126 pounds DeCambra at was certainly no "Moose," despite her nickname. Her won and loss record on the mound was 11-8 and her career batting average was just under 200. Her team was inducted into the Baseball Hall of Fame in Cooperstown shortly after she passed away.

Education

Local Somerset schools and Somerset High School.

Skills

DeCambra loved sports, played golf and was a great bowler as the years went along. When not participating in sports, she worked at Firestone on the Fall River waterfront. After the last great fire at that site, DeCambra worked at Aluminum Processing Corporation. She was inducted into the Somerset High School Sports Hall of Fame.

Information gathered from Girls Professional Baseball League—photo courtesy of Girls Professional Baseball League

BRIAN FOX
Celebrity Artist

Profile
Brian Fox was born in 1967 in Fall River. He and his two siblings are the children of Earl and Pat Wallace Fox. He is married to Sidonia Campos and they have two children.

Experience
Fox is an internationally known artist. His specialty is painting celebrities such as Jackie Robinson, Keith Richards, Michael Phelps, Johnny Depp and Ray Charles, to name a few. He was selected by Major League Baseball to be the official commemorative artist for the 2007, 2008 and 2009 All-Star games. Fox is currently working on projects for New England Patriots' owner Robert Kraft, player Rob Gronkowski, the Disney Company and he has sent artwork to Russian President Vladimir Putin. His work exhibits and sells throughout the world.

Education
Local Somerset schools and a B.A. in Fine Arts from University of Massachusetts Dartmouth.

Skills
In 2009, Fox was commissioned by the National Hockey League to produce original art work for the January 1, 2010, NHL Winter Classic at Fenway Park. He recently collaborated with Olympic goaltender Jim Craig for original art work to commemorate the thirty-year anniversary of the "Miracle on Ice."

Information gathered from Brian Fox—photo courtesy of Mr. Fox

SHIRLEY MAY FRANCE
Long-Distance Swimmer

Profile

Born in Fall River in 1933 to Florence Manchester and Walter J. France, Shirley May France and her three siblings were brought up in Somerset, where she is buried. She died in 2012. The widow of Douglas Smith, who died in 1959, and Donald Setters, she had five children, twelve grandchildren and five great-grandchildren.

Experience

France was an endurance swimming champion who set multiple world records. She swam in various lakes in this country including Lake Sinclair in Michigan, Lake George, New York, and before one million people at Coney Island. Her most publicized swim was her attempt at age sixteen to be the youngest female to swim the 21-mile English Channel. France made three attempts between 1949 and 1950. She gave swimming lessons to locals at the Fall River YMCA.

Education

Local Somerset schools.

Skills

Not only a swimmer, France modeled hats in New York, was a disc jockey for WSAR and starred in a television series on Providence, Rhode Island station, WJAR-TV.

Information gathered from *Wikipedia*—photos courtesy of *Wikipedia*

GREGORY C. GAGNE
Professional Baseball Player

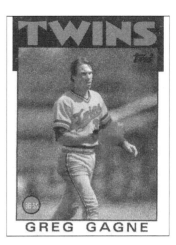

GREG GAGNE

Profile
Born in 1961, Gregory C. Gagne is the son of Elmer "Ike" Gagne. Greg has three siblings and is married to Michele Blais. They have three children.

Experience
Very few of all the great local baseball players from more than 150 years of Greater Fall River baseball history can claim a World Series ring as a player. Gagne has two—1987 and 1991.

Drafted by the Yankees in 1979 right out of Somerset High, Gagne was traded to the Minnesota Twins in 1982. By 1985, he was a permanent fixture between second and third and remained there for eight seasons. He hit two inside-the-park home runs in 1986 and is one of only two major leaguers since 1930 to accomplish the feat. His lifetime batting average is .254.

Education
Local Somerset schools and Somerset High School.

Skills
Gagne played for ten years as a shortstop for the Twins, then played for both the Kansas City Royals for three years and the Los Angeles Dodgers for two seasons before retiring in 1997 to become the baseball coach for Bishop Feehan High School in Attleboro, Massachusetts. He is a member of both the Somerset High Sports Hall of Fame and the Minnesota Twins Hall of Fame.

Information gathered from *Wikipedia*—photo courtesy of *Baseball Almanac*

JAMES MCDERMOTT
Massachusetts Amateur Golf Champion

Profile
James McDermott is one of three children of Carl and Elizabeth McDermott. A lifelong Somerset resident, he married Kathleen Hackett and they have three children.

Experience
McDermott won the Massachusetts State Amateur Golf Championship not once but three times. Very few players in the state have accomplished this feat. His first title, playing out of the Fall River Country Club where he was seven-time champion, took place at the Salem Country Club in 1980. His second title came four years later at the Country Club of Pittsfield and his final was played at the Worcester Country Club, the same year he received the award as the Massachusetts Golfer of the Year.

Education
Somerset schools and University of Massachusetts Amherst, where he was captain of the golf team in 1979 and a member of the East Team for the East-West Division 1 NCAA matches.

Skills
Only two players have won more titles than the Somerset resident. Frederick J. Wright, Jr., won seven times and the famous Francis Ouimet won six times along with the U.S. Open Championship in 1913 and U.S. Amateur title in 1914 and 1931.

Information gathered from Mr. McDermott and the Fall River Country Club—photo courtesy of Mr. McDermott

BEATRICE (ARBOUR) PARROTT
Professional Baseball Player

Profile
Born in 1920 in Somerset where she still lives, Beatrice Parrott is the youngest of four children of Zerlia Roy and Clovis Arbour. She married Donald Parrott and they had four children and seven grandchildren.

Experience
Parrott played for only one year as a shortstop, actually in only one game with one at-bat with the Racine Belles in 1947. She threw and batted right-handed.

Education
Local Somerset schools and Somerset High School.

Skills
Her baseball team was featured in the 1992 film, *A League of their Own*, starring Madonna.

She is a member of the Somerset High School Sports Hall of Fame.

Information gathered from *Wikipedia*—photo courtesy of Girls Professional Baseball League

STEPHEN REBELLO
Author and Screenwriter

Profile
Stephen Rebello was born in Fall River. He is the only child of Arthur and Evelyn Pavao Rebello.

Experience
In 1980, after some years as a Boston clinical and psychiatric social worker and supervisor, Rebello moved to Los Angeles and branched into journalism for top national magazines. As an award-winning, widely quoted feature writer and editor, he interviewed Lee Iacocca, Sandra Bullock and Tom Cruise among dozens of others and became a *Playboy* Magazine contributing editor. In 1980, he became the last journalist to interview Alfred Hitchcock.

By 1988, Rebello had written an award-winning nonfiction book *Reel Art: Great Posters From the Golden Age of the Silver Screen*. Two years later, Rebello followed that book with another award-winning nonfiction book, *Alfred Hitchcock and the Making of Psycho*. He recalls the impact of seeing the film at Fall River's Durfee Theater. The book, now in its fourth printing, has been published in many languages around the world. Unfortunately, the Academy Award and Golden Globe-nominated film *Hitchcock* (2012), based on the book, was not shown at the Durfee, Empire, Capitol, Center, nor the Somerset or Westport Drive-In theaters, none of which are still open. The author of three other books, Rebello is currently writing and developing feature film and television projects for his production company, Fall River Boy Productions.

Education
Somerset schools, University of Massachusetts Dartmouth and masters degree from Simmons College.

Skills
In 2010, Rebello recorded "an intimate conversation" with reclusive star Kim Novak for a five-film DVD box set.

In 2013, Rebello won a Los Angeles Press Club Award for a *Playboy* feature story looking back on "the rise of redneck cinema" typified by the *Smokey and the Bandit* movies of the 1970s.

Information gathered from and photo courtesy of Mr. Rebello

JERRY REMY
Professional Baseball Player, Announcer,
Restaurateur and Author

Profile
Born in Fall River in 1952 to Joseph and Connie Whalon Remy, Jerry Remy married local girl, Phoebe Brum, and they have three children.

Experience
Remy began his baseball career in 1975 with the California Angels. He played three years on the West Coast before coming "home" to Boston in 1978. He played second base and was selected for the All-Star game in 1978. He retired in 1986 and was listed as one of the major league leaders in stolen bases. His career batting average was .275 with over 1,200 hits and 329 runs batted in.

Education
Somerset schools, Somerset High School and graduated from Roger Williams University.

Skills
With major league playing days ended in 1986 by a knee injury, Remy joined the New England Sports Network as the color commentator for the Red Sox. Still providing color to Red Sox Nation, Remy has opened a number of restaurants, including one near Fenway Park and one in Fall River. He has also written four books, including *Watching Baseball*.

Jerry, top right, with Coach Sullivan and teammates in 1969.

Remy is a member of the Red Sox and Somerset High School Sports Halls of Fame.

Information gathered from *Baseball Almanac*—photos courtesy of Somerset High School yearbook and *Baseball Almanac*

JANET L. ROBINSON
New York Times Company CEO

Profile
Born in 1950 and raised in Somerset with her sister by Isaac F. and Louise Cottell Robinson, Janet Robinson was the first woman named as president and CEO of the *New York Times* Company.

Experience
After a short career as a teacher in Newport and Somerset, Robinson moved on in 1983 to advertising sales management at *Golf Digest* and *Tennis* magazine, both part of the *New York Times* Group. From 1990, she served as group senior vice president at the *New York Times* Women's Magazine Group until she joined newspaper operations in 2001. In 2004, Robinson became the president and chief executive officer of the *New York Times*, a position she held until 2011. She is credited with helping to transform the company into a leading digital source of news.

Education
Somerset schools and Salve Regina University. She completed graduate study at the Tuck School of Business at Dartmouth College. She received an honorary doctorate from Salve Regina, Wheaton College, Pace University and University of Massachusetts Dartmouth.

Skills
Robinson began her career as a teacher in the Somerset school system at the Pottersville Elementary School and taught in the Newport, Rhode Island, school system.

She serves on the International Advisory Board of Fleishman Hillard and the board of directors of BankNewport. She is also a member of the Board of Trustees of The Carnegie Corporation of NY, Salve Regina University, URI Graduate School of Oceanography and The Preservation Society of Newport County.

Information gathered from Ms. Robinson, *Wikipedia*, and the *New York Times*—photo courtesy of Ms. Robinson

ANTHONY J. SANTORO, JR., ESQUIRE
University President and Law Professor

Profile

Anthony J. Santoro was born in Melrose, Massachusetts, but brought up in Somerset. He is the son of Samuel S. and Mary Carbonaro Santoro. He married local girl Pauline Plante, and they have four children and ten grandchildren.

Experience
After serving as the CEO of the family needle trade manufacturing firm and as chair of the board of the Fall River Area Chamber of Commerce, Santoro took his legal talents to the College of William and Mary in Virginia before founding the Widener Law School in Wilmington, Delaware. He returned home to Bristol, Rhode Island, and founded the Roger Williams School of Law. In 1993, he was named president of the university, a position he held until 2000 before returning to the classroom at the law school.

Education
Somerset High School, Boston College and both his J.D. and LL.M from Georgetown University.

Skills
Santoro returned to Roger Williams to teach business in the law school after retiring as president.

Information gathered from Mr. Santoro and Roger Williams University—photo courtesy of Mr. Santoro

NEIL SWIDEY
Magazine Writer and Author

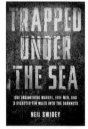

Profile
Neil Swidey was born in 1969. He is the son of Sam and Mary Ridge Swidey and the fourth of five children. He married Denise Drower, chef and TV culinary producer, and they have three daughters.

Experience
As a kid, Swidey wanted to be an architect; big Lego projects instilled that desire in him. High school jobs including picking apples at Del-Mac Orchards in Swansea and selling paint at Sears did little to prepare him for his eventual occupation. Writing, though, was in his DNA; both his grandfather and dad were writers. Swidey formed a new school newspaper at Somerset High School—*The Forum*—when he was not shooting hoops or running track for Mr. Bernardo. Telling stories satisfied his creativity that he originally thought he could only satisfy with architecture.

Swidey landed a writing internship at the Fall River bureau of the *Providence Journal* after his junior year at Tufts University and had two steps up on fellow interns from out of the area—he knew where the Flint was or what was going on "up" the South End.

After graduating in 1991, Swidey was selected as the founding editor of a startup weekly newspaper in Woburn, Massachusetts. After numerous positions in various locations, Swidey joined *The Boston Globe* in 1999 as New England Editor. In his free time, he wrote in-depth articles for the *Globe's* Sunday Magazine. As his family grew, Swidey knew he had to choose between editing and writing. In 2002, he chose the latter, becoming a staff writer for the *Globe Magazine* and he has never looked back.

Education
Somerset schools, Somerset High School and Tufts University.

Skills
Swidey is the author of *Trapped Under the Sea: One Engineering Marvel, Five Men and a Disaster Ten Miles into the Darkness* and co-wrote *Last Lion: The Fall and Rise of Ted Kennedy.*

Net profits from Swidey's book, *The Assist: Hoops, Hope and the Game of Their Lives*, has led him and friends to form a nonprofit scholarship and mentoring organization, Alray.org. Alray helps promising students from inner-city Boston return to college after experiencing a setback on their first try.

Also of Note
His writing has been recognized by the National Magazine Awards and the Society of Professional Journalists and has been featured in *The Best American Science Writing, The Best American Crime Reporting* and *The Best Political Writing.*

"If you approach the world with curiosity and an open mind, you will often find the best stories from the most interesting people,"

-NEIL SWIDEY

Information gathered from the *New York Times* and Mr. Swidey—photos courtesy of Mr. Swidey

DAVID LEITE
Chef and Author

Profile
David Leite is the son of Elvira and Manuel Leite. Born in 1960 in Fall River, where he lived until he was six, he is an only child and grew up on Sharps Lot Road in Swansea, Massachusetts.

Experience
Leite has written about food for nearly every well-known publication here and abroad, including *Bon Appetit, Food & Wine, Martha Stewart Living* and many daily newspapers. He is a regular contributor to the public radio program, *The Splendid Table*, and he authored the award winning book, *The New Portuguese Table* and is a frequent guest on the *Today Show* and other television and radio programs.

Education
Swansea schools and Case High School followed by Rochester Institute of Technology, Carnegie Mellon, University of Pittsburgh and City University of New York. He maintains dual citizenship with Portugal.

Skills
Leite has received the James Beard Award on two occasions for his website Leite's Culinaria, a third James Beard Award for his writing in T*he New York Times* as well as the Bert Greene Award for Food Journalism. He was also the winner of the 2010 First Book/Julia Child Award and is a member of the Culinary Hall of Fame.

SUMNER J. (JAY) WARING, III
Senior Vice President,
Service Corporation International

Profile
Sumner J. (Jay) Waring II, born in Fall River in 1968, is the son of Elizabeth Waring and the late Sumner James Waring, Jr. (also highlighted in this book). Waring married Kristen Moyer and they have three daughters.

Experience
Shortly after Waring joined the family's Fall River funeral business, Waring, Ashton, Coughlin, Sullivan, and Driscoll Funeral Homes, the firm began acquiring Massachusetts funeral homes throughout the area.

Waring joined Service Corporation International (SCI) in 1996 when his Fall River firm joined SCI. SCI owns hundreds of funeral homes, cemeteries and mortuaries in North America.

Education
Local Swansea schools, Friends Academy, Tabor Academy, Stetson University, Mount Ida College and a masters degree from University of Massachusetts Dartmouth.

Skills
Waring has advanced from area vice president in 1996 to President of the Northeast Region in 1999, then President of the Pacific Region in 2001. In 2002, he was appointed vice president of Western Operations. Currently, he is a senior vice president responsible for business development and personnel, a position he has held since 2006.

Information gathered from family members and SCI—photo courtesy of Waring Portrait Art Photography

CHRIS MCDONALD
Olympic Trials Boxer

Chris, left with "Hurricane" Peter McNelly

Profile
Chris McDonald was born in 1963 to William and Carol McDonald. He lived in Tiverton, Rhode Island with his two brothers and two sisters.

Experience
McDonald won the 1980 Golden Gloves New England Heavyweight title and went to the finals of the National AAU Tournament in Las Vegas. The Tiverton pugilist won his Olympic Trial semifinal before finalizing as the heavy weight runner-up. Many who watched the championship fight felt he had beaten James Broad in the finals in Atlanta.

He had 17 professional fights with a record of 15-1-1 and 14 knockouts. It seemed like McDonald lost his enthusiasm after he lost a 10-round bout to James "Bonecrusher" Smith, also a questionable decision.

Education
Local Tiverton schools.

Skills
Managed by the Petronelli brothers, Pat and Goody, McDonald was under the tutelage of the best coaches in boxing at the time. He was often compared to Jerry Quarry. Manny Steward called McDonald the hardest natural puncher he ever worked with.

Information gathered from BoxRec—photo courtesy of BoxRec

JOSEPH "ZAZA" FERREIRA
Olympic Soccer Team

Profile
Joseph "ZaZa" Ferreira was born in Fall River in 1916 and died in Fall River in 2007 at age ninety. He was the son of Mariano and Rose Moniz Ferreira. He married Bellma "Billie" Mello and they had two daughters and two grandchildren. He is entombed in the Notre Dame Cemetery Mausoleum in Fall River.

Experience
Ferreira's illustrious career on the pitch began with the Ponta Delgada S.C., which in 1946 was a dominant team in the soccer world. They lost the U.S. Open Cup in 1946 and 1950 but took home the title in 1947, the same year they won the National Amateur Cup.

Ferreira was also a member of the U.S. Soccer Team at the 1948 Summer Olympics. The team unfortunately lost to Italy in the initial round. He was a member of the local "Fab Four." Ferreira earned three caps* as a member of the US National Team between 1947 and 1948. He was a member of the 1947 Ponta Delgado Open Cup Championship team and went on to play as a member of the National Team at the 1947 NAFC Championship.

Education
Local Tiverton schools.

Also of Note
Joseph in Portuguese is Jose, so the name ZaZa came from that but pronounced more like zusa and for short came his nickname ZaZa.

*A player is "capped" for each international match played. A player who has played in 50 international matches has 50 caps.

Information gathered from *Wikipedia* and his family—photo courtesy of *Wikipedia*

ALLEN LEVRAULT
Professional Baseball Player

Profile
Allen Levrault was born in 1977 to Allen and Elizabeth McCarraher Levrault, and has a sister. Married to Vanessa J. Quirk, they live in Westport with their child.

Experience
After graduating from Westport High School, Levrault was drafted by the Milwaukee Brewers and played for the Brewers in 2000. He played in 37 games over a two year period for the Wisconsin team before he was traded to the Florida Marlins in 2003. Levrault pitched in 19 games for the World Champion Marlins and earned a World Series Championship ring when he went 1-0 with a 3.86 earned run average with less than a half season played. His last big league contest was at Fenway Park, where he finished the game but tendonitis in his throwing elbow sidelined him through the remainder of what proved to be his last season. His career record was 7-11 with a 5.59 earned run average and 110 strikeouts.

Education
Westport schools, Westport High School and Rhode Island Community College.

Skills
Levrault is a member of the Westport High School Sports Hall of Fame.

Information gathered from *Wikipedia* and Mr. Levrault—photo courtesy of Baseball Almanac

JOHN J. "MIKE" MACKOWSKI
Insurance Company Executive

Profile
John J. "Mike" Mackowski was born in 1916 and died
in 2007 at age eighty-one. The son of John and Victoria
Mieczkowski, he was one of three children. Married
to Ruth Williams, they had four children, and retired
to Ponte Vedra Beach, Florida, and Westport over
looking Quicksand Pond. Mackowski knows the pond
well—when he was young, he and his father collected
seaweed there to use as fertilizer for the family farm on
Sanford Road.

Experience
Mackowski left the family produce farm in North Westport and headed to Duke
University, his beloved alma mater, where he played varsity football. His career path
was undetermined but his leadership skills were developed.

Beginning in 1951, Mackowski progressed through the ranks of the Atlantic Mu-
tual Insurance Company until he was elected president and CEO of The Atlantic
Companies. He was a director and chair of the Auditing Committee of Transatlantic
Holding and the Woolworth Company.

Mackowski served on the board of the Insurance Information Institute, the Seamen's
Church Institute of New York and the American Bureau of Shipping. He was also a
member of New York's Trinity Center for Ethics and Corporate Responsibility, which
led to the creation of the Mackowski professorship in Organizational Ethics at Duke.

Education
Westport schools, Duke University and Harvard Business School.

Skills
A member of the Greatest Generation, Mackowski served as a Marine Corps first
lieutenant in World War II.

Information gathered from *Baseball Almanac* and the *New York Times*—photo courtesy of his family

MORE WHO EXCELLED

As well as more than 260 Fall River-educated finest on the preceding pages, there are others who excelled in their fields of endeavors in various categories.

From 1850 to 1925, citizens such as Sarah Brayton* had a tremendous effect upon the city with not only her generosity during her lifetime but with her largess after her passing. If it were not, for example, for the incredible generosity of Mary Brayton Durfee Young (Mrs. Jeremiah Young)*, there would be no high school on the hill named after her son, Bradford Matthew Chaloner Durfee*.

The period between 1926 and the present has also produced some exceptional individuals in various categories of expertise.

Arts: Ted Delaney (writer, educator and brother of Michael, listed below), Joe Duquette (actor), Wendy Moniz (actor), Hank "the Angry Dwarf " Nasiff* (radio personality), James Khoury (musician), Bobby Justin (vocalist), Dania Krupska* (choreographer), and Bonnie Strickman (vocalist).

Business: Ray Cabral* (investments), Bob Fisette (international aircraft executive), Gary Goldberg (manufacturing), Paul Gustafson (technology), John Harding* (national food chain executive), John Harty (turnaround specialist), David Machado (chef) and brother of Barry listed below, John McDonough (financial executive), Brian McGuinness (hotel executive), James Mooney (beverage distributor), and Bob Wood (financial executive).

Education: Professors all: William A. Carroll* (English), Joseph Conforti (history), the Delaney brothers-Edmund, Daniel and Thomas (all brothers of Bishop Delaney*, included herein and psychology professors), Jamie Ferreira (philosophy), Barry Machado** (history) and brother of David above, Joseph E. Magnet (law) and brother of Myron Magnet, Mary Ann Shea (academic affairs), Don Solomon (math) and David Wilner (astrophysics).

Local: Alan Amaral (manufacturing), Tony Cordeiro (developer), J. Thomas Cottrell (historian), Allen Jarabek* (businessperson) and John J.McAvoy* (writer, historian and Durfee Distinguished Alumnus 1999).

Media: J. King Cruger (newspaper bureau chief), Michael Delaney (photographer and brother of Ted, listed above), Rosemary Feitelberg (fashion writer), Vic Palumbo III (advertising), and Rachel McDonald Sanchez (television producer).

Military: U.S. Marine Lt. Colonel Thomas Carroll (Ret.) and member of the Diman Hall of Fame, U.S. Army Lt. Colonel Santi DiRuzza (Ret.) and father of Barry DiRuzza included herein, U.S. Army Lt. Colonel Bruce Hackett (Ret.), U.S. Army Colonel George F. Phelan, U.S. Air Force Colonel David R. Sheahan*, U.S. Army Colonel Ronald Silvia (Ret.) U.S. Navy Commander Teddy Tokarz and U.S. Navy Commander M. Norman Zalkind* (Ret.).

Professional: Peter Collias, Esq.** (Durfee High School Alumni Scholarship Committee, Durfee High Distinguished Alumnus 1997), John C. Corrigan, M.D. *(first local cardiologist and Durfee Distinguished Alumnus 1965), Linda Kaufman Grabiner (computer scientist) and W. Hugh M. Morton,Esq. (partner at Hill & Barlow).

Religion: Rabbi Mark Lipson (religious music composer).

Sports: Anthony Abraham** (football), Gordon "Buddy" Andrews** (basketball), Tommy Arruda** (baseball), Al Attar** (basketball),Ted Darcy* (National Softball Hall of Fame), Bob Farias (coach), Ernie Flemming+ (basketball), Andy Farrissey** (basketball), Mike Pilotte (auto cross), Ruben Rezendes (soccer), Tom Salvo (football), Andrew Sousa (soccer), the swimming Mercer family and the boxing Synnott brothers*, Jimmy and Babe.

Suburbs: Somerset residents Sandy Curt (coach), Warren Hathaway (publishing), and Jacques Steinberg (writer); Swansea resident Judge Antone Aguiar* and Westport resident Douglas Amaral (chef).

*Deceased
**Members of Durfee High School Sports Hall of Fame

ACKNOWLEDGMENTS

This massive (as it turned out) undertaking certainly would never have been possible if it were not for the nearly 100 people listed herein. It took more than two years from germination to harvesting and launch in May 2014. Thanks go to the subjects, many of whom provided me with specific details of their childhood and motivating factors in their lives. The private stuff. Some of it is listed, some not.

My wife, Paula, told me this was going to be quite an undertaking, others have asked how many names: like 25. Ha ha. No, around 250! Take that, ye of little faith. The book took me to nearly every state in the union as well as the far East, Europe and even behind the Iron Curtain. I traveled to the near East and the British Isles. I went by Internet and the old fashioned invention by Alexander Graham Bell to the Pacific and the Caribbean. Contact was made with subjects and family members, most who were not only willing to tell their stories but proud of the achievements of loved ones. It has been quite a trip that I hope you will enjoy as much as I have had on my excursion.

It takes lots of research and even more editing to construct the garden that became this book. What should be capitalized, where do I use the comma or a dash or hyphen? For an author who was more of an advertising creative writer, I needed all the help I could get. I relied on my wife, Paula, to read and reread. My youngest grandchild, Lucy, made changes to the edits during her summer vacation from prep school. The person who I relied upon most is my editor, Dr. Stefani Koorey, who also provided the index.

The research aspect of this effort was by far the most enjoyable. If it was not for Michael Martins and Dennis Binette at the Fall River Historical Society, my efforts would have been thwarted early on. Their historical knowledge of Fall River and the major players of the pre-Great Depression era is remarkable. Special thanks also to Michael Martins for writing the generous foreword to this book. Special thanks also to Mary Faria, the *Herald News* librarian who was always available when I needed her.

Local historian physicians Bruce Derbyshire and Dick Fitton made suggestions as well as the late Durfee High School principal, Jim Panos, Peter Collias and Bernie Taradash. All their leads proved fruitful and accurate. My friend Chris Audet, who often challenged my knowledge of Fall River trivia from the not too distant past also deserves a nod as does Kevin Manning. Both provided names of subjects that I was unaware of. From one week to the next, new suggestions were offered to me and most proved to be completely worthy of inclusion. The committee on inclusion rejected very few suggestions. I am sure there are more who could and should be listed but who are unknown.

Thanks to my "One To One" tutor at the Apple Store, Garry Kashuk, who provided the cover idea, and my printer and artist extraordinaire, Mary Senra at Senco Printing, who put it together with the final touches. Thanks to attorneys Michele and Peter Lando for their advice and counsel and to those who wrote testimonials for the book: author Chris Ogden; Ambassador Bill Middenoff; author Bill Reynolds; Atty. Mark Harty; District Attorney Sam Sutter; Eileen T. Farley, President Emerita of Bristol Community College and; Cardinal Sean O'Malley. I will be forever grateful.

Special thanks to President and CEO of BayCoast Bank, Nick Christ, and his staff for the *big* assist in providing convenient locations to make this book available for purchase. To the *Herald News* and other local print media for making excerpts available in the newspapers prior to publication.

Every effort has been made to identify qualified individuals, and where possible, to contact them or family members for information and or inclusion. We apologize for any errors or omissions.

Finally, the following list of sources deserve special thanks for all their help and information. I could not have done this without you:

ACKNOWLEDGMENTS

Tony Abraham
Keith Allan
Mike Andrews
Charles Auclair
Patricia Bernier
Jim Bjorge
Bob Bogan
Herman Bomback
Dr. Brian Bowcock
Dick Brightman
Nicole Cairamella
Ann Carruth
Kathleen B. Castro
Tony Ciampanelli
Tom Coughlin
Dominic Corrigan, M.D.
J. Thomas Cottrell
John King Cruger
Tom Cuddy
Sue Curran
Bill David
Fire Chief Ed Dawson (Ret.)
Bob Deane
Gloria deSa
Richard Desjardins, Esq.
Dick Dobbins
Blyth Eagan
Tom Eaton
Joe Feitelberg
State Representative Carole Fiola
Paige Green
Marvin Greenberg
Irving and Roberta Metras Goss
Frank "Brud" Hadley
Ray Hague
Maureen Harrington
Theresa Hartnett
Mark Harty, Esq.
Theresa Hennessey
Charles Hickey
Mike Holtzman
Phil Hudner
Kris Impastato
Bob Jenkins
Kim Kaiser
Christine Kearns
James Keeley, Esq.
Eileen Kelly
Eileen Kent
Ann Marvel Kerwin
Rene Kochman
Stan Koppelman
Kyle Kupiec

ACKNOWLEDGMENTS

Maryellen Kurkulos
Aime Lachance
Herman W. Lapointe
William Lapointe
Lorraine Lecour
Tim Lowery
Pina Luciolla
John MacKinnon
Police Chief Frank McDonald (Ret.)
John McDonough
Jane Feitelberg McKean
Anne Marie Medeiros
Debbie Medeiros
Jay Mercer
Jack Moll
Nora Murphy
Pauline Noga
Brian O'Neil
Manny Papoula
Debbie Pelletier
Vic Pereira
Ted Pettine, Sr.
Lois Powers
Renita Presler
Mary Lou Quigley
Mike Quirk
Sara Rabern
Donald H. Ramsbottom
Albert Resnick, M.D.
Pauline Rodriques
Glenn Russell
James Sabra
Justin Shay
Dan Sheahan and the entire staff of the Fall River Public Library Reference Department
Susan Shelby
Arthur Silvia
Dr. Phil Silvia
Nancy Stulack
Bernard Sullivan
Fred Sullivan
Greg Sullivan
Lynne Sullivan
Roger Tache
Robert Taylor
Charlotte Thomas
Lucy Thompson
Christine Vargas
Monsignor Barry Wall
Bunny Wilkinson
Barbara "Bambi" Truesdale Wisbach
Richard Wolfson
Barry and Mick Zais

PUBLISHED SOURCES

Of Men and Money and The Fall River National Bank-1825-1975 – Barbara Ashton

Greater Fall River Baseball – Dr. Philip Silvia

Phillips History of Fall River – Arthur S. Phillips

Parallel Lives – Michael Martins, Dennis Binnett

Victorian Vistas – Dr. Philip Silvia

75th Anniversary Souvenir Year Book – Prevost High School – Aime Lachance

Durfee High School yearbook collection

Images of Fall River – Rob Lewis

Fall River Revisited – Stefani Koorey, PhD.

Our Story: Charlton Health System – David Eske

Fall River: A Pictorial History – Judith A. Boss

The Memorable 1940s – Fall River Herald News

The Fabulous 1950s – Fall River Herald News

Mark Twain Wit & Wisecracks – Doris Benardete

JOHN B. CUMMINGS, JR.
About The Author

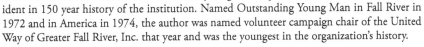

Profile
Cummings was born in Fall River in 1945. He is the only child of Angela King and John B. Cummings, Esq. Spouse of Paula J. Francoeur, he is the father of John B. Cummings, III and David C. Cummings, grandfather of Chloe J. Cummings, Max M. Cummings, Jamie C. Cummings and Lucy T. Cummings.

Experience
Cummings served as a Vice President of the Fall River National Bank between 1974 and 1978, and was the youngest vice president in 150 year history of the institution. Named Outstanding Young Man in Fall River in 1972 and in America in 1974, the author was named volunteer campaign chair of the United Way of Greater Fall River, Inc. that year and was the youngest in the organization's history.

Cummings was selected as the Chief Professional Officer of the United Way in 1978 and served in that capacity until 1995. The funds raised in that period for the betterment of the people of Greater Fall River were double the national average for similar size United Ways in the nation.

Named Endowment and Planned Giving Director at the United Way in 1996, he was recognized by the United Way of America for having one of the outstanding planned giving programs in the nation. He retired in 2006.

Education
Sacred Heart School, Portsmouth Priory School, Regis College, University of Rhode Island and University of Massachusetts Dartmouth.

Also of Note
Cummings was elected the youngest president in the history of the Acoaxet Club in Westport, Massachusetts, in 1984 and served for many years as an honorary governor.

He is a licensed real estate broker in Massachusetts and Rhode Island and is the owner of Cummings Group Realtors in Westport with his wife.

His civic work included President of the Greater Fall River Development Corporation between 2001 to 2002 as well as chair of the Fall River Conservation Committee and Fall River Task Force on Sports and Recreation.

He is the recipient of various awards for advertising excellence and his first book, *The Last Fling, Hurricane Carol 1954, Stories from Westport, Massachusetts,* was recognized with awards from The New England Book Festival and the Beach Book Festival in 2012. He was also the producer of a documentary film by the same name and coauthored a book, *From Little Acorns to Giant Oaks*, about the history of the Greater Fall River Development Corporation and the economic development in Fall River between 1954 and 2004.

INDEX

Entries are arranged in letter-by-letter order, using the *Chicago Manual of Style, 16th Edition.* References to page numbers for photographs of the person indexed are indicated in italics type. When an individual is the topic of an entire or half-page biographical entry, the page number is in bold type.

This index covers named individuals in the text who were born or attended school in Fall River, Mass., with the following exceptions: family members who are related by birth or marriage to the subject of the biographical entry are excluded if their names appear only in the profile section. Military ranks, honorary titles, and medical and education standings are omitted, while religious designations are included.

All businesses, institutions, organizations, sports teams, and government entities are located in Fall River, Mass. All other references in the text are excluded. In cases where the text of the book differs from the index entry, the entry reflects the official or standardized usage or name.

354

357

Rezendes, Ruben, 338
Rhythm Makers (band), 81
Richard Borden Post No. 46 G.A.R., 76
Richards, J., *296*
Richardson, Arthur, 220
Richardson, Douglas J., 186
Richmond, Arthur D., 43
Rigby, Alston, 186
Riley, Martin, **68**
Riley, Richard P., **166**
Rippon, William, 40
Rivers, Herbert P., 218
Riversi, Steve, *302*
Roach, Richard, 218
Roberts, George, 43
Roberts, Joseph A., 220
Robeson, John F., 41
Robidoux, Adjutor, 218
Robin, Joseph E. W., 218
Robinson, Alfred, Jr., 43
Robinson, Arthur, 43
Robinson, Janet L., **328**
Robinson, Mindy, **100**
Rochefort, John R., Jr., 220
Rockett, Edward Francis, 43
Rockett, George, 40
Rockett, Patrick Lewis, Jr., 43
Rodgers, Edward A. "Ted," 183, **212**
Rodgers, Thomas A., Jr., **183,** 212
Rodrigues, Aliva, 43
Rodrigues, George, *302*
Rodrigues, John, 43
Rodrigues, Richard, 221
Rogers, Francis J., 218
Rogers, William, 218
Romano, Aime, 220
Romano, J., *300*
Romanowicz, Walter, **289**
Rooney, Hugh, 40
Root, Waverly, **195**
Rosa, Louis, 43
Rose, Gerard, 218
Rose Hawthorne Lathrop Cancer Home, 163
Rosenberg, Jacob, 43
Rosenberg, Richard M., **132**
Ross, J. Maurice, 218
Rouke, Patrick, 40
Roundsville, Cyrus, 187
Rousseau, Henry R., 218
Routhier, Armand, *294*
Rowcroft, Thomas, 40
Roy, Adam, *312*
Roy, Amber, *309*
Roy, Charles E., 218
Ruel, Jason, *310*
Ruel, John, *310*
Ruggles, Micah, 17
Ruggles Park, 110, 164, 277
Ruggles School, 282
Ruthman, Orville H., 43

Ryan, James, 40
Ryan, James T., 218
Ryan, Patrick, 40
Ryan, Thomas J., 218
Ryder, Herman Kenneth, 43
Ryley, Francis J., 218
Rzasa, John I., 218

S
Sabik, Joseph F., III, **246**
Sabra, James, 246
Sabra, Philip F., 218
Sacred Heart Parish, 63, 65, 238, 239, 275
Sacred Hearts Academy, 172, 242, 257
Sacred Heart School, 89, 90, 93, 96, 110, 127, 129, 164,
    165, 166, 200, 238, 239, 247, 254, 257, 277
Saint Jean the Baptiste's School, 174
Saint Louis Parish, 34
Saints Peter and Paul School, 86, 183, 212
Salmond, Doug, 299
Salois, Ann, *304*
Salvo, Tom, 338
Sample, Dick, *295*
Sampson, Orrie D. W., Jr., 220
Samson, Ray, *295*
Samuel Watson School, 81, 159, 271
Sanchez, Rachel McDonald, 337
Sanders, Jessica, *309*
Sanford, Abram, 40
Santo Christo Parish, 54
Santoro, Anthony J., **329**
Santoro, Jack, 315
Santos, Adelino M. L., 218
Santos, Albert Willard, 221
Santos, George F., 218
Santos, John, 307
Santos, Rudolfo S., 218
Saraiva, Ashley, *314*
Sardinha, Lori "Chick," **100**
Sardinha, Rui, 307
Sardinha Plumbing and Heating, 100
Saucier, Octave J. B., 218
Saulnier, Roland G., 218
Savoie, J. Raymond, 218
Scanlon, John, **101**
Schieri, Vin, 300
Schmoke, Ed, *296*
Schraer, George, 218
Schwartz, Albert, 218
Schwartz, Jerry, *298*
Scrivo, Ferdinand J., 218
Searil, Elmer, 218
Seligman, E., *301*
Senay, John F., 220
Senay, Joseph C., 218
Seneca, Russell P., **247**
Senior League CYO, 277
Senra, John, *310*
Shallow, Jeremiah Charles, 43
Sharkansky, Ira, **150**